Corrigenda

p. 61, line 11. for Edward I read Edward III
p. 152, line 13. for once read twice
p. 153, line 30. for Bacon read Bryan
p. 176, plate caption. for Antelope read Boreyne
p. 177, plate caption bottom right. for Earl of Eglinton
read Lord Avandale and Ochiltree
p. 199, line 10. for Cambrensio read Cambrensis
p. 212, heading. for Terms read Treatises

The Heraldic Imagination

Rodney Dennys

BARRIE & JENKINS
COMMUNICA - EUROPA

First published in 1975 by
Barrie & Jenkins Limited
24 Highbury Crescent
London N5 1RX

Copyright © Rodney Dennys 1975

ISBN 0 214 65386 2

Printed by Cox & Wyman Limited, Fakenham, Norfolk.

TO MY BROTHER OFFICERS,
THE KINGS, HERALDS AND PURSUIVANTS OF ARMS OF ENGLAND
WITHOUT WHOSE ENCOURAGEMENT AND HELP
THIS WOULD HAVE BEEN A MUCH WORSE BOOK

Contents

Acknowledgements

Where so many have helped, advised and criticised, it would be invidious to single out one rather than another. All my brother heralds, from the senior King of Arms down to the most junior Pursuivant, have put me individually in their debt; and collectively, as the Chapter of the College of Arms, I also owe them my warmest thanks for so generously allowing me to include so many photographs from the unique records and collections of the College, many of which have not hitherto been published. Individual acknowledgements will also be found in the footnotes.

We should be lost indeed without the resources of the splendid library of the Society of Antiquaries, and the limitless patience and ready and understanding help of our Librarian, Mr John Hopkins, to whom and to the Society I most gladly express my grateful thanks. The remarkable manuscript collections of the British Library have provided considerable material used in this book, and I am much indebted to the Board of the British Library. My thanks also go to the Keeper of Manuscripts and Egerton Librarian, and to all the members of his Department, whose help and kindness have put me in their debt. The Bodleian Library has, of course, been a similar mine of source material, which has been extensively quarried; and my warm thanks go to Dr R. W. Hunt, M.A., D.Phil., F.B.A., Sub-Librarian and Keeper of the Western Manuscripts and, in particular, to Dr W. O. Hassall, M.A., D.Phil., F.S.A., whose patient and ready help has been invaluable, while the subject card index over which he presides is unrivalled anywhere. So too do my thanks go to Mr E. B. Ceadel, M.A., the Librarian of the University Library, Cambridge, and to his staff. Finally, I must express my warmest thanks to M. Marcel Thomas, Conservateur-en-Chef, Département des Manuscrits at the Bibliothèque Nationale in Paris, for whose kindness and help I am deeply grateful. The footnotes will make it clear where I have drawn on their resources, and the list of plates and illustrations will indicate which have been published with their permission.

My most grateful thanks must also go to the Duke of Buccleuch and Queensberry for his great kindness in allowing me to use some of the splendid and enchanting illustrations in the *Wrythe Garter Book*, none of which has hitherto been published, for some of the colour-plates.

I am much indebted to the Directors of Faber & Faber Ltd. for permission to quote from *The Works of Sir Thomas Browne*, edited by Sir Geoffrey Keynes (Faber & Faber Ltd., 1964). To David Higham Associates Ltd., my thanks go for permission to quote from *The Book of Beasts* by T. H. White (Jonathan Cape, 1954 etc.). The footnotes will make it clear to which of them I am indebted for some delightful quotations. Others, too numerous to mention here, have been equally helpful, and I hope they will forgive me if I express my indebtedness to them generally.

This book could not have been written without recourse to the works of all the many writers, past and present, on heraldry and its allied subjects, and my indebtedness to them will be recognised in the references to their works in the footnotes. At the same time, any deductions I may have made or opinions I may have expressed are my own, and I must also admit paternity for any errors which may have crept in.

Without its illustrations this book would have been much duller, and I would therefore like to record my gratitude to Mr A. C. Cole, M.A., B.C.L., F.S.A., Windsor Herald of Arms, for allowing me to use some of the line drawings which he made some years ago for *The Coat of Arms*, and also to the Herald Painters of the College of Arms, notably Mr Gerald Cobb, M.V.O., F.S.A., Mr Geoffrey Mussett, Mr Norman Manwaring and Miss D. Corner, and also to Miss A. Urwick, for the many lively drawings they contributed.

Finally I must thank my publishers for their remarkable patience, encouragement and guidance; in particular John Bunting, formerly editorial director of Barrie & Jenkins Ltd., and Ursula Owen, who succeeded him as the midwife for this book, without whose help it would not have been born, and to Michael Carter who designed the book.

But the book would not have got that far had it not been for the encouragement and help given me by my wife and family, both with typing and with candid but constructive criticism; nor would it have been possible for me to devote the time to research and writing, had it not been for the ungrudging and loyal help of my Personal Assistant, Carol Hartley, who not only coped with much of the typing of the book, but also kept a large and busy heraldic practice ticking over smoothly, with remarkable calmness and efficiency.

List of colour plates

List of monochrome plates

Introduction

CHIMERICAL creatures, compounded of incongruous elements, have peopled the imagination of men in all parts of the world since the earliest times. Some of the mythological beings, who were believed by our distant ancestors to inhabit the earth and its ambient air and the waters under the earth, were evolved to explain the frightening and perplexing phenomena of nature. Others of these fabulous beasts and 'mix't four footed creatures' may have derived from hazy folk memories of the prodigious monsters of prehistoric times, whose fossilised remains still excite our wonder and awe. Most of them, however, were the result of imperfect observations of wild animals, birds and reptiles, and the garbled tales of too-trusting travellers.

Most of these creatures found their way into the pages of Herodotus, Aristotle, Pliny and other classical writers, and thence into the Septuagint, the Vulgate and Isidore of Seville. The authors of the bestiaries and encyclopedias of the Middle Ages, such as Alexander Neckham and Bartholomew the Englishman, drew on these and added much new lore, which the medieval heralds and writers on armory used extensively and themselves embellished. In more recent times, however, writers on the fabulous creatures of heraldry have tended, almost without exception, to relate them to the chimerical creatures of classical antiquity, and it is on this view of them that the imaginations of modern heralds have been fed.

Consequently, when I was asked to write an illustrated book on heraldic monsters I agreed, because I then thought I probably knew as much as most of us about them; an attitude which I subsequently discovered to be unduly hubristic. Further consideration of the problem soon made it clear that it would be no contribution to heraldic studies to produce yet another book on armorial monsters, on the lines of those which have been published in recent years. Others, such as John Vinycombe, whose *Fictitious and Symbolic Creatures in Art* was published in 1906, have done it as well as any of us could on these lines.

The obvious approach, therefore, was to see how the medieval heralds and writers on armory viewed them, and this sent me to the medieval treatises on armory, which have not hitherto been studied in depth and as a whole. It soon became clear that these drew their inspiration mainly from the encyclopaedias and bestiaries of the twelfth and thirteenth centuries and their copies and derivatives of the later Middle Ages, rather than directly from the classical authors.

Heraldry, or more correctly armory, was mainly evolved and brought into flower during the exciting renaissance of the twelfth century, the age which embraced the early crusades and the troubadours, the schoolmen and the saints, and saw the foundation of the great churches and universities of Europe – the bright morning of chivalry. Its more flamboyant characteristics, which included the incursion into badges and supporters, crests, and finally shields, of the bizarre and chimerical creatures, were developed during the renaissance of the fifteenth and sixteenth centuries – the golden sunset of chivalry.

In order to relate the literature of heraldry to the heralds, it becomes necessary to touch lightly on the origins of the heralds and of armory. This modest foray does not presume to be more than a background to what follows, for none of us can pretend to hold a candle to the two incomparable books by Sir Anthony Wagner, Garter King of Arms, *Heralds and Heraldry in the Middle Ages* (O.U.P. 1939; 2nd ed. 1956), and *Heralds of England* (H.M.S.O. 1967), which will remain classics on this subject for many generations to come. Complementing these are the invaluable books by Professor N. Denholm-Young, *History and Heraldry 1254 to 1310* (O.U.P. 1965) and *The Country Gentry in the Four-teenth Century* (O.U.P. 1969); while Professor Gerard J. Brault, *Early Blazon* (O.U.P. 1972) and *Eight Thirteenth Century Rolls of Arms in French and Anglo-Norman Blazon* (Pennsylvania State University Press 1973), has opened a new door to any serious study of early armory.

Nevertheless, it seemed to me that not enough weight has been given to the military aspects of the early heralds. Even in modern armies, where the general staff are far more highly organised, it is the deeds of the commanders which are chronicled, while the work of the staff officers is taken for granted. In the first part of this book I am, therefore, suggesting very tentatively that this may have been the case too in the Middle Ages when, in the military society of the time, the staff duties of the heralds would be taken for granted and would not normally merit mention in the medieval chronicles and romances. The fact that the heralds, minstrels and household clerks of the King were lumped together in the royal accounts does not necessarily make this suggestion untenable.

That dedicated armorist, the late Oswald Barron, F.S.A., Maltravers Herald of Arms Extraordinary, taught us to go back to first principles, to the sternly functional simplicity of the early Middle Ages, and to ignore all armorial develop-ments since the end of the fourteenth century. His view was that 'armory was stricken when the medieval period had its death wound, and as a living thing it cannot be said to have survived our last civil war'. Indeed, he felt that a study of armorial practice 'in its native age, an age which has passed utterly away, is all that remains for the student of armory'. His chilly blasts did the modern heralds much good, for it made us turn to the source material of English heraldry, in its widest aspects, with increasing curiosity and deeper understanding and, as a result, to question some of his assumptions.

Oswald Barron worked largely on the early medieval rolls of arms, those catalogues of real and fabulous sovereigns, barons, bannerets and knights, with blazons or paintings of their arms. These were compiled by heralds for practical purposes. The 'general rolls' were probably memoranda of arms most likely to be met with in the course of their work, while some may have been compiled by pursuivants on completing their apprenticeship before being christened by their masters and promoted herald and others for the delectation of a lordly patron. 'Occasional rolls' were records of those who were gathered together for a particular occasion, such as a military expedition or a tournament. One would not, therefore, expect such manuscripts to contain explanatory matter, for that was not their purpose, any more than one would expect the armorial shields upon a tombstone to be accompanied by an explanatory gloss. These severely practical documents were the end product of the herald's work, and we must look deeper to see if we can discern what led up to them.

For the period before 1300 we can only make the most tentative inferences from a study of the early seals and the few remaining rolls of arms, and must rely largely on the romances of the troubadours, trouvères and minnesingers. From these one gets the impression that heraldry was a gay and cheerful art, untrammelled by the guide-lines laid down by the pedants of later ages, and certainly nothing like the starkly serious science that Barron would have us believe. It is therefore not without significance that the earliest factual herald known to us was the young minstrel lately made a herald, who sang so persuasively to William the Marshal, while the earliest herald of romance appears on the scene clad only in his shirt, having pawned his clothes at the local pub. The early heralds, like their modern successors, were the products of their age and society, and we must assume that they were as deeply influenced by their education and environment as we are today.

They would have listened to the same songs and stories as their masters, have read the same books and have accepted the same conventions and beliefs. They would have been reasonably well acquainted with the Vulgate and have read the contemporary and earlier encyclopedias and bestiaries. Unfortunately no heraldic treatise has survived from before 1300, but with *De Heraudie* the series begins, and after Bartolo di Sasso Ferrato they appear with increasing frequency. Barron was inclined to dismiss these treatises, and particularly those of the later Middle Ages, whose authorship he contemptuously ascribed to 'Master Mumblazon', declaring that none of them were written by heralds. We now know that this is not correct, for some were certainly written by heralds, like the *Blason des Couleurs,* while the other fact which has emerged is that the authors of the remainder of the medieval treatises, where they can be identified, were people of some weight, who moved in the military society of the knights and magnates, and were on close terms with the heralds. Wherever it has been possible to identify the contemporary owners of these treatises, we find them to be the very people who were making practical use of armory, in the field of battle, in tournaments and in the embellishment of peace.

This leads us to the second part of my book, a preliminary study of such medieval heraldic treatises as I have been able to examine. While the late Hugh Stanford London, Norfolk Herald of Arms Extraordinary, Professor Evan J. Jones (whose invaluable *Medieval Heraldry* did much to trigger off this inquiry), Mr. Cecil Humphery-Smith, and others have discussed individual heraldic treatises in some detail, and the first produced a most useful short list of them, no one has so far tried to consider them as a whole and in relation to each other and the setting of their time. While the principal libraries in England have been searched pretty thoroughly, time has not permitted more than the most superficial searches in private libraries. By the same token, only preliminary searches have been possible in the Bibliothéque Nationale in Paris, and I have left European libraries virtually untouched. The present study has brought out the close connection between the English and French medieval heraldic treatises. These links must also exist in the case of the Empire and the Burgundian lands, and would well merit further study.

Heraldry comprises all the duties of a herald, of which armory was, and still is only one, but for the purpose of this book I have narrowed the definition of a heraldic treatise to one which is wholly devoted to armory, or to a military treatise which contains a number of chapters or sections on armory. It is a rather arbitrary definition, because many of the treatises on tournaments contain important references to the armorial practice of the time, as indeed do those treatises, written by heralds for heralds, on the organisation of ceremonies, and the like. Any serious study of heraldic treatises should, therefore, include these, and this would be a pretty formidable task.

As this part of my book is breaking new ground, I have changed the tempo because this is not a subject which can be treated quite so lightly as the first and third parts of the book. Those who are only interested in the colour and sparkle of heraldry may, therefore, prefer to skip part II, but I hope it will encourage those who are interested in armory to explore the matter further.

The heraldic treatises bring us to part III of this book, which discusses the heraldic imagination in some of its wilder flights. In order to keep the scope of it within reason, I have confined myself to a consideration of the celestial beings and chimerical or fabulous creatures which have excited the imagination of the medieval and later heralds, and have been used as charges on shield and banner, or as supporters and badges in European and particularly English heraldry, or which have some connection with it. Thus most of the mythological beings and creatures of Asia and the Egypt of the Pharoahs will find no place here, because few of them have been used in European heraldry and those only in recent times. The New World and Australasia have contributed even fewer beasts to the heraldic zoo.

It was when I was rounding up the fabulous and monstrous creatures of heraldry that some of the Angels first flew into my net, because they were, or perhaps I should say are, composed of incongruous elements, a human form with the feathered wings of a bird, which brings them technically into the category of monsters. Nevertheless it is difficult to think of the several ranks of Angels, sometimes benevolent but more often the implacable ministers of God's terrible wrath, as monsters. Clearly they had to be treated as a separate category of beings and this made it possible to consider the heraldic function of all the heavenly host. Most of them, from the Holy Trinity to the Devil, have such heraldic connections. The former was represented and identified by an ingenious heraldic diagram and this, as well as anthropomorphic representations of the Trinity, was carried in state on the great ceremonial banners used in peace and as battle flags in war by our pious ancestors, whether to bolster the morale of a Crusade or in the solemn obsequies of a grand funeral; while Satan, that monster to out-monster all monsters, turns out to be a respectably armigerous gentleman.

When one comes to the earthbound beings and creatures of heraldry the problem of their classification arises: they must be grouped in a way that is both logical and easy of reference, yet any such grouping must in the nature of things be rather arbitrary. Are the Harpy, the Pegasus and the Dragon creatures of the land or air; and where should one put the Winged Sea-Lion or the Winged Sea-Unicorn? I have, therefore, placed them according to their most notable characteristic; thus a fairly large group of land, sea and air creatures can be grouped together because they have some prominent human characteristic, if only a head and face, in their make-up. For this reason the Griffin comes among the fabulous birds because his foreparts and wings are those of an eagle, while the Harpy rubs shoulders with the Mermaid, the Mantyger and the Satyr.

There are, however, certain creatures whose physical forms are credible but which have some fabulous attribute, such as the Panther Incensed, the Phoenix and the Salamander, who are not really chimerical monsters; but I felt one could be forgiven for stretching a point by regarding the flames with which each is indissolubly associated as an incongruous juxtaposition of elements. Anyway they are among the most decorative of the creatures which have excited the heraldic imagination and it would be a pity to let them escape. While the Bonacon is somewhat lacking in charm, his truly remarkable defensive mechanism has ludicrously incongruous if incendiary characteristics, so he too has been included. By the same token, although the Beaver of the Middle Ages is based on a garbled version of the real thing, his heraldic appearance and his curious method of escaping his foes demands his inclusion too. As the purpose of this book is to illustrate the heralds' approach to their art by examining their employment of these fabulous beings and creatures in heraldry, it is not my intention, nor is there the space available, to do more than touch briefly on their mythological or literary origins nor indeed do I pretend to include all of them in my survey; but the provenance of these creatures will be apparent in the passages which discuss them. I have sought, whenever possible, to illustrate my subject matter with the best and earliest examples available, so that the reader may have some idea of the way in which they were rendered during the golden age of armory. Only if a later example is of particular interest or artistic merit have I included it.

So much for the contents of this book. It has attempted a new approach to an old subject, which my limitations prevent me from treating as comprehensively as it deserves. One must, therefore, regard this as a pilot operation, which one hopes will encourage others to follow up. As a working herald, like all one's predecessors since heralds first appeared on the scene in the twelfth century, one is better able to discuss armory in its many manifestations and applications and to talk about the heralds in action, so I have tried to illustrate the problem by looking at it through eyes of the medieval heralds and the writers of the early heraldic treatises. A consideration of the heraldic imagination helps to give us a pointer to the wider question of the place in medieval society and literature of the heralds and armory, and as an indication of what made the heralds tick.

There are some who believe heraldry to be a subject fit only for pedants and snobs, but armory and its allied art of genealogy are more than the footnotes to history. Not only have the colourful threads of heraldry run through the fabric of European history from the earliest times – they still bring a lively significance to state occasions and the daily activities of corporations and the lives of individuals – but there is a growing awareness of the light heraldry can cast on many a murky corner of past politics. Naturally there is an aristocratic undercurrent to it, but there is also a freedom of imagination and expression and a certain inconsequential abandon, together with an uninhibitedly robust approach which the heralds have always had towards their art. While they have always been conscious of the dignity and importance of 'the noble office of arms', our predecessors have usually approached the subject of armory itself in a fairly light-hearted way, for it has always been a cheerful as well as weighty matter.

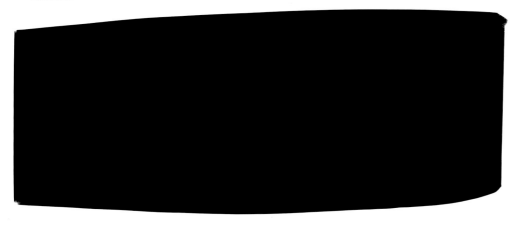

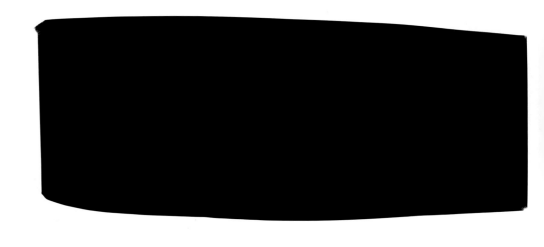

Part I
The Heralds and Armory

1
The Beginninge and Grownde of Armes

ERALDRY, strictly speaking, embraces all the duties of a herald, although 'heraudie' was already acquiring its modern connotation as early as the beginning of the fourteenth century. Throughout the Middle Ages we find the heralds employed as staff officers in war, directly responsible to the constable (the commander-in-chief) and the marshal (roughly corresponding to the adjutant-general of modern times), as well as being more or less permanently employed in the households of all the European kings and greater barons. In peacetime they proclaimed and organised tournaments, those colourful schools for war, where they also assisted the judges. On many occasions we see them acting as envoys between sovereigns or the commanders of warring armies, when they enjoyed diplomatic immunity and their persons were sacrosanct – indeed, even today it is still treason to kill an English herald when he is wearing his sovereign's tabard. The concern of the heralds with the personal devices and cognisances of the nobility and gentry, now one of the principal activities of the English and Scottish heralds, arose from their armorial duties in wars and tournaments; while their present-day responsibility for the planning, organising and marshalling of the great ceremonies of State grew from their duties as royal officers.

It is these men whose imagination was responsible for the development of later medieval armory and its flamboyant growth in the sixteenth century, and it is their hands which we can detect in the employment of the fabulous and chimerical creatures of heraldry. Let us, therefore, glance briefly at these colourful, efficient and sometimes eccentric men, to see how their origins and their many different duties and activities, so closely interwoven with the military, social and literary life of the times in which they lived, influenced their approach to armory.

By the time of the First Crusade the normal tactic of European warfare was the massed cavalry charge of the mail-clad horsemen, the knights, and mounted men-at-arms who, with lance 'of ash and apple beam' held under the right arm (although earlier they were often thrown over-arm) and shield and reins held by the left hand, would thunder down upon the enemy, relying on the combined weight of horse and rider behind the lance to shatter him. *The Chanson de Roland* has many references to the deadly effect of the Frankish lance:

> Buckler nor byrny avails against him now,
> Into the midriff lance point and pennon plough,
> From breast to back the shaft runs through and out,
> A whole spear's length he hurls him dead on ground.[1]

Duke William at the Battle of Hastings with his standard-bearer beside him (drawn by N. Manwaring from the Bayeux Tapestry)

The renowned Frankish charge (Anna Comnena, who was living in Constantinople at the time of the First Crusade, described it as irresistible) was feared and respected by all Saracen armies, but it was essentially a movement which could be executed only once. If the enemy had not been shattered and scattered, the broken lances would be thrown aside and the line of battle dissolved into a mêlée of loose individual hand-to-hand engagements which the army commander was unable effectively to control since he was usually fighting in the thick of it himself.

In these circumstances, it soon became obvious that a simple system of personal devices, or 'conoisances' as they were termed, was essential if the commanders of armies and of subordinate units were to exercise any control over the knights, men-at-arms, archers and infantry under their command. A flag was necessary in order that the scattered members of the unit could re-form around it. The *Chanson de Roland* describes an early Geoffrey of Anjou as carrying into battle the Oriflamme, the sacred red flag of the Abbey of St. Denis which was used as the battle flag of the French, and last carried in war at the Battle of Agincourt. The *Chanson* also relates that the Moorish Emir had his Dragon standard borne before his army, but that Ogier the Dane 'the dragon-bearer with furious force assails and sends him crashing Dragon and ensign and all upon the plain'.[2]

When Duke William of Normandy was planning the invasion of England he enlisted the support of the Pope, who sent him a consecrated banner, but unfortunately its design is not known. The Bayeux Tapestry illustrates William, accompanied by a banner-bearer holding a lance-flag, or gonfanon, with a cross upon it, during his invasion of Brittany in 1064. This was evidently his battle flag for it is shown carried by his banner-bearer two years later at the Battle of Hastings. We also know that King Harold marked his command post at the Battle of Hastings with the Dragon standard of Wessex and his personal banner of the Fighting Man; the former being shown in the Bayeux Tapestry in the scene in which he is struck down by the Norman knights at the end of the battle.

That these command flags were sufficiently distinctive to be readily recognised in the heat of battle is illustrated by Anna Comnena's account of a battle in 1083 between a force commanded by Bohemond of Taranto and an Imperial force under Ouzas, which was routed. In the fight Ouzas speared Bohemond's standard bearer and, snatching the banner from his hands, waved it round and then pointed it towards the ground. The Normans, puzzled by the sight of the lowered banner, turned in confusion along another route and the resourceful Ouzas escaped.[3] The anonymous knight who wrote the *Gesta Francorum*, that

Death of King Harold beside the Dragon Standard of Wessex (drawn by N. Manwaring from the Bayeux Tapestry)

lively eye-witness chronicle of the First Crusade, tells us that Bohemond had his own distinctive banner, as did his nephew Tancred, and Raymond of St. Gilles and Gaston of Bearn, but, alas, no precise description is given of any of them. In the early Middle Ages these command flags were usually in the form of a lance-flag or gonfanon, with little streamers from the fly; by the end of the twelfth century the command flags of knights-banneret and higher commanders were in the form of a banner – which was at that time a rectangular flag, the height being almost twice its width; but by the later Middle Ages they had become more nearly square – while the pennon remained the flag of the ordinary knight.

Before long the kings, army commanders and barons were painting personal devices on their shields and using similar emblems on their seals. Later in the Middle Ages these personal devices were also painted on the front and back of the linen surcoats which they wore over their armour – hence the coat of arms or coat armour. This would enable a commander's men to keep an eye on him in the heat of battle, and so observe and follow his hand signals or shouted orders. Without the aid of such cognisances, any cohesion or control would have been almost impossible to maintain and the distinction between friend and foe difficult to establish, since, on European battlefields, all were encased in similar armour.

The Bayeux Tapestry shows us many Norman knights holding shields, some of which are decorated with wavy geometrical designs and others with designs somewhat resembling curious dragon-like creatures; but neither William the Conqueror nor any of his subordinate commanders used devices that later became hereditary in any of their families. It is, however, not without interest that the Great Seals of the Conqueror's younger son, King Henry I, and Henry's successor on the throne, King Stephen, show them holding lances with gonfanons bearing somewhat similar crosses to that depicted on William's gonfanon in the Bayeux Tapestry. It would seem, therefore, that these were command flags and that the design painted on them in these early days was not necessarily the same as that painted on the shield. An interesting early example of this is to be seen in the *Eneide des Heinrich von Veldeke,* written about 1180, in which knights are depicted carrying banners with devices which are different from those on their shields.[1] A later example is that of Simon de Montfort, Earl of Leicester (d. 1265), who used a simple banner, *Party per pale indented argent and gules,* while the arms painted on his shield were *Argent a lion rampant queue fourchée gules.* A stained-glass window in Chartres Cathedral depicts two members of this family with these arms and a banner *Party per pale indented gules and argent.* In his seal John, King of Bohemia

27

De Montfort arms and banner (drawn by N. Manwaring from a window in Chartres Cathedral)

(a) Seal of John, King of Bohemia and Poland, and Count of Luxembourg (1296–1346)
(b) Seal of Rudolf IV, Archduke of Austria (1358–65)
(c) Seal of Ernest, Duke and Elector of Saxony (1464–86)
All these show them carrying banners which are materially different from their personal arms on their shields (Society of Antiquaries Collection of Seal casts)

and Count of Luxembourg (1296–1346), holds a shield of an Eagle displayed and a banner of a Lion rampant, while the seal of Rudolf IV, Archduke of Austria (died 1365) shows him with a shield of the Hapsburg arms, *Gules a fess argent* and holding a banner of a Lion rampant.

At first only the kings and commanders-in-chief of feudal armies and the counts and barons commanding subordinate contingents appear to have used devices on their shields, while the ordinary knights used plain shields. Anna Comnena, who met the leaders of the First Crusade (her description of Bohemond is one of the most arresting thumb-nail sketches of any man), described the armour of the crusaders, and added that it was 'supplemented by a shield, not round but long, broad at the top and tapering to a point; inside it is slightly curved; the outside is smooth and shiny and it has a flashing bronze boss.' It seems unlikely that such an acute observer would have omitted to mention it if their shields had been painted with different identifying devices, for her detailed descriptions of battles show a keen appreciation of military

(a)

(b)

(c)

matters.[5] The anonymous author of the *Gesta Stephani,* describing the siege of Exeter Castle in 1136, tells us how Joel of Totnes slipped in unnoticed through the king's men surrounding the Castle, 'for among so many clad in mail it was impossible easily to distinguish one from another' and brought reinforcements to the garrison.[6] It is clear, therefore, that the ordinary knights, who were not army or divisional commanders, were not then, in England at any rate, using personal or group armorial devices on their shields and surcoats, even if they did so on their pennons.

Sir Anthony Wagner, Garter King of Arms, has defined true heraldry as the systematic use of hereditary devices centred on the shield, with the corollary that national and personal devices without the element of inheritance are therefore not heraldry.[7] With the exception of the royal arms of the United Kingdom, which are not automatically inherited by the children of the Sovereign, but have to be specially assigned by Royal Warrant with suitable differences in each case, this definition is basically true of modern European armory, and has probably held good since the early years of the thirteenth century, if not earlier. Before that, however, there was quite a long period during which the laws and usages of armory were being evolved, and during which it is impossible to say with any certainty when devices used on seals, for example, became used on shields and banners, or in what order this happened. There is an appreciable length of time before we can say definitely that these early devices, depicted on banners, lance-pennons, and shields in a recognisably heraldic manner, actually became hereditary. It would seem, therefore, better to call this early formative time the period of proto-heraldry, whose tentative beginnings can be faintly discerned in the latter half of the eleventh century and which overlapped true heraldry into the thirteenth century. This in turn has, of course, some bearing on the earliest heraldic use of the fabulous creatures of armory.

That there should be a period of some confusion and contradiction in armorial practice is, after all, not surprising, for human institutions usually take time to develop and become systematised. Many modern writers on heraldry have been too apt to assume that it was the knights who evolved the rules of armory; but those of us who took part in the last war know that soldiers are not particularly interested in the finer points of heraldry; all they want is a distinctive device to put on shield and banner, or on battle-dress and army vehicles. The majority of the signs adopted during the last war by the divisional or corps commanders in the British armies flouted one or more of the rules of heraldry, and it was, surely, no different in the early formative years of proto-heraldry.

The Arthurian romances of Chrétien de Troyes, for example, show a remarkably untidy approach to heraldry, and they were written for the delectation of the barons and knights who were using armory in a practical and functional way in their daily lives. It was the tidy minds of the heralds, the lawyers and the writers of heraldic treatises which gradually brought order to the rather haphazard armorial practice of the early knights and evolved in time an internationally recognised system and terminology.

The important part which knighthood played in the social and military life of the Middle Ages had, by the early twelfth century, given rise to an appropriately solemn and dignified ceremonial for the creation of the new knight. Not only did the lord who dubbed him present him with his armour and weapons, but he also invested him with a shield painted with the new knight's heraldic device. An early illustration of this was the knighting of young Geoffrey of Anjou (he was only fifteen at the time) by King Henry I in 1127, prior to his marriage to the Empress Matilda, Henry's daughter. Geoffrey came to Rouen accompanied by five barons and twenty-five squires. On arrival he was examined by Henry on the duties of a knight and then

The armorial shield with which Geoffrey of Anjou was invested in 1123 by Henry I of England (drawing by N. Manwaring from his memorial brass, now in Le Mans Museum)

29

conducted to his rooms, where he took a ceremonial bath, after which he was clothed in gorgeous robes and shoes on which had been embroidered golden lions. The next day the ceremony took place, when Henry invested him with a hauberk and shoes of mail and hung a shield painted with little golden lions about his neck; thereafter he was presented with a spear, a magnificent sword, and a war-horse. The ceremony was followed by much jousting and junketing. The enamel portrait of Geoffrey, who shortly afterwards succeeded as Count of Anjou, holding his blue shield with the six rampant golden lions upon it, which was placed on his tomb in 1151, is now in the Museum at Le Mans in France. The interesting thing about this knighting of Geoffrey Plantagenet is that it seems to indicate that even so great a magnate as the Count of Anjou had at that time no definitely established hereditary armorial device of his own, indissolubly associated with his family and his county.

This blue shield with the six golden lioncels (as they were called when more than three) is frequently quoted as the earliest example of true hereditary heraldry, but it was clearly not so regarded at the time. There is no evidence that Geoffrey's eldest son Henry, afterwards King Henry II of England, ever used these arms (although there is some indication that he may have used two lions), nor does it seem that his younger son Geoffrey used them. Henry's bastard son by the fair Rosamund, William Longespee, Earl of Salisbury, at first used a single lion rampant for his arms (possibly based on those of his father-in-law, William fitz Patrick, the late Earl) and only later adopted his grandfather's coat of the blue shield with the six little lions; so Geoffrey of Anjou's shield must really be regarded as typical of the period of proto-heraldry, when armorial bearings were being evolved and used in a recognisably heraldic way without necessarily being hereditary.

Even King Richard I had no hesitation in drastically changing his arms, after his first Great Seal had been 'lost for a time and was in another's power while we were in captivity in Almaine'. His arms had probably been two lions combatant, rampant and facing each other,[8] which he changed in about 1195 to the three gold leopards on a red field : these have remained the royal arms of England ever since. There are other examples of lords and knights altering their arms, well into the fourteenth century, and this must make us cautious in thinking of early armory as a precise science. The more rigid rules and procedures which we know today were evolved by later generations.

Probable arms of Richard I, as borne by him on the Third Crusade (drawing by Miss A. Urwick)

From an early period the Emperor and the other European kings were granting arms as a corollary to ennoblement; and there is evidence that army commanders also granted arms on the field of battle, evidently in connection with knighting a retainer for valour. The judges of tournaments, with the advice of the heralds, could also assign arms to those wishing to take part and who were not already armigerous. In 1389 an English soldier, John be Kyngeston, had been challenged to a joust by a French knight and, in order to enable him to accept it, King Richard II 'received him into the estate of Gentleman and have made him Esquire, and will that he be known by Arms and bear them henceforth'. In England the armigerous gentleman and esquire has always been regarded as the equivalent of the continental nobleman.

There is an interesting early Tudor example of arms being conferred as a corollary to knighthood. Wiston Browne, of Rookwood Hall in Essex, was a soldier of fortune who took service under King Ferdinand of Spain and fought with distinction against the Moors. As a result of his outstanding services King Ferdinand knighted him and granted him, on 15 September 1511, an augmentation of honour to his arms of a black Spread-eagle facing to the sinister, crowned and armed gold. Browne returned to England and lost no time in regularising the position, matriculating the text of Ferdinand's letters-patent in the official registers of the College of Arms. The kings of arms were, however, somewhat at a loss as to the family arms, upon which the augmentation of honour had to be

First and Second Great Seals of Richard I (F. Sandford, *op. cit.*, p. 55)

placed, but they managed to discover a typically Tudor coat which they 'confirmed' to Sir Wiston Browne – namely, *Gules a Chevron between three Lion's gambs erased, a Chief and a Bordure argent* – and then placed the black Spreadeagle on the Chief. They made no difficulty about recognising his knighthood. Sir Henry Guilford, of Haldon in the parish of Rolvendon in Kent, a friend of King Henry VIII, who later held many important official appointments in England, similarly 'had his Armes enobled with a Canton of Grenado by Ferdinand, King of Spayne, for his worthy service in that Kingdome when it was recovered from the Moores'.[9] He too hastened to get this confirmed by the English kings of arms, and we find his arms recorded in the College of Arms with the pomegranate of Grenada on an argent canton.

As early as 1375 Parliament had enacted that troops raised for the French wars were to be dressed in a uniform manner, and some ten years later, at the Battle of Poitiers, the army of the Black Prince wore uniforms of green and white. At the Battle of Agincourt in 1415, Henry V ordained that 'every man, of what estate or condition, that be of our partie, [should] beare a bande of Seint George sufficient large' upon his clothes.[10] The commanding officers, bannerets, and knights would also wear a surcoat of the family arms in battle: there are many references to them putting on their surcoats of arms, on the orders of the King or commander-in-chief just before battle was joined, and they took off their coats of arms directly they were stood down. In the same way, the banners were unfurled at the beginning of a battle and furled again when it was over.

While the kings, dukes and greater tenants-in-chief, who enjoyed almost sovereign powers within their own territories, undoubtedly assumed arms of their own volition, it is clear that the proliferation of armorial devices soon led to a growing measure of control. The great popularity of tournaments, in which knights of every degree took part, as well as the increasingly weighty and enveloping armour which totally hid the knights' faces, no doubt also led the junior

Sir Simon de Felbrigge, K.G., standard-bearer to King Richard II, showing the proportions of banners in the late 14th century (from his brass in Felbrigg Church, Norfolk)

Opposite page
The melee of an early medievel battle, depicted by Matthew Paris in the *Chronica Majora,* compiled shortly after 1245. It purports to show King Harold defeating Tostig and the King of Norway at the Battle of Stamford Bridge in 1066, but the armour and attributed heraldry are of the 13th century. This scene includes the earliest appearance of a Mermaid in armory, on the shield and horse-trapper of the central figure, but it is not known who is supposed to be indicated by this. (Cambridge University Library ms. Ee. iii, 59, f. 32ᵛ)

knights to use, both in battle and in tournament, some kind of personal identifying device, and this soon needed to be regulated. During the latter half of the thirteenth century there were only about 2,000 men who would qualify for knighthood, while the 'strenuous knights' – those regularly on active service – were even fewer. The Parliamentary Roll, compiled about 1310, gives only the names and arms of 1110 throughout the kingdom.

There are many instances, from early in the Middle Ages, of quarrels between knights who found themselves bearing identical arms on campaign or at a tournament, and these bitter bickerings would have led to a breakdown in good order and military discipline. Such cases would normally be tried by the Court of the Constable and Marshal (also known in England as the Court of Chivalry, and which is still in existence and still presided over by the Earl Marshal) with the heralds as expert witnesses, who also proclaimed its judgements.

So much for the origin of armorial devices, or the 'beginninge and grownde of armes', as several of the fifteenth-century heraldic treatises described it. The origin of the heralds must next engage our attention, and we will see how their development of the art of armory eventually led to the extravagant flowering of the heraldic imagination.

Murat
du lac
deuon
Browne
hardy
Jernyghan
lucy
brise
pethin
Beaumont
Descarb

vrses
Lescu
Montagu
momorancy
haward
broke
ŷbrise
choiſy
beaumont

le Duc de vendofme
le Duc de Suffolke
le conte de Sht pol
le marquis Dorset

la Rochepot
Meſſire William Kyngeſton
Grpon
Meſſire Rychard Je

2
The Heralds
as Army Staff Officers

FIFTEENTH-CENTURY writer on armory believed that 'in the early days of heraldry comely girls were appointed to run to and fro between the opposing armies as messengers, whom everyone favoured because of their sex, but as these girls were often pregnant it was arranged that the older soldiers, riding in chariots, should mediate between contesting armies in place of the girls. Nevertheless, when they in turn said they could not stand the pace, it was arranged that noble and distinguished young men should assume the duties of heralds instead.'[1] The origins and occupational hazards of the heraldic profession are, fortunately, somewhat different today, although equally fascinating.

It is just possible that the earliest European herald to be mentioned in history was Male Couronne (*Mala Corona*), a serjeant on the staff of Bohemond, who was commanding the crusading army at the assault on Antioch on 2 June 1098. Having secretly arranged with a disaffected Turkish captain of a section of the walls to admit his men that night, Bohemond sent Male Couronne 'as a herald' round the camp, to order the various units of the army to be ready at sunset, giving as a reason that they were to set out on a raid into enemy territory. This tantalising reference cannot, alas, be accepted as firm evidence that Male Couronne was actually a herald, but it does seem odd that this serjeant (the rank below a knight) should bear a name similar to the heraldic titles which we find regularly bestowed on pursuivants later in the Middle Ages, such as Bon Rapport, and Sans Repose Pursuivants. Whatever he was, the author of the *Gesta Francorum*, who was himself a knightly vassal of Bohemond and formed one of the selected band who accompanied him at the assault, uses the word *preco* in describing Male Couronne's duties, a word which was normally employed in the twelfth century for a herald of arms.[2]

It has been persuasively argued by the two foremost authorities on the early heralds, that they were recruited from the ranks of the minstrels. It has, too, been shown that some thirteenth century Kings of Heralds are found in other contemporary account rolls in receipt of royal largess and described as Kings of Minstrels. Obviously not all minstrels would either wish to become heralds or be qualified to do so, for no doubt the famous troubadours, whose songs so enchanted the courts of love over which Queen Eleanor of Aquitaine presided, would find sufficient employment there and, in any case, would probably have been too unreliable to be used as military staff officers. On the other hand the minstrels who specialised in the bardic kind of songs, reciting the family

Jousting-cheque or score-sheet for one of the jousts held during the festivities at the Field of the Cloth of Gold in June 1520. The score-sheet is headed by the Royal Arms of King Francis I of France and King Henry VIII of England, with below them the arms of some of the jousters. The top of the sheet shows the method of scoring. (Soc. Antiqs. ms. 136, part 2, f. 1)

33

histories of their patrons and the great deeds of arms done by contemporary and past heroes, would have knowledge which could be put to good purpose in the field of battle.

While the heralds of the early Middle Ages would no doubt have been recruited from several different walks of life, the essential requirement was that they should be literate, which is why one of the obvious sources for their recruitment would be the minstrels, the troubadours of the sunny southern lands of Provence and Aquitaine and their later followers the trouvères of Normandy and northern France, and the minnesingers of the Empire and the German principalities. These minstrels played a large part in the literary life of the twelfth century, under the active patronage of people like that brilliant and wayward character William the Troubadour, Duke of Aquitaine, his granddaughter Queen Eleanor of Aquitaine and her son King Richard the Lion Heart, himself an accomplished troubadour. Before long the heralds, because of their close and constant association with the feudal leaders in peace and war, developed separately from the minstrels, and we find some jealousy among the latter at the success of their erstwhile colleagues.

This brilliant and imaginative society of the troubadours, minstrels, scholars and clerks would be the common experience of the early medieval heralds, and piety, symbolism and lively design would be mingled in the heraldic imagination to serve the stark and practical necessities of war. Bertrand de Born, one of the most famous of the knightly troubadours who then graced Queen Eleanor's sophisticated court at Poitiers, has left us an echo of this colourful and exciting age.

> I love the medley of blazons
> Enamelled scarlet, gold and blue,
> The standards and the gonfanons
> Painted every vivid hue;
> I love the tents that decorate the field,
> I love to break a lance or pierce a shield,
> Or cleave a helm and call on foes to yield.[3]

The troubadours were only one aspect of a remarkable and exciting century, a century in which the foundations were being laid on which the universities

Creation of a Pursuivant in the 15th century. A drawing by Robert Glover in his copy of Baddesworth's version of *De Studio Militari* (Coll. Arms ms. Vinc. 444, f. 163)

34

Creation of a Knight in the 15th century. A drawing by Robert Glover (*op. cit.*, f. 171)

of Bologna, Paris and Oxford were to grow and the building of the great cathedrals and churches of Europe was begun. The twelfth-century renaissance also called into being the colourful and vigorous designs of heraldry, to adorn and unite the worlds of action, piety and scholarship.

The world in which the heralds lived was an aristocratic world, the world of rights and duties, chivalry and romance. When the feudal concept of society was emerging towards the end of the Dark Ages, the bearing of weapons was the prerogative only of free men, and the bestowal of weapons on a young man symbolised his acceptance into the military society of Europe. In the early centuries of chivalry any knight could dub and invest with sword, lance, shield, hauberk and spurs any other free man. As time went on knighthood became regarded as a chivalric confraternity, as 'an honourable office above all offices, orders, and estate of the world'.

Ramón Lull, a Spanish knight who was Seneschal of King James II of Aragon for many years, and subsequently entered the Church and became a missionary to the Moors of North Africa, being martyred there, wrote the *Book of the Order of Chivalry* in about 1280, a work which remained popular throughout Europe until the sixteenth century. According to Lull, a knight should be nobly born, and also rich enough to bear the expenses of his rank, lest he be driven by need to crime; nor should he be maimed or over-fat. He should be lord over many men, 'for in seygnorye is moch noblesse'. While he had rights and privileges, he also had duties and responsibilities and must therefore be just and humble, but few of us manage to live up to our ideals and Lull already lamented the shortcomings of the knights of his time.[4]

As warfare became more sophisticated it became essential for the commander of an army to build up a picture of the enemy's order of battle if he was to fight him effectively, and this entailed the correct identification of the enemy commander-in-chief and his subordinate commanders. In the early Middle Ages the feudal service by which the barons held their fiefs of their King would be generally known; thus, if the King of France went to war

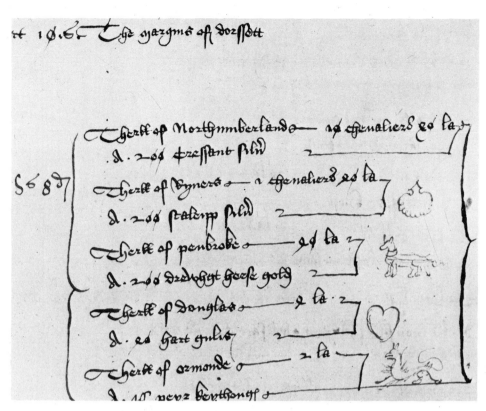

A page from Barnard's Book of Badges, the muster roll of Edward IV's expedition to France in 1475 (Coll. Arms ms. 2nd M.16, f. xvi)

and called up half the feudal service, it would be possible to deduce the size of the force brought into the field under the command of a particular baron.

This the heralds were able to do through their expert knowledge of the banners, armorial devices and badges used by the feudal leaders. Later, when contract service superseded feudal service, it would become important to discover the terms of the contract between the King and his commanders, and this the heralds could no doubt do, by reason of the fact that they were constantly travelling about Europe with contacts in every court. So here again the correct identification of the enemy commanders would enable the herald to brief his own commander on the strength of the force opposed to him. The heralds were also employed in drawing up the muster rolls of their own side; these were sometimes in the form of written lists of names, with the arms blazoned (that is, described in heraldic terms), sometimes in verse and sometimes with the arms beautifully illustrated in colour.

This close association of armory and warfare is also brought out in many of the earlier treatises on war and armory. *L'Arbre des Batailles,* written between 1382 and 1387 by Honoré Bonet, which became almost compulsory reading for medieval heralds and was extensively copied over the next century, consisted of four parts: the first of twelve short chapters, mainly introductory; the second of nineteen chapters, mainly historical; the third of eight chapters, dealing with the qualities of a soldier; and the fourth of one hundred and thirty two chapters, dealing with the laws and customs of war. This last part contains only six chapters dealing with the rules and usages of armory. *Le Livre des Faits D'Armes et de Chevalerie,* which that formidable woman Christine de Pisan wrote some thirty years later, also consisted of four parts, each divided into a large number of chapters on the laws and art of war; but again, with only a few chapters on armory tacked on at the end. With Nicholas Upton, who wrote the *De Studio Militari* about 1446, we still have the treatise arranged in four books, the first and second dealing with military matters and the laws and usages of war; but now the whole of the third and fourth books deal with armorial matters.

Although the heralds still continued to act as military staff-officers, they were increasingly employed as ambassadors, enjoying diplomatic immunity, and

36

the two functions were becoming incompatible. The dilemma is well illustrated by a letter written in about 1400 by Anjou King of Arms, deploring the way in which pursuivants abused their immunity to spy out the military plans of their masters' enemies. He evidently felt that collation and analysis of information on the enemy's order of battle was permissible, but that obtaining it by spying in person was carrying things too far and did not become an officer of arms. He laments the fact that in France the captains of every little castle and even petty knights now appointed their own pursuivants: the country, he felt, was going to the dogs.[5]

The diplomatic status of the heralds gave them a community of interest that transcended national frontiers, and, like diplomats today, they regarded heralds of other countries as *chères collègues*. Jean le Fevre, afterwards Toison d'or King of Arms, who was present at the Battle of Agincourt in 1415, tells us that the French and English heralds stood in a group together, observing the battle and keeping the tally of the lords, knights, and squires who were killed.[6] At the end of the battle King Henry V sent for the principal French herald, Montjoye King of Arms, and asked him to whom the victory belonged, to himself or the King of France; Montjoye replied that 'the victory must be attributed to him and not to the King of France'.[7] When King Edward IV mobilised his army in 1475 'in his service of Guerre into his Duchie of Normandye and his Realme of Fraunce', the muster roll shows that Garter, Clarenceux, Norroy, and March Kings of Arms, together with an unspecified number of heralds and pursuivants, formed part of his staff. Garter's pay on active service was 4s. a day, the same as a baron and a banneret, while the three other kings of arms received 2s. 4d. a day; the heralds' pay was 2s. a day, the same as a knight's; and the pursuivants got 1s. 6d. a day, rather better than a squire or man-at-arms, who got 1s. a day.[8] While the heralds of England by this time were undoubtedly playing a very active part in the granting and control of arms, it seems unlikely that they were mobilised for active service, at rather high rates of army pay, only for armorial duties, and we must conclude that they were there as military staff-officers as well.

3
Tournaments
and the Heralds

KNIGHTS need regular training in the handling of their weapons and horses, and in fighting in formation, if they are to play their part effectively in war. The tournament, which was early believed to have been invented by Godfrey de Preuilly, (who was killed taking part in one in 1062), served just this purpose, and by the middle of the twelfth century it had become so popular in France that it was called, for long afterwards, the *conflictus Gallicus.* The contemporary biographer of William the Marshal tells us that an enthusiastic knight-errant could travel around Europe attending a different tournament every two weeks.[1] In 1177 William and another knight, Roger de Gaugi, entered into a partnership and travelled from tournament to tournament for two years, gaining much renown and capturing no less than one hundred and three knights in ten months – and incidentally making a handsome profit, as the defeated knight usually had to surrender his armour and horse and pay a ransom.

The heralds were given all the broken armour as their perquisite, which explains why William the Marshal was so popular with them and why he was usually followed, from one tournament to the next, by a group of heralds extolling his merits. From an early period we find the heralds responsible for proclaiming and organising tournaments, and they soon became the experts whose job it was to identify the contestants from the devices painted on their lance-pennons, banners and shields. One can see how these ever-moving groups of knights and heralds would soon spread the usages and conventions of heraldry to all European countries.

The earliest definite mention of a herald in an armorial context is by Chrétien de Troyes, who wrote his Arthurian romance, *Le Chevalier de la Charette,* between 1164 and 1172 at the behest of Marie, Countess of Champagne, a famous patron of the troubadours. The story goes that Lancelot, having been released on parole from durance in order to take part in a tournament, arrived at the place of assembly and lodged in a small and lowly house, as he did not wish to be recognised, for his prowess was such that few would otherwise challenge him. He placed the vermilion shield lent him by his captor's lady outside the door of his lodging, as was the custom, and then lay down on the bed, A herald of arms (*héraut d'armes*) arrived running barefoot and clad only in his shirt, because he had pledged his clothes and shoes at the tavern. He saw the shield hanging outside the door but did not recognise it, since the arms were not Lancelot's own; however, he immediately recognised Lancelot, and rushed out crying 'Now has come one who will take the measure of everyone!' but at Lancelot's request refused to divulge his name.[2] Chrétien de Troyes adds in an aside, 'this herald was the master of us all, when he taught us to use the phrase, for he was the first to make use of it', which suggests that the story was based on an actual incident. It even led Gaston Paris to suggest that Chrétien himself may have been a herald, but this seems to be stretching it too far.

There is more of armorial interest in this story, a little further on in the action, when the Queen, her damsels and knightly onlookers are discussing the contestants. 'Do you see that knight yonder with a golden band across the middle of his shield? That is Governauz of Roberdic. And do you see that other one, who has an eagle and a dragon painted side by side upon his shield? That is the son of the King of Aragon, who has come to this land in search of glory and renown.' So they continue, identifying the different shields, including 'yonder shield [which] is of English workmanship and was made at London; you see on it two swallows which appear as if about to fly, yet they do not move, but receive many blows from the Poitevin lances of steel; he who has it is poor Thoas'.

It is interesting that Chrétien de Troyes' fictional herald, living from hand to mouth like the wandering students and minstrels of the twelfth century, was already described in about 1165 as a *héraut d'armes* and was expected to be knowledgeable about armorial cognaisances and devices. Clearly the heralds of arms had been in existence for some time, because the writer makes no attempt to explain him more fully, obviously taking it for granted that his readers will know all about heralds and enjoy the rather disreputable reference. We can, therefore, assume that heralds of arms, and not just heralds in the narrower sense of messengers or criers, were part of the medieval scene before the middle of the twelfth century. Now this is only some two generations after the First Crusade and one is emboldened to think that Male Couronne may, after all, have been a herald of arms – and his name suggests that he may have been as scruffy as the herald who was baffled by Lancelot's shield.

Our earliest herald in literature has a factual contemporary, who also makes his appearance in connection with a tournament: the young minstrel, lately made a herald of arms, who sang so persuasively to William the Marshal, at the tournament held at Joigny in about 1180, and was rewarded with a captured horse. Too much weight should not be given to the fact that the earliest references to heralds are in connection with tournaments. If, as has been suggested, their primary duties were those of military staff-officers, these would be taken for granted in the military community of the feudal barons and knights for whom the troubadours wrote, and would not merit particular mention. The tournament, however, was not only a training ground for knights, but also an exciting social occasion, when gaily-dressed ladies were present as spectators, with troubadours, minstrels and other hangers-on; and in consequence, the heralds, who were early involved in the arrangement and marshalling of tournaments, would attract attention because they were so much in evidence.

By the later twelfth century, we already find the lesser freemen and the burghers excluded from knighthood in most of the Continental countries, but in England there was always much more social mobility, even if the structure of society tended to be strongly hierarchical, and by the thirteenth century only the sons of knights, with rare exceptions, were eligible for the honour. Before long it became necessary to prove that all four great-grandfathers had been knights, if one wished to be of sufficient standing to take part in the major tournaments. Thus the equation between nobility of blood and armorial bearings was established, and what had been a by-product of the heralds'

Sir Edmund Tame, of Fairford, Gloucestershire, d. 1534, wearing his jousting coat of arms, from his brass in Fairford Church (Society of Antiquaries Croft-Lyons Bequest of armorial rubbings)

earlier military duties in war and tournaments became one of their principal concerns.

In the later Middle Ages, when the tournament had become a more formal social occasion, it was preceded by an inspection by the judges, assisted by one or more heralds of arms, of the crests of the participants: what the Germans called a *Helmshau*. There is a lively illustration of just such an inspection in the *Traité de la Forme et Devis d'un Tournoi*, written by the good King René in about 1465, which also gives an admirably detailed description of the duties of the heralds on these occasions.[3]

The nobility and gentry maintained an unabated enthusiasm for tournaments and jousts until the end of the sixteenth century; but by that time the armour and equipment had become so elaborate and costly, and the attendant pageantry and junketing so expensive, that only the very wealthy could afford to take part. The jousting cheques or score-sheets, kept by the English heralds and still among the archives of the College of Arms, indicate this, the names of the same men recurring time after time; and this state of affairs had probably existed since the late fourteenth century. The elaborate and flamboyant crests worn by the jousters were, therefore, heraldic status symbols, which indicated not only that the wearer was of tournament rank, with the requisite number of noble ancestors, but also that he could afford the expense. This explains why very few of the lesser gentry in England had crests before 1530, and it is mainly as crests, supporters, and badges that we find the fabulous and chimerical creatures of heraldry first making their appearance.

In his will, the Black Prince mentions his shield for war and his shield for peace: the former was the quarterly Royal Arms of England, with his label across it, while the latter was black with his three ostrich feathers shown separately upon it. The shield for peace was presumably used in jousts and tournaments and, as the Prince was widely regarded by his contemporaries as the pattern of chivalry, it is likely that this fashion of using two shields was followed by his friends and close adherents. It is possible that much the same thing happened with badges, the traditional family badge being used on the liveries of the family retainers and troops in war, while the more bizarre and fanciful creatures were used in tournaments and jousts.

4

Armory and Symbolism

HE literature of the Middle Ages contains many references to the symbolic importance of the shield and the device painted upon it. The anonymous author of *The Ancrene Riwle*, or Rule for Anchoresses, writing shortly after 1200, observes that 'in a shield there are three things, the wood, the leather, and the painting. So too in this shield (of Christ's Body): the wood of the cross, the leather which was God's Body, and the painting, the red blood which coloured it so fair. Then after the death of the brave knight, his shield is hung high in the church in his memory. And so is this shield, the crucifix, set in the church, where it may be most easily seen, that it may remind us of Jesus Christ's deed of knighthood on the cross'.[1] Ramón Lull, himself an experienced knight, writing about 1280, has much to say about the symbolism of knighthood, including the knight's shield and the armorial ensigns painted on it, 'wherefor every knyght ought to honoure his esseygnal, that he be kept fro blame, the whiche blame casteth the knyght and putteth him out of chyvalry'.[2]

In the eleventh century, and the beginning of the twelfth century, knights used long, narrow, kite-shaped shields, which covered most of the body. At first these shields had rounded tops (this type was used at the Battle of Hastings and in the First Crusade); later the tops were flat. They were made of wood covered with boiled leather – which dries very hard – the surface of which was painted with the knight's cognisance. We also know, from the story of *Sir Gawain and the Green Knight,* that knights sometimes painted the inner side of the shield with religious symbols, such as the image of the Virgin Mary.[3] Geoffrey of Monmouth, who wrote his *History of the Kings of Britain* in about 1138/39, also says that Arthur bore 'the shield that was named Pridwen, wherein, upon the inner side, was painted the image of holy Mary, Mother of God, that many a time and oft did call her back unto his memory'.[4]

The ensigns or cognisances painted upon their shields had a much greater significance to the men of the Middle Ages than we, in this less imaginative age, usually appreciate. Ramón Lull laid great stress on the significance and symbolism of knighthood. The ceremony of creating a new knight had, by his time, taken on something of the nature of a sacrament, in which the Church took an active part; and the ceremonial presentation to the new knight of his sword, spurs and shield, such as took place when King Henry I knighted Count Geoffrey of Anjou, gave rise to a particular symbolism in which feudal obligation, the calls of religion, and social duty were interwoven. It can

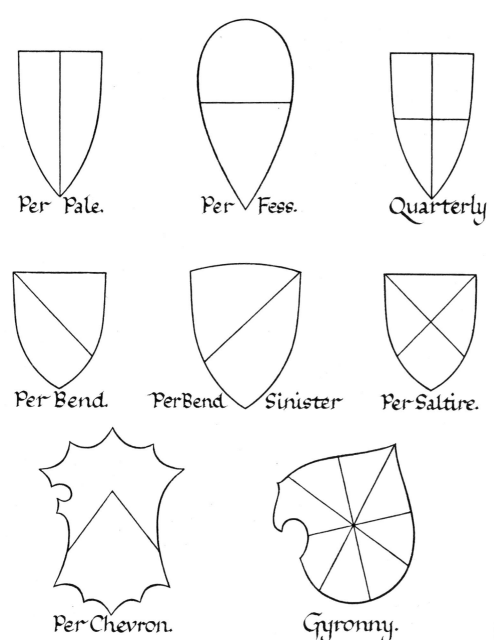

Per Pale.

Per Fess.

Quarterly

Per Bend.

Per Bend Sinister

Per Saltire.

Per Chevron.

Gyronny.

Shield shapes and party lines (drawn by G. Cobb)

therefore be seen that the device on a knight's shield would have a special significance and be regarded by him and his followers as his 'alter ego'.

In this connection, it is interesting that in the twelfth century the London craftsmen had a reputation for making good shields. Not only does Chrétien de Troyes make one of the onlookers at the tournament in which Lancelot distingushed himself say, 'Yonder shield is of English workmanship and was made at London', but in the romance of *Cligés,* the hero sends his squires to London to buy three suits of armour, together with three shields, one painted black, another red, and the third green.[5] These early romances show that shields rarely lasted long, usually being hacked to pieces by the end of a battle or tournament; this explains why no shields of the twelfth century have survived, in England at any rate.

By the thirteenth century, shields had become smaller and, with the more general use of plate armour in the following century, they continued to diminish. The all-enveloping heavy armour of the fifteenth century made shields unnecessary, while the greater penetrating power of the long-bow and the crossbow made them largely useless; but heraldic devices continued to be displayed on the knight's surcoat, on his lance-pennon and, when he was promoted to knight-banneret, on his banner. Although shields were seldom, if ever, used in battle after 1360, they continued to be used ceremonially, on parade, in tournaments and in jousts until the sixteenth century. As a consequence shields of more fanciful shape were developed, some of them very attractive; but the plain, simple lines of the fourteenth century shields maintained their popularity and they have continued to be used in heraldic art to the present day.

Completely plain shields or banners, with no charges upon them (the Oriflamme, the scarlet war flag of the French, is the most famous example), are extremely rare in heraldry, since the possibilities of differentiating the arms of one knight from another are too limited. In consequence, a method was soon evolved of dividing the surface of the shield by means of partition lines, so that when knights wished to use two or more different tinctures in their arms, either alone or in combination with one or several charges, they could do so in a systematic way. The partition lines of a shield readily lent themselves to further development: by turning them into broad bands they formed the Ordinaries, the basic geometrical figures charged upon the shields. The principal Ordinaries are the Pale, the Fess, the Cross, the Bend, the Bend Sinister, the Saltire, the Chevron and Gyronny, to which were added the Chief, the Canton, and the Pile, plus about two dozen Subordinaries. Most of the Ordinaries have diminutives which can be used in any reasonable number, while both the partition lines and the Ordinaries and Subordinaries can be further differentiated by making them wavy, nebuly, indented, engrailed, embattled, raguly, and so on, in a dozen or more different ways.

Before long, armory became a more precise science. By the thirteenth century, arms were becoming regarded as the property of a person or family, as incorporeal hereditaments, as well as being ensigns of hereditary noblesse. In consequence the heralds and lawyers found it necessary to describe a shield of arms in such a way that there could be no shadow of doubt as to what and whose it was, and thus a technical language, readily understood in all Western European countries, was evolved.

When blazoning a coat of arms one starts first with the tincture of the field, then the principal charge upon it, followed by charges of lesser importance, then any minor objects or figures which may be placed upon the principal charges, and finally marks of augmentation, cadency or distinction. The colour of the field of a heraldic shield is blazoned, or stated, first, because the symbolism of the colours used in heraldry was of considerable importance to the medieval mind, and it is here that we begin to enter the fanciful and allegorical world of the Middle Ages.

Thomas of Lancaster, Duke of Clarence, who was Constable of the Army in 1417, with authority over the heralds, is said to have ordained that the officers of arms were to apply themselves, inter alia, to the study of the properties of colours, herbs, and precious stones, so that they might be able properly and suitably to assign to each person the arms that should appropriately belong to him. We shall see that this echoes closely the views expressed in the heraldic treatises written at that time and earlier.

From very early times, certain qualities and attributes were assigned to particular colours. In the heraldic treatises of the fourteenth century, planets and jewels are associated with different tinctures and, by the following century, it became a regular convention to equate the metals and colours of heraldry with the sun, moon and planets, as well as with certain precious stones, and even with the days of the week.

The Anglo-Norman lapidaries were inspired by the *De Gemmis,* a late eleventh century Latin poem by Marbode, Bishop of Rennes, which enjoyed an immense vogue throughout the Middle Ages (more than one hundred and forty manuscript copies of it are still extant in English and Continental libraries). As such literature was mainly Anglo-Norman, it would tend to have

44

its greatest influence on the heralds of England and Normandy, and the symbolism of the precious and semi-precious stones would, in turn, exert a great influence on the colours of heraldry with which they were equated.

By the flamboyant days of the sixteenth century, the symbolism of heraldic colours had exploded into improbable fantasy, and the conventions by which they were blazoned had become so convoluted that the system eventually died of ridicule. Gerard Legh, in *The Accedens of Armory*, written in 1562, takes forty-eight pages to discuss it. In consequence, heraldic writers for the last two generations have tended to decry the importance of colour symbolism in the Middle Ages, taking the line that most of the early heraldic treatises were written by men who were not working heralds. We now know that most of these treatises were written either by heralds, or by clerics who were civil lawyers closely associated with heraldry. Moreover we shall see in the following chapter that heralds read these books, as did their masters. Although we need not go all the way with Gerard Legh and his complex system, by which each metal or colour has a different significance when combined with another in the same shield, there is no doubt that far more weight should be given to the importance of colour symbolism in heraldry in the Middle Ages.

The earliest heraldic treatise, the Anglo-Norman *De Heraudie,* originally written about 1300 and known to us from a late fourteenth-century transcript,[6] begins with the colours used in arms and states that it was the heralds' business to know the properties of these colours. By the time of Bartolo di Sasso Ferrato, whose *De Insigniis et Armis* was written about 1354, the properties and significance of the heraldic colours had become well established, and their use in arms systematised. In almost every heraldic treatise written subsequently, until well into the seventeenth century, the colours of heraldry are discussed, often at considerable length, and their symbolism and significance treated in detail.

The most important treatise produced during the Middle Ages on this subject was *Le blason des couleurs en armes,* written before 1437 by Jean Courtois, of Mons in Hainault, Sicily Herald of Arms and Marshal of Arms of Hainault, a herald of Alphonso V, King of Aragon and Sicily. His book enjoyed great

Sicily Herald of Arms, from *Le Blason des Couleurs en Armes* (drawn by N. Manwaring)

popularity at the time and subsequently, and a recent edition was produced, with a most useful introduction, by Hippolyte Cocheris. In his prologue, Sicily Herald tells us that he had composed his treatise at the request of his brother kings of arms and heralds. As one might expect, he draws on the Bible, Isidore of Seville, and the usual medieval sources. The treatise consists of two parts: the first describes how to blazon colours in armory, and the second defines colours in general and in particular, and discusses their properties.[7]

The principal tinctures used in medieval heraldry consisted of two metals, five colours and two furs: gold and silver; red, blue, black, green and purple; ermine and vair. By the fifteenth century we find tenne or orange, and murrey or sanguine added to the list of colours, together with some extremely rare and curious colours such as cendree or ash, and brunatre or brown; while the two furs could be depicted in half a dozen or more different ways, by changing the tinctures. A glance at each of the principal colours will give us a better idea of the medieval approach to heraldry.

GOLD

Usually blazoned as 'or', but in English heraldry it is also often blazoned as 'gold'. Bartolo di Sasso Ferrato describes gold as a nobler colour than the others, representing the light of the sun, and says that no-one is allowed to bear gold in his arms except princes. Honoré Bonet, writing some thirty years later, between 1382 and 1387, follows Bartolo and declares that 'the colour gold is the noblest in the world, because gold, of its nature, is bright and shining and full of virtue, and so comforting that the doctors give it as a sovereign cordial to the man who is sick unto death'. He too adds that 'the ancient laws ordained that no-one but a prince should bear this colour'. John de Bado Aureo, whose *Tractatus de Armis* was written in the late fourteenth century, puts gold third, but Sicily Herald puts it first and equates it with the sun and the precious stone topaz, and with Sunday among the days of the week. He says that its properties are those of the age of adolescence and faith, and that it corresponds to the virtues of richness and noblesse. Nicholas Upton, who wrote the *De Studio Militari* in 1446, follows Sicily Herald, while Gerard Legh, writing in 1562, devotes some six pages to a discussion of gold.

SILVER

Normally blazoned as 'argent', although several of the later medieval English rolls of arms use the term 'silver'. Both Bartolo and Bonet place it fourth in order, after gold, red and blue. Sicily Herald, however, places it second, and says that is corresponds to the virtues of purity and justice, to the age of childhood and hope. It is appropriate for those of phlegmatic temperament, and should be equated with the pearl and the moon, and with Monday. This very curious practice of blazoning colours by the day of the week is said by Gerard Legh to have been invented by Falcon King of Arms in the time of King Edward III, but, luckily for modern heralds, it never became popular.

RED

Invariably blazoned as 'gules'. While the shade is not laid down, it should of course be a clear and unambiguous red, although in the early Middle Ages no distinction was made between red and purple. Both Bartolo (who described it as *color purpureus sive rubeus*) and Bonet place it second, immediately after gold, and Bonet has this to say: 'the second colour is purple, that we call in French red or vermilion, and it represents fire . . . . This colour too, according to ancient laws, should be rarely worn except by great princes or those nearest them in blood'. The *Llyfr Dysgread Arfau,* a Welsh treatise on heraldry probably written between 1394 and 1410, is even more explicit: 'This colour is forbidden by civil law to be worn without permission, except by a prince; and whoever transgresses may be executed. And why is this colour ordained to a prince more than white or black or blue or golden colour? Because this colour represents cruelty, and a prince ought to be cruel to his enemies, and it behoves him to punish disorder.'[8] This restriction, however, appears to have been disregarded fairly early on in the Middle Ages, and red was used pretty widely among all levels of the knightly class. Sicily Herald equates it with the ruby, fire, the planet Mars, and with Wednesday and summer, and considers it symbolic of a sanguine temperament, nobleness, boldness and the age of virility.

BLUE

Invariably blazoned as 'azure'. Here again, the exact shade is not laid down, but it should not be too dark for 'this colour Blew doth represent the Sky in a clear Sun-shining day, when all clouds are exiled . . . . and signifyeth Piety and Sincerity.'[9] The treatises of both Bartolo and Bonet place this colour third. Nicholas Upton says 'thys colowre ys callyd the hevenly colowre bycause ye ayre hathe most dominion . . . as hyt aperyth in saphyres whych preciouse stoones resemble moste trewly thys azoure or blew coloure. The Saphyre hys nature ys to take away envy, to expell fere, to make one hardy and victoriouse, to strength a man hys mind in goodness and to make the berar meke, lowly and jentyll.'[10] This echoes the views of Sicily Herald, who also equates it with the planet Jupiter, with the quality of justice and purity, and with Tuesday and the autumn season.

BLACK

Always blazoned as 'sable', and equated with the diamond and the planet Saturn. Bartolo regards it as the least of all the colours, and Bonet echoes this view, describing it as the lowest and humblest colour, fit only for the religious, who should eschew vainglory. Following Francois de Foveis, Bado Aureo promotes black to the second most important colour, on grounds which seem remarkably abstruse. Sicily Herald, however, puts it firmly back in its place and says it is symbolic of sadness and decrepitude and a melancholic temperament, and corresponds with Friday and the season of winter. One might wonder why anyone ever bore black in their arms after this, but fortunately the Middle Ages had a flexible approach to the problems of heraldry.

GREEN

Always blazoned as 'vert', and in the later Middle Ages also as 'emerald' or 'Venus', that planet which 'exciteth to love wonderfully, especially betweene man and woman'. Randle Holme, writing in 1689, describes it as the colour which signified felicity and pleasure. Neither Bartolo nor Bonet includes green in their lists of heraldic tinctures, although Bonet was writing about the time that *Sir Gawain and the Green Knight* was composed. The *Tractatus de Armis* of Bado Aureo has an interesting comment on it: 'Green colour some men put and adde [i.e. include], the which as I suppose hadde and toke his begynnyng of some knyght mynstrall or bourder [jester], the which was no worthy man'.[11] However, he then depicts, later in the same treatise, the attributed arms of King Arthur – a Cross argent on a green field with the Virgin Mary and Child in the first quarter – which seems to indicate a little muddled thinking on the subject. Sicily Herald considers it symbolic of jolliness and youth, but also of beauty and shame (a rather cynical combination), and equates it with Thursday and spring. Nicholas Upton, writing about the same time, had commented disparagingly on the colour green but, by the time he wrote the *De Studio Militari,* had been persuaded to change his mind. Apart from King Arthur's arms, there are a few other well-known cases of the use of green in heraldry, in particular the attributed arms of Uther Pendragon

Opposite page
Top and bottom left
Sir Thomas de Montacute, Earl of Salisbury, K.G. (died 1428), and his wife Eleanor, daughter of Sir Thomas Holand, Earl of Kent, K.G. Nicholas Upton served under him in the French wars. This gives a good idea of the flamboyant crests used in tournaments during the 15th century. (Buccleuch ms. Wrythe Garter Book, ff. 151, 219)
Bottom right
Squires holding banners of the Trinity and of the Virgin Mary, such as were borne at the Battle of Agincourt. (Buccleuch ms. Wrythe Garter Book, f. 160)

(*Gold, two Dragons addorsed Vert, crowned Gules*) and the famous party arms of William Marshal, Earl of Pembroke and Regent of England (*Party per pale Or and Vert a Lion rampant queue fourchée Gules*), who died in 1219, over a century before Bartolo was writing. Nevertheless, there seems to have been an antipathy towards the colour until well into the fifteenth century, for it is not often found in the earlier armory. This may possibly have been because, in the literature of the time, while bright green was emblematic of spring – like the surcoat, shield and trappings of the Green Knight, 'as green as the grass and greener it seemed' – pale green was regarded as emblematic of death. Even to this day one finds many people who regard green as unlucky. John Guillim, Rouge Croix Pursuivant of Arms in 1613, has the last word on this colour which 'best resembleth youth, in that most vegetables, so long as they flourish, are beautiful with this verdure; and is a colour most wholsome and pleasant to cie, except it be in a young Gentlewoman's face'.

The curious system of blazoning arms in terms of precious stones became quite popular in the fifteenth century and lingered on into Tudor times, but fortunately it then fell into disfavour. There is however one modern instance of it in English heraldry: the grant of arms on 20 February 1967 to the Gemmological Association of Great Britain, whose arms are blazoned in the letters patent as: *pearl, on a Cross Formy quadrate throughout ruby and sapphire, a closed Book bound and clasped topaz the cover set with an Emerald environed of Pearls between two Sapphires in pale and two Rubies in fess, between in chief within an Annulet topaz a rose-cut Diamond proper, in fess two Lozenges pearl each charged with a Cross diamond, and in base a Ring topaz gemmed pearl.* This is, of course, a most complicated example, because one has to think carefully in order to sort out which are the real gems (here given with initial capitals) and which the colours expressed in terms of precious stones; generally it is not quite as difficult as this.

ERMINE

The principal fur of heraldry is ermine, and it is so blazoned. It consisted originally of the white winter coats of stoats, with the black tips of the tails sewn on. As stoats in Western Europe do not normally turn white in winter, these skins had to be imported in the Middle Ages from as far away as Muscovy, at great expense, and consequently were only within reach of the purses of the great. Ermine was, therefore, highly regarded, and we find the Dukes of Brittany using it for their arms, without any other charges upon it. The heralds of the fifteenth and sixteenth centuries invented several variations of ermine by reversing or changing the colours: thus white tails on black become 'ermines', while a gold ground with black tails is 'erminois', and the last reversed becomes 'pean'.

VAIR

This fur is also of some antiquity in heraldry, being originally composed of the skins of a kind of squirrel, blueish-grey on the back and white underneath, sewn together and producing an alternate blue and white appearance. Sudak, on the southern shores of the Crimea, was the main emporium where Russian vair was traded to Venetian merchants, Marco Polo's father among them, and thence found its way to the west. Later the ingenuity of the heralds produced variations of these colours, so that we get *vairy gold and azure,* or *vairy argent and gules.*

The evidence of the earliest French seals and enamels, between 1127 and 1300, shows that the Ordinaries and Subordinaries are by far the commonest charges, the Fess and its derivatives being most popular by a long way. Of the beasts, the Lion rampant heads the field, with two hundred and twenty examples as against forty Lions passant, the next most numerous beast. Of

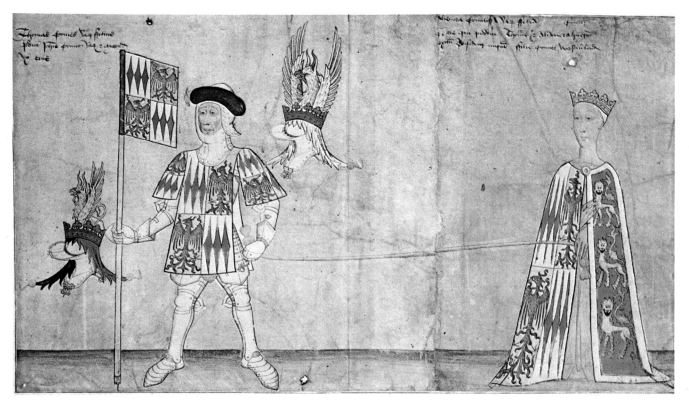

par le coc en lerbre est signifie le precheur
qui defule e le peie adespire·

par lentree est munde·

par langle remuctur le muschet od le muscher le cude dantgle qui est gardein de chescun home·

e les muschet les uenies pensees qui desturbent le repentantorum·

par langle od lespee qui est pres del hatterel· la destresce del deuin iugement·

par le diable setant· les suggestions del diable·

par la dame est signifie repentant·

par le columb li saint esprit qui eschauue la sainte escriture·

par le pere· le pere qui est sainte fei·

par lessul la fei·

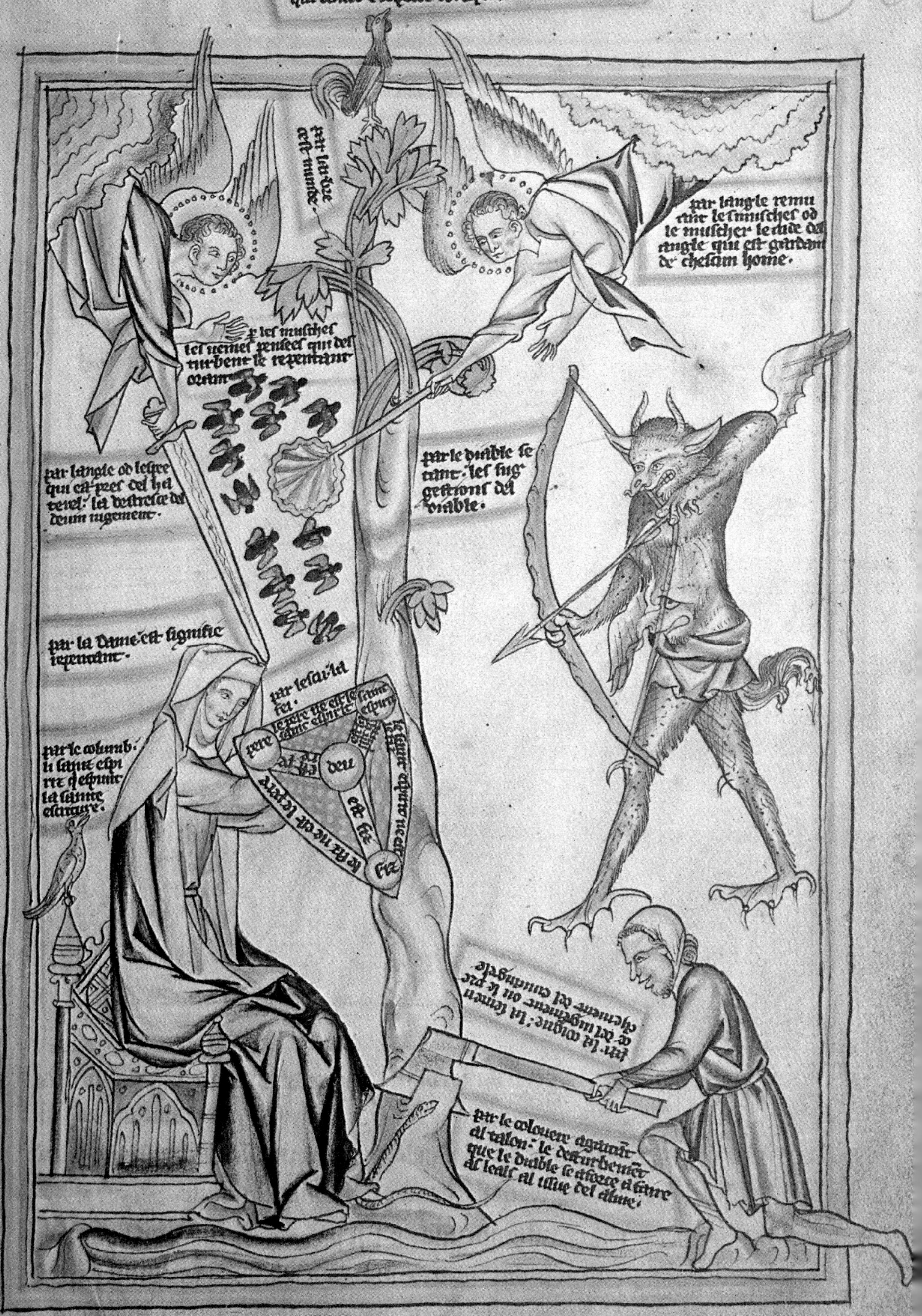

le fuiz qui est sainte esprit·

li pere nen est le fuiz· ne le fuiz nen est le saint esprit· le quel esperit nest· ne le pere ne le fuiz· ne le fuiz nen est deu·

en la uigne· la terre ou il laborenur ot del laborement· on le pre· le chemin del champeistre·

par le colouere aguisant al ualon· le desturbement que le diable se afforce a faire al ostel al tiede del esme·

par lewe· deuine escriture la quele le precheur demustre·

birds the Eagle, with forty-eight examples, leaves the rest far behind. The fabulous beasts produce, unexpectedly, one chimera, while several of the Lions rampant may have been queue-fourchee or double-tailed. Fabulous birds consist of five double-headed Eagles (which for convenience I shall call Double-Eagles), one Alerion and one Griffin. The earliest Dragon makes his appearance in about 1165, if we omit the earlier literary and historical references.[12]

The three earliest English rolls of arms, the Matthew Paris Shields, Glover's Roll, and Walford's Roll, compiled between 1244 and 1275, give a similar picture. Again the Ordinaries and the Subordinaries are by far the commonest charges in arms. Here we get our first Mermaid in heraldry, but fourteen Lions rampant queue fourchee are the only fabulous beasts, while there are no more than six Double-Eagles among the fabulous birds. Apart from the occasional Griffin, a similar pattern recurs throughout this century.

Dragons, however, make their appearance from time to time as decorative adjuncts to shields if rarely as actual charges, from the twelfth century onwards. In the Barons' Letter to the Pope, written in 1301, dragons appear in some profusion on twenty-two of one hundred and seven seals, as decorations or quasi-supporters beside the shields. This suggests that the fabulous creatures were considered inappropriate as charges on banners or shields, but acceptable as gay and fanciful adjuncts to armory to be used as crests in tournaments, or as supporters to banners and shields, particularly when the latter were used architecturally or depicted in manuscripts.

De Heraudie is the earliest treatise to discuss the use of natural and fabulous creatures in heraldry. The beasts then customarily borne in arms are said by the author to be the Lion, the Leopard, and the Griffin – *Gules a Griffin Argent* being the arms attributed to King Alexander the Great. The birds customarily borne in arms were the Eagle, the Martlet, the Popinjay, the Crow, the Swan and the Heron. The Double-Eagle was said to be borne only by the Holy Roman Emperor, because all the kings of Christendom ought by right to be subject to him. Bado Aureo gives a rather conventional list of natural beasts, birds and fishes, but gives only the Double-Eagle, the Griffin and the Dragon as acceptable chimerical creatures to be borne in arms. Nicholas Upton accepts the Harpy as an armorial charge, with the Panther (incensed), the Tyger and the Unicorn as fabulous beasts to be met with in heraldry. He mentions only three fabulous birds – the Double-Eagle, the Griffin and the Calader – that mythical bird with remarkable healing properties – and the Dragon completes his list.

Although it was not until the end of the fifteenth century that human monsters and fabulous beasts, birds and reptiles became common in heraldry, the qualities and attributes of the real creatures gave the early heralds plenty of scope for an imaginative use of symbolism. Bartolo laid it down that animals, whenever represented in heraldry, must be depicted in their most noble aspect and furthermore must exhibit their greatest vigour. He goes on to say that the Lion, for example, should be painted erect, rampant and snarling, with gnashing teeth and clawing feet, and the same holds good for other fierce animals. Those which are not fierce, such as the Horse or the Lamb, should be depicted more conventionally.[13]

The early heralds would have searched the bestiaries for information on the beasts and birds of the world. Bado Aureo was clearly influenced by them in describing, in his *Tractatus de Armis*, the various beasts, birds and fishes which are borne in arms. The 'sweetness of music with melodious notes', which the Swan was said to pour forth, is echoed by Bado Aureo who tells us that singers, when dubbed knights or otherwise raised to eminence, ought to bear a Swan in their arms. He goes on to say that he had, nevertheless, seen unmusical men bearing Swans in their arms, and he therefore asked a 'King of the Heraulds why he assigned to such men to bere swannes in armys, which

The Virgin Mary defending Herself from an attack by Satan, with the shield bearing the device of the Arms of the Faith, while one of Her guardian Angels sweeps away with a fly-swatter evil thoughts depicted as flies; from the Lambeth Apocalypse (Lambeth Palace Library ms. 209, f. 53)

49

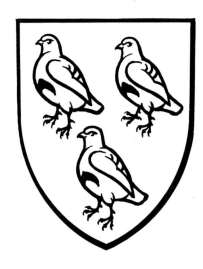

Gules three Partridges (drawn by G. Mussett)

were no syngers'. The king of arms replied that one reason could be that 'they were passing faire men', and another that 'they had longe nekkes'. It is interesting that by 1394 it was apparently accepted in English Court circles that a king of arms was the appropriate authority for designing and assigning arms.[14]

The influence on the heralds of the bestiaries, those splendid natural-history books of the Middle Ages, which drew a moral from the characteristics of every beast, bird and reptile, was profound, and their significance was accepted without question. The twelfth century bestiary (known as the Cambridge Bestiary) which T. H. White translated in such a lively way,[15] tells us that the Partridge 'is a cunning, disgusting bird. The male sometimes mounts the male, and thus the chief sensual appetite forgets the laws of sex. Moreover, it is such a perverted creature that the female will go and steal the eggs of another female. . . . The Devil is an example of this sort of thing. . . .' Nicholas Upton was evidently well acquainted with the bestiaries and, among the birds sometimes borne in arms, he mentions the Partridge: 'to bere therfore partryches in armes hytt betokenyth the fyrst berar to be a gret lyar or a sodomyte. Ther was a certain gentylman, whose name I woll not shew, which by the reason of hys manhode [i.e. valour] was made a noble man by my lorde and master, and he gave iii partryches in hys armes in a redde fylde'.[16] Alas, I have been unable to identify this grantee of arms, over whose name Upton draws a discreet veil, but who was knighted on the field for bravery in France about the time that Joan of Arc was rallying her country-men. It is obvious that the recipient can have had no idea of the significance of Partridges, so we must suppose from this and the example of the Swan in arms, just quoted, that the medieval heralds were given to rather donnish 'in-jokes', the allusions being readily appreciated by other heralds though not necessarily by the less-educated knights and squires.

Although badges, or devices akin to heraldic badges, were used by the early Plantagenet kings and later by the magnates of the realm, their use did not become widespread until the reign of King Edward III, and even then it remained restricted. By the middle of the fifteenth century they were widely used on the liveries of retainers and army contingents. This was no doubt due to the greater professionalism of warfare and the mustering of men from many different places and lordships, previously unknown to one another. Barnard's Roll of Badges,[17] the muster roll of King Edward IV's expedition to France in 1475, is a most important source of information on the badges in use at the time, and from this it is clear that all commanding officers used them, irrespective of the size of the units under their command. For example, the contingent of the Duke of Gloucester, afterwards King Richard III, which comprised ten knights, one hundred lances (squires and men-at-arms) and one thousand archers, wore his badge of the White Boar; while the contingent of Sir Humphrey Talbot, banneret, consisting of ten lances and one hundred archers, wore his badge of the Silver Talbot courant; and that of Sir John Ferrers, knight, which consisted of only two lances (one of which was himself) and fifteen archers, also wore his badge. Even John Smert, Garter King of Arms, is recorded as using his badge, a Broad Arrowhead ermines, presumably on the liveries of his servants, since he was not holding a fighting command – but we have seen that he ranked with the barons and bannerets, so this is understandable. The interesting point about the badges in this roll is that there are only five examples of fabulous creatures: a Lion rampant queue fourchée, two Unicorns, one Unicorn's head, and one male Griffin.

Fenn's Book of Badges,[18] which is almost contemporary, gives the badge of William Hastings, Lord Hastings, as a Mantecora, but Barnard's Roll gives his badge, when on active service in command of his contingent of forty lances and three hundred archers, as a Black Bull's Head. Similarly Sir Thomas

Borough, banneret, is recorded in Barnard's Roll as using an Arm-guard with its gauntlet as his badge on active service, while Fenn's Book of Badges gives him a Boreyn as a badge. Altogether Fenn's Book records two human monsters (a brace of Mantecoras or Mantygers) and five fabulous beasts, among whom the Alphyn and the Ypotryll make their first appearance in heraldry.

It was during this period that the lively imaginations of the Tudor heralds began to conceive strange and wonderful creatures which were unknown even to the credulous compilers of the bestiaries. The need to create new chimerical creatures to fit particular or unusual armorial circumstances sometimes still arises even today but, by and large, we can usually find a suitable solution to a problem of heraldic symbolism by drawing on the inventions of our predecessors. New chimerical creatures should only be evolved if there is nothing in our stables which will fit, and then they should be apt and have a reasonably plausible pedigree.

That urbane and civilised commentator on the wonders of the natural and metaphysical worlds, Sir Thomas Browne, writing in the middle years of the seventeenth century,[19] when the heraldic imagination had temporarily exhausted itself, observed: 'We shall tolerate Flying Horses, Black Swans, Hydras, Centaurs, Harpies and Satyrs; for these are monstrosities, rarities, or else Poetical fancies, whose shadowed moralities requite their substantial falsities.' He added: 'although there were more things in Nature than words which did express them; yet even in these mute and silent discourses, to express complexed significations, they took a liberty to compound and piece together creatures of allowable forms into mixtures inexistent. Thus began the descriptions of Griphins, Basilisks, Phoenix, and many more; which Emblematists and Heralds have entertained with significations answering their institutions; hieroglyphically adding Martegres, Wivernes, Lion fishes, with divers others. Pieces of good and allowable invention unto the prudent Spectator, but are looked on by vulgar eyes as literal truths, or absurd impossibilities, whereas indeed, they are commendable inventions, and of laudable significations'.

Even in the jaded world of today, symbols and symbolism play a part in our lives; but in the ages of intense faith symbolism was seen everywhere, for, if there is a God in heaven, there must be a reason for everything and everything must have a meaning. As T. H. White so aptly put it, 'A true symbol is not only a badge, it is a brief sermon, a shorthand way of saying something . . . . A symbol is a metaphor, a parable, a parallelism, a part of a pattern . . . . The meaning of symbolism was so important to the medieval mind that St. Augustine stated in so many words that it did not matter whether certain animals existed, what did matter was what they meant.' This view was echoed by St. Bonaventura, some six hundred years later when heraldry was in full flower: 'The creatures of this sensible world signify the invisible things of God; in part because God is the source, exemplar, and end of every creature; in part through their proper likeness, in part from their prophetic prefiguring.'

With the coming of the Renaissance in the fifteenth century, symbolism and religion parted company, and in these exciting and colourful years we find the heralds and their patrons regarding the fabulous with less awe. In consequence the chimerical creatures of heraldry make their appearance in growing numbers, especially in German heraldry, at first to satisfy the demand for ever more bizarre crests and badges, and later creeping on to shield and banner as well.

In the bustling sixteenth century, the lively imaginations of the Tudor heralds opened the gates, and the fabulous and chimerical beasts, birds and reptiles jostled each other into the many new arms granted to the rising new men looking for new worlds to conquer. They cemented those conquests with a grant of arms, and rounded them off finally with a grand heraldic funeral

51

and a baroque monument in the parish church, decked out with the pomp of armory. The Tudor heralds, although influenced by the infectious brashness of the age, were very conscious of the dignity of 'the noble office of arms', with its roots in the Middle Ages and its origins ascribed to Alexander the Great. It is possible, therefore, that those more complicated sixteenth-century arms may have been deliberately designed to distinguish the new men from the old feudal families, with their very simple, functional coats of arms.

From the fourteenth century onwards the heralds were becoming important royal officers in all Western European countries, and there are frequent references to them in the records and chronicles of the time. By the beginning of the fifteenth century, the English kings of arms were confirming arms to individuals and corporate bodies; and soon afterwards we find them granting arms on behalf of the Crown, which led fortuitously to the continued vitality of the English and Scottish heralds to this day. The memory of their ancient military origins is still very much alive, and the Earl Marshal of England remains responsible for the heralds. The brave days of William the Marshal do not seem so very far away.

A Herehaught in hafte muft thus be clad,
vntill fuche tymes as mo clothes bee had.

Part II
The Literature of Heraldry

5
Some Heralds and their Libraries

THERE is some doubt about the authenticity of the 'Ordinances and Statutes . . . for the good Government of the Office of Arms', said to have been promulgated by Thomas of Lancaster, Duke of Clarence, when Lieutenant-General of the army in France and Normandy between 1417 and 1421; but it is probable that those parts which do not concern the office of Garter were based on genuine originals of the fifteenth century. The passage with which we are concerned laid down that at convenient times the officers of arms were to apply themselves to the study of books of good manners and eloquence, chronicles and accounts of honourable and notable deeds of arms, and the properties of colours, plants, and precious stones, so that they might be able most properly and appropriately to assign arms to each person.[1] Officers of arms would, of course, be familiar with the whole range of medieval literature, but a glance at such early heralds' libraries as are known to us will give us a better idea of the kind of books they actually read.

In 1484 the heralds obtained from King Richard III a charter creating them a body corporate and granting them a house in the City of London called Coldharbour, to enable them to establish a library, common to all the heralds, under the control of Chapter. There each king of arms 'had his place several for his own library'. The next year Richard III, who had always taken a close interest in the heralds, was killed at the Battle of Bosworth, and Henry VII took the house away from them. There is some conflict of evidence as to what happened to the heralds' corporate library, but it seems that all the books were taken to the house of John Wrythe, then Garter King of Arms.

In 1555 King Philip and Queen Mary granted the heralds a new charter of incorporation and a new house (the present College of Arms being built on the ashes of this, which was destroyed in the Great Fire of 1666, though all their records and books were saved). In this house they were directed by the Earl Marshal, in 1568, to establish a library, but little seems to have been done immediately to give effect to this and the kings of arms continued to maintain their separate libraries. Sir William Dethick, appointed Garter in 1586, is said to have appropriated much of Robert Glover's personal library on his death in 1588, but in 1597 the ancient records and books of the kings of arms and heralds were acquired by Chapter, and the nucleus of the College's unique library was established.[2] Unfortunately the earliest full catalogue of the College Library is that made in 1618 by Samson Lennard, Bluemantle Pursuivant,[3]

White Boar badge and White Rose en Soleil of King Richard III (drawn by Miss A. Urwick)

55

and by that time it had become very much a professional library, reflecting the heralds' day-to-day work.

Fortunately inventories exist of the libraries of two of the sixteenth-century English heralds, those of Thomas Benolt and Robert Glover, and we will begin with the latter. Robert Glover was born in 1544, appointed Portcullis Pursuivant in 1568 and Somerset Herald in 1570, a position he held until his death in April 1588. A man of great learning and a scholarly and critical antiquary, he was the first to appreciate the value of early rolls of arms, of which he copied no fewer than thirty. In 1584 he compiled *Glover's Ordinary,* comprising some fifteen thousand coats of arms, each neatly 'tricked' by himself. His enormous collection of books and manuscripts was dispersed after his death; many items are now in the Philipot Collection in the College of Arms, some are in the Vincent Collection, also in the College, while others are in the British Museum, the Bodleian Library, Queen's College Oxford, Caius College Cambridge, Trinity College Dublin, and elsewhere. On 1 June 1588 an inventory was made of Glover's 'Bookes, Rolles, and Papers of Heraldry placed in the Upper Study towards the gardin' and 'In the great Study next the Streat' and 'In the Gallery'. Altogether sixty-nine items were catalogued, but since about half of these each comprise two or more books, rolls, or papers, it is clear that Glover's library was considerably larger than at first appears. Unfortunately the description of the books is not always clear, so that it is not possible to identify them all with certainty, but we have enough to give us a good idea of the private library of an active Tudor herald.[4]

As might be expected from the 'Ordinances and Statutes... for the good Government of the Office of Arms', Glover possessed some thirty-six *'cronicques, actes et gestes d'honneur [et] faictz d'armes'.* These ranged from a copy of Eutropius's History of Rome, Bede's *Historia Ecclesiastica,* the *Historia Anglorum* of Henry of Huntingdon, the *Gesta Regum Anglorum* of William of Malmesbury, the *Historia Regum Britanniae of* Geoffrey of Monmouth, the *Expugnatio Hibernica* of Giraldus Cambrensis, a copy of Gildas, three copies of the *Flores Historiarum* (a popular history from the Creation to 1326), 'The Historie of Enland Called Brut' (now Vincent MS. 421), and a number of other chronicles covering various periods, mostly of English history. The *'livres de bonnes moeurs [et] elequence',* which the heralds were enjoined to read, are few, but a copy of John Gower, the 'moral' poet and philosopher, and friend of Chaucer, would perhaps fall into this category, together with a copy of the Bible and 'a Booke of cardinoll vertues'. Of his other books at least six concerned matters of law or state, and four concerned coronation, funeral, or other ceremonies. It is impossible to estimate either the number of books, rolls, or notes of arms, or the number of his books, rolls, or sheets of pedigrees.

Among his books were four treatises on heraldry. There was a copy of Bado Aureo's *Tractatus de Armis,* and a copy, made by Glover himself in 1572, of Baddesworth's version of Nicholas Upton's *De Studio Militari* (now Vincent MS. 444), beautifully illustrated. There was also a book of the statutes of the Order of the Golden Fleece and another book described as 'Of Heraldry et aliis'.

Although Glover acquired his library in the mid-sixteenth century, it is clear that all the chronicles and heraldic treatises were either originals or copies of works compiled at a much earlier period; so it might well have been the kind of library that a fifteenth-century herald would also have collected and used. A glance at the library of Thomas Benolt, who was already a herald in the late fifteenth-century, will support this view.

Thomas Benolt is believed to have been a pursuivant in the reign of King Edward IV, and was created Windsor Herald in 1504, Norroy King of Arms in 1510, and Clarenceux King of Arms in 1511. He died in May 1534, and in his will bequeathed his library to Thomas Hawley, then Carlisle Herald and later Clarenceux, for life. After his death it was to pass from Clarenceux to Clarenceux, for 'every one in his own tyme to use occupy and Enjoye as his owne during his Naturall Life'. Thomas Wall, Windsor Herald, made an inventory of Benolt's library, dated 30 June 1534, for the executors, and a copy of this remains in the College of Arms (printed in full by Sir Anthony Wagner as Appendix F to the second edition of *Heralds and Heraldry in the Middle Ages*).[5] His library comprised fifty-four manuscript books or sheets, seventeen rolls of pedigrees, seven rolls of arms, thirteen narrative or record rolls, and twenty-three printed books. A considerable number have been identified as still remaining in the College of Arms and they formed the foundation of the College Library.[6]

Arms of Thomas Benolt, Clarenceux King of Arms (drawn by Miss A. Urwick)

Benolt possessed thirteen chronicles and histories, of which one of the more interesting was 'a booke wrythyn by Willm. Whityng alias Huntingdon herauld, after Chester, of Cronicles in frenche of popes, emperours & Kinges of England wt. the armes of divers gentilmen painted', for William Whiting was probably Chester Herald around the middle of the fifteenth century.[7] Benolt's four volumes of the first edition of Froissart's *Chronicles* were also specially mentioned in his will. There are several volumes, some manuscript and some printed, of chronicles of England and France, and 'a litell pamphlet of fetes of armes'.

Of books on good manners and eloquence we find a printed copy of Boethius's *De Consolatione Philosophiae,* and another volume called *Le coeur de philozophie.* A number of volumes which appear to fall into this category cannot be clearly identified from their description in the inventory, but the printed volume of Cato was possibly the aphorisms on conduct and morals. There was also an Old Testament in French and 'a boke of Tailes or miracles writtin in ryme in Frenche'. A book on the Nine Worthies of the World, *Le livre de ix preux,* completes this section, while a volume of Boccaccio attests to the variety of Benolt's tastes.

Six volumes concerning law and matters of state are what one might expect to find in the library of a herald who was a very active diplomat. Benolt was constantly being sent on missions abroad between 1505 and 1533, and it may have been on one of these occasions that he acquired the Hyghalmen Roll (now College of Arms MS, 1st M.5). Benolt had two bestiaries, one printed and described as *Le propriete de bestes* and the other listed as 'A booke of the propertie of beestes writtin in Latin', but both have vanished.

There are fourteen volumes of treatises on heralds, heraldry, chivalry, and war. Those which deal specifically with the officers of arms include 'a frenche booke concernyng many notes neccessary for officers of armes, writyn in frenche with divers noble mens armes of the reaulme of Fraunce', and 'a litell Booke writtyn in basterd hande & well illuminyd concernyng the droites and custumes of the office of armes wt. many other goodly maters'. Two volumes concern 'the othes of kinges of armes', while another item consists of 'xj rowles in paper bounde in oone bondell wherof ys mynutes and greves of all the office of armes against Garter', which evidently refers to Benolt's bitter controversy with Garter Wriothesley in 1530.[8] A copy of the *Epitome Rei Militaris* of Flavius Vegetius, the celebrated military writer of the fourth century, whose work on the art and science of war maintained an unrivalled popularity until the time of Frederick the Great, would have been normal reading for any herald throughout the Middle Ages, and it finds a place on Benolt's shelves. There is also a volume listed as a 'Traietie sur le f[aic]t de la guerre', which may be another copy of the *Epitome Rei Militaris.*

We have seen that when on active service in the fifteenth century, heralds ranked with knights, and the standard works on chivalry would be read and followed by any man who lived in the aristocratic world of the Middle

Ages; so we also find on Beholt's shelves a copy of the *Livre de chevalerie* of Geoffroi de Charny, one of the most distinguished and experienced French knights of the fourteenth century. There are five treatises specifically on heraldry and war in Benolt's library and the standard authorities are among them. There is a volume listed as 'Des blasons d'armes', and two manuscript copies of the *Arbre des batailles* of Honoré Bonet, first written between 1382 and 1387, and widely read and copied during the next two centuries. There is a volume of the *Tractatus de Armis* of Bado Aureo, written in French (possibly College of Arms MS. 1st M.18), and a volume of *Le livre des faits d'armes et de chevalerie* of Christine de Pisan, written around 1400, which achieved an equal popularity.

As Thomas Benolt was already a herald in the late fifteenth century, we can take it that this would be the sort of library that an average herald would have collected at that time and, as many of them are originals or copies of much earlier works, we are fairly safe in assuming that these are the kind of books which earlier heralds would also have read.

6

Early Medieval Treatises on Heraldry

SWALD BARRON dismissed the medieval heraldic treatises as the compilations of 'Master Mumblazon', the concoctions of people who were not heralds, and that they did not reflect the views of the professional heralds on their subject. We now know that the standard medieval works on heraldry formed part of the libraries of two heralds of standing and repute, and there is reason to think that other heralds before them would likewise have read and been influenced by these early treatises. Books were costly in the Middle Ages, and copiously illustrated and illuminated books would not have been bought, or new hand written copies commissioned, unless they were considered of sufficient importance.

Apart from this, a study of these early treatises shows that some at least were indeed written by heralds while in every case where we can identify the author, the rest were written by men who were closely associated with the military commanders, or moved in the society of the 'strenuous knights', those whom we would today regard as professional officers.

The late Hugh Stanford London, Norfolk Herald Extraordinary, gave a 'List of some Medieval Treatises on English Heraldry' in the *Antiquaries Journal* (vol. XXXIII, p. 182). This consisted of twenty separate treatises, but it has now been possible to extend this list and a 'Preliminary List of Medieval Heraldic Treatises' will be found in the Appendix. Further research, particularly in Continental libraries, could probably extend this list still more. One problem to contend with is the medieval habit of copying manuscripts without making any acknowledgement of their source and sometimes copying only parts and adding further matter, and so on. This is very much the case with the heraldic treatises, and it is sometimes difficult to decide whether a manuscript should be regarded as just a copy of an earlier treatise, or whether the interpolated matter is sufficient to enable one to regard it separately. Until the treatises can be studied in greater depth, the 'Preliminary List' printed here must be regarded as very preliminary. Meanwhile it may be interesting to look closely at some of the most important of them.

DE HERAUDIE

The earliest of all, so far discovered, is the Anglo-Norman *De Heraudie,* which was copied into the 'St. Alban's Formulary' at some date after 1382. It is written in a small business hand of the late fourteenth century, and begins with fifty-three lines of verse in octosyllabic rhymed couplets, then continues in

59

First page of *De Heraudie*, from the St Albans Formulary (Cambridge University Library ms. Ee.iv.20, f. 160ᵛ)

prose. It is, in effect, a grammar of armory and quotes thirty-four coats of arms, over half of them English, as examples of the way in which particular charges are blazoned and borne in arms. Almost all the examples given, with a few possible exceptions, due to the fact that the same christian names continued in some of the families for several generations, were borne by men living in the last quarter of the thirteenth century.[1]

Professor Gerard J. Brault (who has named this the 'Dean Tract' from the fact that Dr. Ruth J. Dean was the first to draw attention to it), suggests that it can be dated between 1341 – 1345, and that the author drew the bulk of his examples from the Heralds' Roll, which was compiled about 1270-80.[2] The original certainly dates from before 1382 because the author states that the arms of the King of France are blazoned as 'floretty', whereas they were changed to three fleurs de lys in 1376.

In discussing the flowers customarily borne in arms the author states that the 'flour de gley' is gold, whereas the 'flour de liz' is argent. Elsewhere he blazons the arms of the King of France as *d'azeur florettee ove flure de gley d'or*. Cotgrave's Dictionary (published in 1660) gives *glaye* as 'the blew lily or flower de luce' and *glayeul jaulne* as the yellow wild iris. *The Medieval Latin Word List* gives 'glegellatus' as ornamented with a fleur de lys. I have not come across any other example of the use of the term 'fleur de glaye' or 'fleur de glaieul' for the gold or coloured fleur de lys of heraldry after 1300. There are, however, four examples in the Camden Roll, which was compiled about 1280, namely '*Munsire William Peynferer, l'escu d'argent od treis flurs de glagel de sable*'; '*Munsire Jorge de Kantelo, l'escu de gules a treis flurs de glagel d'or*'; '*Munsire Robert Agilun, l'escu de gules a une flur de glagel d'argent*'; and '*Munsire Robert de Cokefeud, l'escu de gules a une flur de glagel d'ermine*'.[3] The white lily was, of course, emblematic of the Virgin Mary, so it would seem that in the thirteenth century all other similar flowers, of whatever colour, borne in arms by humans were regarded as some kind of

60

iris. The author also uses the term 'gasteul' for the red roundel or torteau. This form is found in Walford's Roll (c.1275) and the Camden Roll, but not much later. The use of these terms by the author of *De Heraudie* makes one wonder whether he was not, in fact, writing around 1300 or earlier.

The more one reads *De Heraudie* the more one feels it was written by a herald, probably for heralds. It is a straight-forward, down to earth treatise, which omits the kind of explanatory matter which would be included if writing for readers who are not specialists or already reasonably knowledgeable. If I am right in thinking this, then one would expect the author to quote contemporary examples, because this was the age of the great captains of Edward I and the Black Prince and their arms would have been very well known to his readers. If the author was writing around 1300 or before he might have drawn on the Herald's Roll (was he its compiler? a fascinating thought), but could equally have drawn on his own knowledge. On balance, I am inclined to place *De Haraudie* between 1280-1300.

The treatise is headed *De Heraudie* and, since the word is used in the opening line of the verse, this was probably its original title. It is of considerable interest that the science of armory was already, by 1382, and probably from about the beginning of that century, becoming known as 'heraldry', the special skill of the heralds. In the margin is written: *'Descripcio armorum sive scutorum diversorum in Gallicis'*. It begins:

> De heraudie le mestier
> Si est les armes diviser,
> Les colours et lez proprotees
> Q'en armes sount trovez.
> Primer vous dirray les colours —
> Ore l'entendez par amours —
> Et puys des armes le devis
> Des heraus come l'ay apris.
> Or, azeure, argent et gules,
> Sable et vert, pluys sount nulles
> Forsque purpre soulement :
> De cele penserount poy de gent.

The treatise then treats of the problems of blazoning arms, quoting among others the arms of Mortimer as a particularly difficult example, mentioning that the heralds (*heraus des armes*) had disputed over the correct blazoning of them.[3] Ermine and vair are given next, with examples. Then follow twelve examples of chequy, masclée, barruly (burlee), vairy, paly, bendy, quarterly, indented (endentee), undy (oundee), gyronny (gerounee), dancetté (dauncee), and chevronny shields.

Next come five examples of fretty, billety, floretty, crusilly, and bezanty shields. The King of Jerusalem bears a shield *'d'argent croiselee d'or a une croise potente d'or'*, and the author comments that it is a bad practice to put the colour gold on argent. Reverting to roundels he adds, *'Quant ils sount d'or, sount besauntz* [Bezants]; *quant ils sount d'argent, platz* [plates]; *quant ils sount de goules, sont gasteuls* [now called a torteau]; *quant ils sount de sable, sount pelots* [pellets]'.

The author goes on to say that the beasts customarily borne in arms are the Griffin, the Lion and the Leopard, and *'quant il y a un leoun, cy est un leoun; quant il passe iij, sount leoncels'*. King Alexander has arms attributed to him of *gules a Griffin argent*.

The birds customarily borne in arms are stated to be the Eagle and the Martlet (called 'Merle' here), the Popinjay (Papejoye) and the Crow (Corf), the Swan and the Heron. The King of Germany bears a shield of gold with an Eagle sable Double-Beaked (i.e. Double-Headed). When there is one

61

'Merle' in a shield, it is 'a Merle'; when three or more, they are 'Merles'. Birds always depicted in their proper colours are the Popinjay green, the Crow black, and the Swan and Heron white.

The leaves and flowers used in arms are next discussed. They are the Trefoil, Quatrefoil, Cinqfoil, and Sixfoil. The Rose, the 'Flour de Gley' and the 'Flour de Liz' are always shown in their proper colours, namely the Rose red, Fleur de Gley gold, and the Fleur de Lys argent. There are also other leaves borne in arms, the 'Foile de Meller', 'Lorer' and Olive.

Then follow examples of Saltires (Sautours), Escallops, and Lozenges entire and pierced (i.e. Mascles). The 'greygnours' borne in arms are the Quarter, the Canton, and the Chief. The author explains that when Rowels, Molets, and Estoiles are gold they are blazoned as Rowels, when gules they are Molets and when argent they are Estoiles. When more than one Fess is depicted it is blazoned as 'fessée'; when there is more than one Bend or Bar one says that the shield is bendy or barry. The Fess can be engrailed and also 'engravelée' (possibly invected). The 'Peus' (i.e. the Pale) is next mentioned, quoting as example the arms of the Earl of Athol: *'l'escu d'or ove iij peus de sable'*. The Gemelle is mentioned, with an example, as are Crescents.

The treatise ends with Crosses of twelve kinds: the Cross 'passaunt' (passion cross?), Cross engrailed, Cross 'percee' (voided), Cross recercelee (moline), Cross formy, Cross 'a les degrees' (cross calvary), Cross croiselee (crosslet), Cross potent, Cross 'pomelee' (pomme), Cross floretty, Cross patee, and a 'Croice entier saunz nulle diversitee qe seint George porta'.

In spite of the fact that a few fabulous and chimerical creatures are found in French seals of the twelfth and thirteenth centuries, used in a more or less heraldic way, here we find only a Griffin and a Double-Eagle; both are so illustriously borne that clearly they were regarded as unsuitable for ordinary barons, let alone knights.

DE INSIGNIIS ET ARMIS

The next heraldic treatise, which was until recently regarded as the earliest, is the *De Insigniis et Armis* of Bartolo di Sasso Ferrato. Bartolo was born in 1313 in Italy. At the age of fourteen he studied law at Perugia, graduating D.C.L. in 1334, and he practised law first at Todi and later at Pisa. He then became a judge at Bologna, where his severe sentences attracted so much opprobrium that he retired in 1340 and returned to Pisa. Here he studied and taught law, but although regarded as the foremost jurist of his day, with an international reputation, he remained unpopular with his colleagues. Shortly after 1351 he was sent on a mission to the Emperor Charles IV, who ennobled him and granted him arms. He returned to Perugia in 1355, the year in which some authorities think he died (it may have been a little later), and was buried there. The *De Insigniis et Armis* was evidently written about 1354 and published posthumously by his son-in-law.[4]

Although very much a lawyer's treatise, the *De Insigniis* achieved immediate popularity, and for the next three centuries it was extensively copied and quoted by writers on warfare and heraldy. It consists of thitry-three short chapters and, as it has played such an important part in the forming of heraldic law and practice, it is worth glancing at the gist of the chapters.

1. Insignia granted in connection with the holding of a dignity or office are borne by the one who holds that dignity or office, and may not be borne by others.
2. Special insignia of dignity, such as belong to a king, may not be borne by any other person, nor any of the devices or appurtenances of a prince displayed.
3. Only those who have been granted insignia and arms may use

Arms of Bartolo di Sassoferrato
(drawn by N. Manwaring)

them. [Bartolo adds that he and his descendants were granted arms by the Emperor: *Or a Lion rampant queue fourchée gules*].

4. Anyone may assume arms and insignia, which may be borne and displayed in his own property. [But this is qualified by the subsequent chapters and by the references he quotes].

5. Whoever assumes the arms or insignia of another, who has borne them from ancient times, may only do so if the first bearer is not harmed or injured thereby.

6. The bearing of arms, or insignia alone, anywhere and in any way, must be strictly controlled. [Bartolo quotes as example the case of a German knight, on a visit to Rome, who finds he is bearing the same arms as an Italian knight, but concludes that this is permissible as they come from different countries.]

7. An individual's trade-mark, such as that used on a sword and other products, is prohibited by law for any other worker's use, in any place at all, once it has been exhibited three times.

8. A notary may not adopt the seal of another and if he does he may be prohibited. A paper-maker may be prohibited from using the mark of another maker.

9. It is useful to have a grant of arms from a prince, because they are thereby publicised and cannot be prohibited by another. They are also of greater dignity and, if two men bear the same arms, the preference is given to him who had them from a prince.

10. Arms or insignia of a house are inherited by all descendants on the father's side.

11. Bastards do not use insignia by right, and the custom of permitting them to do so is not observed in Tuscany.

12. It may be asked with whom the seal of a society or corporate body should remain after dissolution.

13. How insignia or arms should be painted, affixed, or borne.

14. Animals which are borne in arms, if painted on banners, should be facing the staff; likewise if a part of the animal is borne.

15. Animals, whenever represented, must be depicted in their most noble act, and furthermore must exhibit their greatest vigour.

16. The Lion, Bear, and similar creatures are painted erect, rampant, with gnashing teeth and clawing feet.

17. The Horse should be depicted correctly, standing or salient.

18. The Lamb is shown as if walking gently along the ground.

19. The dexter foot should always be in front when an animal is depicted.

20. The part of a banner which faces its bearer should be looked at, not the other side [in fact both sides should show the arms, each facing towards the staff].

21. When the figure of an animal is depicted on trumpet banners it should not face the trumpet. [Because then it would be upside down when the trumpet is being blown.]

22. If two animals are borne regarding one another, it does not matter in what manner they are painted on banners.

23. How should insignia consisting of a variety of different colours be depicted? The first and higher place is more noble than the following and lower. The noble colour should be placed next to the banner staff.

24. Gold is a nobler colour than the others and represents the sun. Nothing is nobler than light.

25. Red, otherwise purple (*rubeus seu purpureus*), represents fire and is noble.

26.   Blue comes third and represents the sky (*aerem*).
27.   The colour white is nobler than black, and black is the lowest.
28.   When arms are borne on clothing, the more important part should be towards the head and the inferior towards the feet.
29.   Arms painted on surcoats, when viewed from behind, must show the more noble parts respecting the left-hand side of the man.
30.   Letters and arms on seals are cut backwards.
31.   When arms are depicted on shields, the nobler part should face towards the part of the shield which, when carried, is on the bearer's right side.
32.   When arms are depicted on the caparisons of horses, the nobler parts should face the horse's head.
33.   Arms are painted in any manner on the coverings of beds, on walls and on other fixtures.

The *De Insigniis et Armis* had an immediate influence, not only because its author had an international reputation as a jurist but also because it is a very sound treatise which met a need. We shall find Bartolo's words echoing down the centuries, being quoted and misquoted, usually without any acknowledgement, in treatise after treatise. A complete translation and edition of this important treatise, together with a detailed consideration of the sources quoted by Bartolo, would be invaluable for any study of early medieval heraldry.

ARBRE DES BATAILLES

The next important heraldic treatise was the *Arbre des Batailles,* or Tree of Battles, of Honoré Bonet. Born in the second quarter of the fourteenth century, Bonet went to Rome in 1368 and by 1382 was Prior of Salon in Provence. He tried hard to exchange this benefice for a better one and consequently spent the next few years at the University of Avignon and about the French court, in the attempt to interest a powerful patron in his behalf. In or shortly before 1387 he wrote the *Arbre des Batailles,* which he dedicated to King Charles VI of France, and this later brought him employment in a minor administrative capacity in Languedoc and elsewhere. He also produced several other works. In 1390 he was driven from his priory by the Vicomte de Turenne, whose enmity he had incurred, and he retired to Paris, where he was still alive in 1405, but died before 1409. Bonet was widely travelled in France, Italy and Spain, and well acquainted with many of the great men of his day, and he himself says that he had many discussions in his youth with knights about matters of war and chivalry.

The Arbre des Batailles, which has been translated in full by Professor G. W. Coopland,[5] comprises a Prologue and four Parts, each consisting of a number of chapters. Part I is of twelve chapters; the first two deal with the definition and origin of war and the subsequent chapters lament the tribulations of the Church in times past and recount certain angelic visions. Part II is of nineteen chapters, mainly recounting the fall of the Empires of Babylon, Macedonia, Carthage and Rome. Part III is of eight chapters, discussing battles in general and the virtues and qualities of a good knight. Part IV consists of one hundred and thirty-two chapters, and discusses in a discursive way the laws and tactics of war and the respective duties of kings, commanders, knights, vassals and serfs; whether priests may take up arms; the rules for recompense for loss during war; questions of pay and ransoms and whether soldiers should receive pay when on leave; paroles and safe-conducts; the granting of letters of marque; the treatment of prisoners; trial by battle and duels; and the like.

Only Chapters 124-129 of Part IV deal with matters of heraldry and armory and, with certain omissions, are based almost verbatim on Bartolo's

De Insigniis et Armis. As Professor G. W. Coopland remarks, 'All that the *Tree* contains on the subject of heraldry is to be found in the *De Insigniis;* the general doctrine of arms, the authority whence the right to bear them may be derived, the topic of the German knight who finds a foreigner wearing the arms of his house, the examination of the virtues of the various colours, and their precedence, and so on. Much as usual is omitted, notably the problem of the allotment of the trade sign on a dissolution of partnership, as also much curious lore bearing on the correct method of depicting and wearing arms on shields, garments, hangings, or elsewhere. Needless to say, there is no acknowledgement of the origin of all this on Bonet's part'. The six heraldic chapters deal with the following matters:

124. *Concerning coats of arms and pennons in general.* Discusses arms of dignity, such as royal arms, and arms of office.

125. *Concerning the arms of all gentlemen in particular, whether barons or small landowners, and whether another, not of their blood, may bear their arms at will.* 'Our masters' [evidently referring to Bartolo di Sasso Ferrato] said that arms given by the Emperor or a king should not be borne by one not of that blood. On the other hand, providing it is not for purposes of fraud, a man may assume what arms he wishes.

126. *Concerning the arms of all gentlemen, both barons and others.* The immediately preceding view is qualified by the statement that 'on this question our masters come to the following conclusion: if a man, or his house, has adopted a new coat of arms and has worn it publicly, lords should not support any other man of that town or region who desires to adopt it, for such arms are adopted for the sake of distinction and difference, and in such a case we should have no distinction by which to recognise people, and the result would be confusion'.

127. *Is a German who finds a Frenchman bearing his arms free to offer him wager of battle?*
'Our masters' conclude [after a spirited vignette of knightly life] that as 'the two men do not belong to the same kingdom there can be no confusion between them in warfare, nor can any great harm result to the King'.

128. *Those who wear the arms of another in order to commit a fraud must be punished.* This is pretty straightforward and further qualifies, the view at the end of Chapter 125.

129. *Of the colours of coats of arms.* Gold 'is the noblest in the world, because gold of its nature is bright and shining and is full of virtue, and so comforting that the doctors give it as a sovereign cordial to the man who is sick unto death. The ancient laws ordered that no man but a prince should bear this colour'. The second colour is 'purple, that we call in French red or vermilion'. It represents fire and 'this colour too, according to ancient laws, should be rarely worn except by great princes or those nearest them in blood'. The third colour is azure, which represents the air 'which, after fire, is the noblest of the elements'. White is the fourth colour and signifies purity and innocence. Black is the last colour, 'which stands for the earth and so signifies grief and it is the lowest and humblest colour'.

Chapters 130–32 return to questions of trial by battle, the qualities of a good Emperor, and the things it behoves a virtuous, wise and discreet king to do.

Professor G. W. Coopland has traced forty-nine manuscript copies of the

Arbre des Batailles, of which the only known English version is that of Sir Gilbert of the Haye, made in 1456; the majority of them are in French. Because Bonet wrote for the ordinary knights and laymen in the common tongue, his book was immediately popular and was extensively copied and widely distributed. 'It is to be found in the gentleman's library, royal or noble, in France, Burgundy, England, Spain.' Professor Coopland has produced an admirable translation of the treatise with an invaluable introduction, which is essential reading for any study of this work and of the fourteenth century heraldic treatises, from which later writers on heraldry drew so copiously.

Le Livre des Faits D'Armes et de Chevalerie

Christine de Pisan wrote *Le livre des faits d'armes et de chevalerie* in about 1409. Born in Venice in 1364, she was the daughter of Thomas de Pisan who had a considerable reputation as a scholar and astrologer. In 1364 he accepted an invitation to serve King Charles V of France and moved to Paris. his family following him four years later. He gave Christine the kind of upbringing and education normally given to boys in the Middle Ages. When fifteen she married Etienne de Castel, the King's secretary, who died in 1389, leaving her with three young children. To keep her family, she began writing, and from then until her death produced a remarkable variety and number of works, both in verse and prose. The former included a hundred ballades dedicated to Queen Isabeau, while the latter ranged from a spirited championship of womens' rights, through romances to her famous treatise on the tactics, customs and laws of war and heraldry. She died shortly after 1429. A. T. P. Byles has edited William Caxton's 1490 edition of *The Book of Fayttes of Armes and of Chyualrye,* and has written a most helpful introduction, which includes a brief biography of Christine de Pisan, together with a detailed examination of the manuscript copies and printed editions. and a critical appreciation of the sources she used.[6]

Christine de Pisan's treatise is divided into four parts; Book I, of twenty-nine chapters, deals with general war, and the qualities and duties of kings, commanders, knights and vassals, the greater part being based on the *Instituta Rei Militaris* of Vegetius, whose treatise on the art of war was closely studied and followed throughout the Middle Ages. Book II, of twenty-eight chapters, deals with sieges, stratagems, and the like, and Christine again draws on Vegetius, and also on Frontinus, although throughout she makes some original contributions. Book III, of twenty-four chapters, deals with the laws of war, the rights and duties of lords, commanders knights and vassals; pay and compensation; mercenaries, prisoners of war, and ransoms. Most of this is based on Honoré Bonet's *Arbre des batailles.* Book IV, of seventeen chapters, deals with safe conducts, truces, letters of marque, trials by battle and duels. Chapters 15-17 repeat very closely the heraldic chapters of the *Arbre des batailles,* as the author herself acknowledges.

The very large number of manuscript copies of Christine de Pisan's book bear witness to its widespread popularity at the time and until the sixteenth century. It would, of course, have been read mainly for its military interest, but the heraldic chapters would undoubtedly have carried great weight with the readers, so that their importance in moulding heraldic thought in the fourteenth and fifteenth centuries must have been considerable. So great was her reputation that at some time between 1400 and 1402 King Henry IV sent Richard Bruges, Lancaster King of Arms, and John, Falcon King of Arms, to Paris to try to persuade Christine de Pisan to come and settle in England. She tells us that she refused this invitation because of her disgust at Henry's treatment of King Richard II.

DE PICTURIS ARMORUM

Franciscus de Foveis, whose name is sometimes rendered as Francois des Fosses, evidently exerted a considerable influence on subsequent writers of heraldic treatises, but no copy of his work has so far been discovered. We know that John de Bado Aureo said that his own treatise followed in part the doctrine and information of 'my most excellent Doctor and master, Master Fraunceys de Foveis'. We also know he was a Frenchman, because Bishop Sion Trevor remarked that 'the bearing of flowers in arms is a sign of instability, for flowers do not last long. These arms belong to the King of France, and this is what Franciscus in a French book writes about his own country'. Finally, John's *Tretis on Armes* (discussed in Part II, Chapter 3) contains the statement that 'This litill tretis [was made] oute of latyn into englissh, suyng the fote steppes of the right nobill predecessour Ffraunces de Ffoueys in his boke intitled *De Picturis Armorum*.' It is to be hoped that these clues will one day lead to its discovery, because clearly it had a great influence on later writers.

TRACTATUS DE ARMIS

John de Bado Aureo wrote his treatise, *Tractatus de Armis,* as he himself says in the introduction, 'atte the instaunce and prayer of some my souveraynes and desirers, and specially of Dame Anne, sumtyme queen of England' (she was the wife of King Richard II). He says that he had 'compyled and drawen this present tretes, following in parte the doctryne and the information [*dogmata ac traditiones*] of my moost excellent Doctour and maister, Master Fraunceys de Foveis'. It is thought that the *Tractatus* may have been completed towards the end of 1394 when Queen Anne died, or soon afterwards, probably in 1395.

The identity of the pseudonym Bado Aureo has been a matter of conjecture ever since his day. Professor Evan J. Jones suggested, after much careful and ingenious research, that he was Sion (or Ieuan) Trevor (d. 1410) a Doctor of Laws and one of the Commissioners appointed by Richard II in 1389 to hear and determine an appeal by Sir John Dynham of Devon against a judgement awarded to Sir William Asthorp by the Court of Chivalry (the military court with jurisdiction in heraldic matters, although in this instance it was not a strictly heraldic or armorial case). Sion Trevor was Precentor of Bath and Wells until 1393 and then Bishop of St. Asaph in Wales. Employed on several diplomatic missions abroad by Richard II and Henry IV, he broke with the latter king and sided with Owain Glyndwr in his rebellion. *The Llyfr Dysgread Arfau* (Book of the Description of Arms), a Welsh treatise on heraldry (of which more will be said later) was probably written by Sion Trevor; he could, therefore, also have been the author of the *Tractatus* and although one is very tempted to accept this most persuasively argued theory, there are still grounds for caution.[7]

The Tractatus de Armis is, after Bartolo di Sasso Ferrato's *De Insigniis et Armis*, the next important milestone in heraldic literature, because it breaks new ground. While Bado Aureo was clearly influenced by Bartolo, his own treatise represents a new approach to armory, and the book became immediately popular and widely copied, influencing all subsequent writers on heraldry. Not only did Bado Aureo draw on Bartolo and Francois de Foveis, but he also goes behind the bestiaries and quotes copiously from Ovid, Pliny, Aristotle, Isidore of Seville, Averroes, Bartholomew the Englishman, and others, in a way which presupposes his readers' familiarity with them. The version printed by Sir Edward Bysshe, Garter King of Arms, in 1654, differs in some respects from the fifteenth century English translation (Bodleian Library MS. Laud. Misc. 733), and the Welsh version, the *Llyfr Dysgread Arfau;* but, in view of its importance, a detailed look at the treatise is called for, and we will consider the three versions simultaneously.

The *Tractatus* is divided into three Parts. The First Part begins with the origin of armorial insignia – that thereby knights and their heirs might be distinguished from others – and adduces their beginnings from the remotest times. It shows that at first it was sufficient to make distinctions by means of different colours, but later, as the number of knights increased, it became necessary to adopt other distinctions such as animals, birds, trees, flowers and inanimate objects like crosses of different kinds, and other charges. We shall first examine the colours used in heraldry and assess their respective values, since some colours were held to be more honourable than others.

The heraldic colours are arranged by Bado Aureo in the following order: white, black, blue, gold, red and green. Here he specifically rejects Bartolo's order in favour of that evidently put forward by Francois de Foveis.

i) White is the noblest tincture, for the curious reason that white and black are the primary colours, from which all the other mediary or mixed colours are derived.

ii) Black is, therefore, the second worthiest colour.

iii) 'The next colour, as my maister Fraunces [de Foveis] seith, is the colour of Azour.'

iv) 'Among the meen (mediary) colours the goldyn colour is second.' It is forbidden by law to anyone to assume it except a prince.

v) 'Than next is Rede colour . . . . it is not leeful [lawful] to no man to bere but of speciall licence, except he be a prince alloon . . . . and they that repugne or disobeye this constitucion and ordenance should be heded [beheaded] . . . . And the cause whye that this colour is gyven to a prince rather than another, as white or blak, azour or goldyn, is for this colour betokeneth feersenesse.'

vi) Some men would include another colour, namely green, 'the which as I suppose hadde and toke his begynnyng of some knyght mystrell or bourder [jester], the which was no worthy man, as seith Barth [Bartolo] in the chaptre of dignitees in the first booke about the myddes of his tretys'.

It must have been very confusing for the late fourteenth century heralds, having conscientiously followed the teaching of Bartolo, to find the significance of the colours and their degree of importance altered by Foveis and Bado Aureo. Fortunately the heralds of today can take a more detached and flexible view of this armorial problem.

In the Second Part, Bado Aureo deals with the symbolism of beasts, birds and fishes in arms, and the influence of the bestiarists and writers like Bartholomew the Englishman can be readily seen. He declares that living things are more honourable than inanimate objects, beasts more honourable than birds, and males of greater dignity than females. He concludes that it is important to study the characteristics of heraldic charges, because these should recall the qualities of the original possessor of the arms. The following real or fabulous creatures were considered by Bado Aureo as suitable for use in heraldry:

(i) *Beasts borne in arms*	(ii) *Birds borne in arms*
Lion	Eagle
Leopard	Hawk or Falcon
Pard	Owl
Hart or Stag	Dove
Boar	Crow, Jackdaw or Chough
Dog	Swan
Horse	Cock
Bear	Griffin
Dragon	Martlet (Blackbird)

<table>
<tr><td>(iii)</td><td>Fish borne in arms</td><td>(iv)</td><td>Flowers borne in arms</td></tr>
<tr><td></td><td>Luce or Pike</td><td></td><td>Fleur de Lys</td></tr>
<tr><td></td><td>Crab</td><td></td><td></td></tr>
</table>

In the Bysshe version the Horse and Bear are omitted from the beasts, and the Dragon hangs uncertainly between the beasts and birds, while the Griffin has been omitted from the list of birds. As will be seen, the list of creatures suitable for bearing in arms was still, at the end of the fourteenth century, fairly short, although we know from some of the early seals and rolls of arms that a limited number of other creatures were employed as well.

It will be sufficient to quote only a few examples to show the way in which these beasts and birds are treated by Bado Aureo.

(i) 'A horse borne in arms signifies a man who is willing and prepared to fight with little cause; for at the faint sound of the clarion is the horse provoked to battle. It also signifies a well formed man, who has four attributes which are found in the horse, namely, form, beauty, prowess and colour . . . . Thus whoever bears this charge should have a corresponding nature in terms of human qualities.'

(ii) 'A dog borne in arms represents a loyal man who will not desert his lord and master in life or death, but will willingly die for his master. This is testified by Bartholomeus [Anglicus] *De Proprietatibus Rerum;* and thus it often happens in the case of other animals that the bearer has the same habits as the animal which he bears, because whenever a man makes petition for arms or some device, it is necessary to know about the man's habits, and thus can arms be suggested for him, as the Civil Law testifies in the book called *Digest.*' [This seems a fairly clear indication that by 1395 one no longer assumed arms of one's own volition.]

(iii) 'A hawk borne in arms signifies that the first to assume it was a slender, weak and daring man, better armed with courage than with bodily strength; for this bird is armed rather with courage than might and talons, and what it lacks in strength is made up in skill, cunning and courage. This is maintained by Isidore [of Seville], Pliny and Aristotle. Alexander [Neckham] too, in his *De Naturis Rerum,* states that on a cold night in winter the hawk seizes a bird and keeps it under its feet until the next day to save being cold, and then sets it free. And if during the next day it should meet that bird several times, it would not cause it any harm because of the help and comfort derived from it, and because of that noble nature the hawk is superior to the lords and proud men, as Alexander says.'

(iv) 'The dove is a gentle bird, free from guile, and it loves the companionship of men and the places which they frequent. It is also forgetful

(a) 1st arms of John Wrythe
(b) 2nd arms of John Wrythe
(c) 3rd arms of John Wrythe
(drawn by G. Mussett)

(a)

(b)

(c)

and timorous, for it seldom feels safe anywhere except in its own hole. A dove borne in arms implies a harmless kindly man, and it implies that the man has more confidence in his companions than in his own might. Arms such as these are appropriate to a herald, who would leave his art and take up arms for himself and his heirs; for Jerome says in his fourth book, that doves are taught in Egypt and in Syria to carry letters from one country to another, and in this Bartholomeus concurs in his *De Proprietatibus Rerum*.'

This last is of particular interest because John Wrythe, the third Garter King of Arms (d. 1504) bore firstly Azure a Fess between three Doves close argent within a Bordure or; then he tried Azure three Doves close argent within a Royal Tressure or; but as Garter he used Azure a Cross or between four Doves close argent, beaks and legs gules. It is possible that he based his Arms on those of the College of Arms, rather than the reverse.

These examples of the heraldic imagination at work may seem quaint or curious conceits to us today, when allegory and symbolism no longer sweep our minds off our very pedestrian ground; but it was not at all odd to our medieval ancestors, and we have only to glance at, say, *The Ancrene Riwle,* or *Sir Gawain and the Green Knight,* to see that. When the *Tractatus* was being written, the famous Scrope vs Grosvenor heraldic lawsuit as to which of them should bear the arms, *Azure a Bend or,* had just been concluded with a personal judgement by King Richard II, and heraldic matters would be much in people's minds in court circles at that time, so we can assume that Bado Aureo was expressing the heraldic views of his day.

The Third Part of the book deals with the ordinaries and subordinaries and, by and large, follows normal heraldic practice. The fifteenth century English version and the *Llyfr Dysgread Arfau* give, at the end of this Part, among examples of arms, those of Uther Pendragon: *gold two Dragons addorsed vert crowned gules;* and the attributed arms of King Arthur: *vert a Cross argent in the first quarter the representation of the Virgin Mary and Son.*

LLYFR DYSGREAD ARFAU

The Welsh language version of the *Tractatus* is the *Llyfr Dysgread Arfau* (Book of the Description of Arms). The copy which has come down to us was made in the sixteenth century and the opening paragraph states that 'Sion Trevor translated it into Welsh from Latin and French, and Hywel ap Syr Mathau wrote it in the year of our Lord one thousand five hundred and sixty one'. The only possible candidate, as Professor Evan J. Jones pointed out, is the Bishop Sion Trevor who died in 1410. We are indebted to Professor Jones for publishing a complete English text of it.[8]

The introductory paragraphs of the *Llyfr Dysgread Arfau* differ somewhat from those of the *Tractatus,* because Sion Trevor was writing for a particular readership, and it is worth repeating some of his opening remarks.

> Arms were ordained and assigned to warriors and gentle folk to be borne by them according to their natures and customs, so that they and their heirs might be distinguished from others by these charges; for charges were appointed to all according to their nature and customs whether good or bad : but there were some of whom nothing good or bad was known, and for these there was granted the use of crosses and chevrons and pales and such charges, as will be treated more clearly later.
>
> Wherefore it was both proper and necessary that every gentleman of noble birth of Welsh stock should know the charges which he could rightly bear without hurt to anyone, and be able

to classify them and describe them in Welsh as in other languages, lest this science of arms be lost to the people of this age, as seems likely to happen through lack of use in the language of the Britons [i.e. Welsh] who may not be well versed in other tongues; for by coats of arms can each gentleman be recognised and his family distinguished, and the reason for the elevation of his ancestor to allow him to bear arms, whether it be prowess, or numbers of near kinsmen, or bravery, or wisdom, or wealth . . . . Wherefore I have essayed to translate from Latin and French into Welsh, portions of the works of various authors who have dealt with this art.

The text of the *Llyfr Dysgread Arfau* thereafter follows closely that of the *Tractatus*.

7
Later Medieval Treatises on Heraldry

ROM *De Heraudie* to the *Tractatus de Armis* we find the grammar or science of armory well established and fairly consistent, and the clear conclusion is that its basic tenets had already been formulated well before 1300. What is beginning to emerge is that the English heralds and writers on armory during the thirteenth and fourteenth centuries played a prominent part in formulating and codifying the law and practice of armory. Obviously a proper study of the early medieval treatises on armory, which must have been written in France and Burgundy, in the Empire, and in Italy, in Spain and Portugal, is now necessary, if we are to get a balanced view of the development of European armory as a whole, for the later English writers on heraldry were influenced by them.

Although the *Tractatus* represented a milestone in heraldic literature, it was no isolated literary development, for interest in heraldry was as keen in France as it was across the Channel. The close contacts between the English and French heralds, which we saw at Agincourt, would have been even more cordial during the earlier reign of King Richard II, and more professionally intimate during the English occupation of France in the reigns of King Henry V and King Henry VI. Two French heraldic treatises, dating from about this period and now in the College of Arms, throw an interesting light on the French approach to heraldry.

MOWBRAY'S FRENCH TREATISE

The earlier is College of Arms MS. 2nd L.12, which is a large vellum book consisting of two independent parts mixed up together. One is a general roll of 2,098 arms, mostly French and almost all depicted in banner form, well painted in colours, a form otherwise unknown in French armorials. Dr. Paul Adam-Even considered this part to be a French compilation of about 1365-1370, and the name 'Mowbray's Roll' (after an earlier owner) has been assigned to it.[1] The other part is a heraldic treatise in French, in a fifteenth-century hand, written on all the blank or partially blank pages among the banners of arms, and bearing no recognisable relationship or reference to them. For convenience, I propose to call this part 'Mowbray's French Treatise'. There is reason to think it may have formed part of the College's 'owld Lybrary' at its first foundation in 1484. The heraldic treatise falls into the following parts:

(i) The characteristics, properties and symbolism of beasts borne in arms, beginning with the Lion and the Leopard, and comprising some eighteen in all, including three fabulous beasts – the Leucrota, the Manitcora and the Unicorn. Apart from the more obvious beasts, there are several unexpected ones like the Hyaena, the Parandrus, the Monkey and the Ant.

(ii) The characteristics and properties of 'serpents', some six in all, including the Dragon, the Amphisboena and the Basilisk.

(iii) The characteristics and properties of fishes, some five in all, including the Mermaid, the Dolphin, the Whale and the Escallop.

(iv) The characteristics and properties of birds, some twenty-three in all, beginning with the Eagle and including the Calader and the Phoenix.

(v) A long passage on the properties and symbolism of precious stones ('ensuit de la vertu des pierres precieuses').

(vi) A complete French translation of the *Book of the Order of Chivalry*, originally written by the Spaniard Ramón Lull in about 1280, which enjoyed unflagging popularity in France and England throughout the Middle Ages.

(vii) A list of trees.

(viii) The rights, dues and largess belonging by ancient custom to the officers of arms, according to the English usage. [This suggests that the treatise may have been compiled in France during the English occupation].

(ix) The *'colores principales'* of heraldry, listed as argent, sable, or, azure, gules, vert and purpure, with their equivalents in precious stones, planets and so on.

BANYSTER'S FRENCH TREATISE

The other French treatise is also a vellum volume consisting of two parts: College of Arms MS. M. 19. The armorial portion has been given the name 'Banyster's Roll' (after an earlier owner), so it will be convenient to call the heraldic part 'Banyster's French Treatise'. It is written in an early fifteenth-century hand, and Dr. Paul Adam-Even considered it was probably compiled during the English occupation of Normandy, by a Norman employed as a herald or pursuivant by one of the English governors or commanders. The heraldic treatises falls into the following parts:

(i) A heraldic visitation of the Pays de Caux, in Normandy, including the abbeys, priories, towns and gentry.

(ii) A complete French translation of Ramón Lull's *Book of the Order of Chivalry*.

(iii) A lengthy description of the coronation ceremonies of French kings.

(iv) An interesting section on the 'office des heraulx et pours[uivants]', their duties and responsibilities.

(v) A short grammar of heraldry, in which are discussed the two metals and five colours of armory, their relative importance and symbolism and to whom they should be assigned. The Ordinaries and Subordinaries and rules for marshalling of arms complete this section.

(vi) A list of the beasts borne in arms, some twenty-seven, beginning with the Lion and Leopard, and including the Dragon, the Griffin and the Unicorn.

(vii) A list of the birds of heraldry, some twenty-six, beginning with the Eagle ('l'aigle est oysel Royal'), and including the Phoenix, the Flying Antelope, and the Flying Stag, as well as some unexpected natural birds such as the Ostrich.

(viii) The reptiles, which comprise five sorts, including the Basilisk and the Crocodile.

(ix) Some eighteen or so fishes, including the Dolphin and, surprisingly, the Hippopotamus, as well as the Mermaid, the 'chevalier de mer' (Merman?) and the Monk-fish.

(x) A general roll of arms, beginning with the Pope, Prester John, the Emperor of Constantinople, the peers of France, the Christian kings and the arms of French families.

What is noteworthy about these two French treatises is the sudden increase in the number of beasts, birds and fishes which are regarded as suitable to be borne in arms; indeed, one gets the impression that there is virtually no limit. While the Dragon, the Unicorn and the Griffin had been well established since the twelfth century, we now find the Manticora, the Amphisboena, the Calader, the Phoenix and the Mermaid, together with Flying Antelopes and Stags becoming established. The greater use of heraldic devices by the junior knights and even squires towards the end of the fourteenth and early fifteenth centuries, is borne out by the need which King Henry V found in 1417 to clamp down on the indiscriminate and unauthorised use of armorial devices. As arms were used in war and tournaments, it was necessary to keep the design of a shield as simple as possible and, as the Ordinaries and the traditional creatures of heraldry were used up, the newly armigerous gentleman had to make do with the more unusual creatures and fabulous beasts.

PRINSAULT'S TREATISE

At about this time – in the early part of the fifteenth century – an important French treatise on heraldry, Prinsault's Treatise, was compiled, which achieved instant popularity in France and was widely copied. One such copy[2] bears an interesting dedication: 'Cy commence certain traitié du blazon d'armes, composé et donné a Jacques, monseigneur, filz de monseigneur le duc de Nemours, conte de la Marche, par Clément Prinsault, très obéisant de mondit seigneur le duc et très humble serviteur de très révérend père en Dieu monseigneur de Castres, oncle dudit Jacques monseigneur.' A delightful miniature in colour shows the author, on bended knee, offering his book to the infant Jacques, who lies in his cot with a coverlet over him embroidered with arms, *Azure semee de Lys or, a Bendlet gules:* the arms of the Bourbon Dukes of Nemours. The only child of tender years who fits is Jacques, son of Bernard d'Armagnac, Duc de Nemours and Comte de la Marche, and his wife Eleonore (the daughter and heiress of Jacques de Bourbon, Duc de Nemours and Comte de la Marche and de Castres, King of Naples and Sicily), whom he married in 1429. Bernard d'Armagnac became Duc de Nemours in 1438/9. It seems a little unusual that only the Bourbon arms are depicted, but it may have been in compliment to the child's mother. This puts the probable date of Prinsault's Treatise at 1439 or soon after.

Prinsault's Treatise consists of twelve brief chapters on the basic elements of heraldry:

(i) The origin of armorial bearings, which were originally ordained by 'le très vaillant et victorieux Alixandre, roy de Macedoyne, le très puissant troyan Hector, le très prudent empereur Jules César, et plusiers aultres nobles princes'.

(ii) The composition of armorial devices.

(iii) Description of the metals, colours and furs used in arms and how they may be blazoned.

(iv) The symbolism of the metals and colours of heraldry and their equivalents in precious stones, the planets and the days of the week.

(v) Description of the nine Ordinaries: the Chief, the Pale, the Bend, the Fess, the Chevron, the Gyron, and Orle, the Cross and the Saltire.

(vi) How one should blazon charges when there are more than one.

(vii) The rules of blazon and the need to avoid placing a metal on a metal, or a colour on a colour, and how 'on peut discerner les faulses armes des vrayes'.

(viii) The order in which the fields and charges in shields should be blazoned.

(ix) Certain differences in the blazoning of birds as compared to beasts.

(x) How one blazons Lions, Leopards and other beasts in arms and the difference between Lions and Leopards.

(xi) Description of the Subordinaries and the different kinds of crosses.

(xii) Demonstration of how fifteen different examples of arms should be blazoned, ending with the arms of Presigny.

The copies of Prinsault's Treatise fall into three main types. The first, like that which Clément Prinsault compiled about 1439 and dedicated to the son of the Duc de Nemours, which consists only of the twelve chapters on the simple grammar of heraldry, is described above. The second, of which the most important example was probably compiled between 1440 and 1447, and was printed by L. C. Douet d'Arcq in 1858, consists of the twelve chapters augmented by a general roll of arms which, for convenience, we can call the 'Augmented Version'. The third type begins with the arms of Christ, followed by the twelve chapters, which are succeeded by a lengthy list describing the properties of beasts, birds and fishes borne in arms, mostly compiled towards the end of the fifteenth century, and which we can call the 'Passion Version'.

PRINSAULT'S TREATISE (AUGMENTED VERSION)
Typical of the Augmented Version is that printed by Douet d'Arcq.[3] The general roll of arms which follows the twelve chapters consists of seven categories of arms, depicted and blazoned, interspersed with comments of an armorial nature, which makes it look as if these general rolls of arms associated with heraldic treatises, which we find on both sides of the Channel, were intended to illustrate the preceding grammar of heraldry. The rolls vary from one copy of the treatise to another, but that in d'Arcq's copy is as follows:

The 'Verger de France'
The arms of certain French cities and towns, duchies and counties
The arms of the eighteen Christian kings
The arms of the twelve peers of France
The arms of the ten 'Nations'
The arms of the nine Muses
The emblems of the seven Arts

PRINSAULT'S TREATISE (PASSION VERSION)
The 'Passion Version', of which two copies are known,[4] is particularly interesting because, after a dedication to some patron (one was dedicated to King Charles VIII of France), it starts off with the arms of Christ, the shield charged with the Symbols of the Passion, followed by a ballade headed 'Cy commence le blazon des armes de nostre Redemption', in which each stanza ends with 'loyaulx amans recongnoissez ces armes'. Thereafter come the twelve chapters of Prinsault's Treatise, followed by a general roll of arms. After that comes a lengthy list of the beasts, birds and fishes borne in arms, which has been taken, almost verbatim, from the *Tractatus de Armis* of John

de Bado Aureo. Among the beasts one finds the Dragon ('porter le dragon en armes signifie le porteur grant et noble veneur, portant que le dragon est une beste ayant soif'), and among the birds the Griffin, while the passage on the Swan in arms is pure Bado Aureo.

Not only in England and France, but also in the Burgundian Netherlands, Spain and elsewhere in Europe, the heraldic imagination had taken wing by the early years of the fifteenth century, and many treatises on the creation, duties and rights of heralds, on armory in all its aspects and on noblesse and chivalry, were being compiled and extensively copied. This, however, is not the place to discuss them in any detail – that is a task for the future, when we have learnt more about them – and it must suffice here to draw attention to only a few of the more important.

Le Blason Des Couleurs En Armes

Jean Courtois of Mons, in Hainault (died 1437), who was Sicily Herald of Alphonso V, King of Aragon, Sicily and Naples, wrote a most important treatise on the heralds, their origins and duties, and another on *Le blason des couleurs en armes*. It deals exclusively with the colours of heraldry, their properties, virtues and symbolism, and their equivalents in the planets, precious stones and days of the week, and it had considerable contemporary popularity.

His contemporary Jean le Fèvre, Sieur de Saint-Remy (died 1468), who was appointed in 1430 Toison d'Or, the first King of Arms of the Order of the Golden Fleece, and was a famous herald of the Dukes of Burgundy, wrote a tract on the creation and duties of Montjoye King of Arms of France, besides other works of a historical and armorial nature. Many of the French treatises produced during this period contain similar chapters on the ceremonial to be observed on the creation of an emperor, king, count, marquis, viscount and baron, and also on the procedure on the promotion of a knight to banneret, as well as passages on military matters.

René of Anjou, King of Naples, Sicily and Jerusalem, wrote the *Livre des tournois,* or *Traictié de la forme et devis d'ung tournoy,* in about 1460 to 1465. Although it focuses on the arrangement, organisation, and conduct of tournaments, these have such a close bearing on the duties of the heralds – from the delivery of the challenge, to attending the presentation of the prize at the end – that the treatise consistutes an important contribution to heraldic literature.[5]

The close international confraternity of the heralds ensured that this heraldic literature passed quickly from country to country. The English occupation of Normandy and parts of France, under King Henry V and King Henry VI, brought the English and French heralds into regular professional contact, while the Anglo-Burgundian alliance would also have brought the English heralds into close relationship with their colleagues in the most brilliant Court in Europe.

De Studio Militari

It is not surprising, therefore, that Nicholas Upton's treatise, *Libellus de Militari Officio,* or *De Officio Militari* – more generally known since the seventeenth century as the *De Studio Militari* – was clearly influenced by the French heraldic treatises which were being produced at the time when Upton was on active service in France, where he may well have met their authors. As the *De Studio Militari* had as great an influence on heraldic thought and practice in England as any of its predecessors, it is worth looking both at the author and his book in some detail.

Nicholas Upton was born shortly before 1400 and is believed (but without actual proof) to have been the second son of John Upton, who held the manor of Puslinch in the parish of Newton Ferrers in Devonshire. He was admitted

Arms of John Rede, of Checkendon, Oxfordshire, the father of Sir Edmund Rede, from his brass in Checkendon Church (Society of Antiquaries, Croft–Lyons Bequest)

to Winchester College as a scholar in 1409, and went from there to New College, Oxford, on 16 December 1413. He became a Fellow in 1415, and graduated a B.C.L. in 1421, which may have given him his interest in heraldry, since it formed part of the curriculum of law students at that time. He was ordained sub-deacon on 8 March 1420/21, deacon on 22 March and a priest on 17 May 1421.

At that time King Henry V was raising a new army in England to take to France, to strengthen his forces already engaged in the French war. The excitement and glamour of service overseas evidently fired the imagination of the young Upton and he, too, went to France soon after taking orders. We next find him in the household of Thomas de Montagu, Earl of Salisbury, recently appointed military governor of Normandy and Maine, and one of the great generals of the Hundred Years' War. It has been suggested that Upton may have been his chaplain, but this seems unlikely because of his youth and because his legal qualifications would have been of more use to Salisbury. Upton himself refers to the Earl of Salisbury as 'dominum meum' or 'meus singularis dominus', and on another occasion speaks of the 'comitava et familia domini mei specialis et magistri'. The fact that he was a trained lawyer and took an informed and knowledgeable interest in military matters, as well as in heraldry, indicates that he was more probably one of the Earl of Salisbury's personal staff-officers and may perhaps have been his personal herald, because we know that he was concerned in two grants of arms by Salisbury.

He evidently accompanied Salisbury on his campaigns and was probably present at the bloody Battle of Verneuil, fought and won on 17 August 1424, which was described by the Speaker of the House of Commons a few years later as 'the greatest deed done by Englishmen in our days, save the Battle of Agincourt'. By his own account Upton designed and granted arms to one of Salisbury's personal squires, who had distinguished himself during the battle. In the passage in his book where Upton treats of the Ox in heraldry, he says that 'the oxe ys a common beeste, and is geldyd', from which it follows that 'to bere therfore oxen or theyr heddes hyt betokeneth that the berer of theym fyrste was geldyd or maymed so in his privi partes that he was unable for generation. And yt was my chance on a tyme to geve to a certen gentilman and squyer of my lord and maysters howsehold iii black oxe heddes to bere in his armes in a feld of silver, bycause at the batell of Vernals [Verneuil] he was stryken wt a spere throughe the privi partes and so thereby made unable to generation ['cum lancia per membra genitalia totaliter transfixus']'. Salisbury commanded the left division of the English army at Verneuil and had a particularly fierce battle against the Scots' division, who were fighting with the French, opposite him, no quarter being asked or given. *Argent three Ox heads sable* are the arms of the family of Walrond, of Bradfield in the parish of Uffculme in Devonshire, and as the family still flourishes today in that county, one can only suppose that Squire Walrond had sired his brood before he met with his unfortunate experience at the hands of a Scottish spearman and was ennobled for his pains.

Upton may have accompanied the Earl of Salisbury to Paris in July 1428 and thence to the siege of Orleans in October – where Salisbury was badly wounded in the face by a cannon ball which struck the lintel of the window by which he was standing; he died eight days later. Master Nicholas Upton was appointed in his Will one of the eight executors – evidence that a close friendship had developed between the Earl and Upton, and that the Earl placed considerable reliance on his loyalty, competence and judgement, for he was mentioned first and appears to have been the most active in dealing subsequently with the estate.

Although Nicholas Upton was admitted rector of Chedzoy in Somerset in

Arms of Walrond, of Bradfield, Devon (drawn by G. Mussett)

77

August 1427, and granted papal dispensation in December 1429, to hold an additional incompatible benefice for three years, he was evidently mainly an absentee, since he was fully employed overseas. He is said to have served under William de la Pole, Earl of Suffolk, and Sir John Talbot, afterwards Earl of Shrewsbury, both outstanding and active soldiers; but further evidence is required before we can accept this. We do know, however, that Upton was granted letters of protection, on 14 January 1429/30, on going overseas in the retinue of Cardinal Beaufort – who had raised an army for a crusade against the Hussites in Bohemia – which on landing in France was diverted to strengthening the hard-pressed English forces there. Three months later Nicholas Upton had transferred to the King's retinue, when letters of protection were issued to him, on 10 April 1430, on going overseas; but a few days later he was appointed to the staff of Lord Tiptoft, who was in command of a division of the army which accompanied King Henry VI to France[6]. The army crossed the Channel on 23 April, and it was during this campaign that their Burgundian allies captured Joan of Arc and the English re-established control over Paris. Presumably Upton was there when King Henry entered in state on 29 July, 1430.

Nicholas Upton evidently returned to England early in 1431, as he became Canon of Wells Cathedral and Prebendary of Dinder on 6 April that year. From then onwards ecclesiastical preferments came steadily, no doubt due to the patronage of Humphrey, Duke of Gloucester, who is said to have encouraged Upton to return to his books. Upton referred to Duke Humphrey as 'domino meo singulari' in his dedication of the *De Studio Militari*. On 10 April 1443 he became Canon of St. Paul's, London, holding the Prebend of Wildland, but he vacated this on being appointed Precentor of Salisbury Cathedral on 14 May 1446. In 1452 Upton was one of the Proxies of the Dean and Chapter of Salisbury to press the case for the canonisation of their founder Osmund, and he was at the Roman Curia from June that year until May 1453; but the mission was not, at that time, successful and he returned to Salisbury, where he remained until his death shortly before 15 February 1456/57, and he was buried at Salisbury.

Upton had evidently been keenly interested in heraldry from an early age, for he tells us in his book, in a disarming passage which claims one's sympathy, that 'Formerly in my youth I wrote on this matter in too dreamy a manner, and in that my writing I must confess to have made many errors, as in condemning the colour green, and I have stated many other matters which are contrary to the truth'. He says he would have liked to burn these early mistakes and now proposes to correct them. Disparaging remarks about the colour green in arms would not have been well received by his master, the Earl of Salisbury, the second quartering in whose arms was that for Monthermer, *Gold an Eagle displayed vert,* and one can imagine a painful and embarrassing interview with the Earl.

Apart from his famous heraldic treatise, Upton is said to have written many other works besides, as well as erudite sermons. His literary tastes ranged from Augustine's *Super Johannem* (a copy of which he gave to Winchester College) and Jerome's *Epistolae* (now in Cambridge University Library, MS. Gg. iv. 2) to the *De Proprietatibus Rerum* of Bartholomew the Englishman (a copy of which also he gave to Winchester), that essential encyclopaedia for every medieval gentleman, which clearly provided much of the material regarding the beasts and birds in Book IV of the *De Studio Militari.* He also owned a fine copy of *La Roman de la Rose* (now British Museum Royal MS. 19. B. xii), that classic allegory of courtly and profane love, which was one of the most popular and widely-read books throughout the Middle Ages. It is not without interest that Christine de Pisan, the indefatigable champion of women's rights, regarded *La Roman de la Rose* as a pernicious book, which tended, she felt, to degrade women.

The picture of Upton which emerges is that of a worldly and civilised cleric, equally at home in the camp, the court or the cloister, capable of making and keeping firm friends with the great in both political factions of the uneasy England in which he lived. He was by all accounts an able lawyer, in both civil and canon law; moreover, his service overseas brought him into close touch with all the great soldiers of the time, and he would have had countless opportunities, not only to discuss heraldic matters with experienced knights, and see their application on the battlefield, but also to know the heralds. We must, therefore, take it that the views he expresses in the *De Studio Militari* are those which would have been held by his contemporaries, and this no doubt explains the immediate popularity of his book, which was to have such an influence on the imaginations of the Tudor heralds.

The *De Studio Militari* was completed after Upton became Precentor of Salisbury, on 14 May 1446, and before the death nine months later, on 23 February 1446/47, of Humphrey, Duke of Gloucester, to whom it is dedicated. Its immediate popularity created a contemporary demand for additional copies and this continued for the next century; so it is difficult to determine which copies most nearly represent the original, for Duke Humphrey's copy has not so far been identified. The difficulty is further aggravated by the fact that the many still-existing copies follow one or other of two appreciably different versions of the *De Studio Militari*, one represented by the text printed by Sir Edward Bysshe in 1654, and the other by the copy made by Baddesworth in 1458.

Bysshe tells us that he examined several different copies of the *De Studio Militari* when preparing the text which he printed. Two he owned himself and 'two most beautiful copies' were lent him by John Selden, one of which is the Morton copy; while Sir Thomas Cotton lent him the Rede copy and Sir William Le Neve lent another.

Of the many copies of the *De Studio Militari* which exist, the Hals copy (Fitzwilliam Museum MS. 324) seems most likely to represent the original text, because there are grounds for believing that it was given to John Hals by Upton himself. Hals was the second son of John Hals of Keynedon in the parish of Sherford, Devon, a Justice of the King's Bench. Like Upton, Hals was educated at Oxford, and he became Provost of Oriel College in 1446 and Chaplain to Queen Margaret. Subsequently he received many Church preferments, becoming Bishop of Coventry and Lichfield in 1459. In 1470 he was Keeper of the Privy Seal to King Henry VI. He died in 1490. Hals, a politically active cleric, was quite possibly a friend of Upton, and there seems to be no good reason for disbelieving the story that Upton gave him this copy, as it is in a hand of about 1450. The interesting point about the Hals copy is that it tallies closely with the printed version and with the Rede copy, and it seems unlikely that a man of Hals's standing would have been given, or would have commissioned, a copy of anything but the original.

This brings us to the magnificent Rede copy (British Museum Cotton MS. Nero C.iii), which is now usually on permanent display in the public galleries of the British Museum. The illuminated capital letter at the beginning of the book contains a quarterly shield of arms, which can only be those of Sir Edmund Rede, of Boarstall in Buckinghamshire, hereditary Forester of Bernwood, who was knighted in 1465 and died in 1487. These arms show Rede quartering James of Boarstall, fitzNiel of Boarstall, and Marmion of Checkenden; and impaling those of his wife Katherine, the daughter of John Cottesmore, Chief Justice of the Common Pleas, namely Cottesmore quartering Bruley. The arms of Rede alone, *Azure three Pheasants or,* are repeated on folio 58, and those of his mother, Christina James, are repeated on folio 52. There can, therefore, be no doubt that this copy was commissioned by Sir

Arms of Humphrey, Duke of Gloucester (drawn by N. Manwaring)

Edmund Rede in about 1450, and he was the sort of man who might well have taken an intelligent interest in heraldry, and was wealthy enough to be able to afford a book of this kind. He moved in the same social, legal and political circles as Upton and could have known him personally, so here too it seems unlikely that Rede would have had a copy of a version which was not the original.

The Morton copy (College of Arms MS. Arundel 64) is in a hand of the third quarter of the fifteenth century. It bears on the flyleaf, in a different and slightly later hand, the shield of arms and rebus (the letter 'MOR' upon a tun, or barrel) of John Morton, who began life as an active lawyer practising chiefly in the ecclesiastical courts, when he would no doubt have known Upton. He became Prebendary of Salisbury in 1458, Master of the Rolls in 1472, Archbishop of Canterbury in 1486 and also Lord Chancellor (of 'Morton's Fork' notoriety), and finally Cardinal in 1493, dying in 1500. The Morton copy tallies with the printed version and with the Rede copy. Here again, it seems unlikely that Morton would have acquired a copy which was not Upton's original.

We now come to the Holkham copy (Bodleian Library ms. Holkham misc. 31), which may possibly be the original which Nicholas Upton gave to Duke Humphrey, although at present there is insufficient evidence to prove this. It is a handsomely produced volume, almost as good as the Rede copy, which it closely resembles both in format and style. A note at the end of the book (on fo. 72) in the hand of James Strang(e)man, the antiquary (died about 1595), tells us something of its provenance. He states that it had formerly belonged to William Hervey, Clarenceux King of Arms (died 1567), whose wife was 'oone of the pryvey chamber of ye late quen Mary', who gave her the wardship and marriage of William, the son of Ralph Latham, lord of the manor of Upminster, Essex, where she died. Strangman was, in fact, wrong, because it was 'Susan Clarenceux', widow, and Gentlewoman of the Privy Chamber to Queen Mary, to whom this wardship was given on 22 December 1557, (see Cal. Pat. Rolls, 1557–8, p. 302); so the book must have belonged to Thomas Hawley, Clarenceux, who died on 22 August 1557. He made William Hervey his executor and left him his books, but Susan appears to have taken this copy with her. William Latham, of Sandon in Essex, subsequently married James Strangman's sister Anne, and Strangman says he obtained the book as the result of a family arrangement. It later came into the possession of Sir Edward Coke (died 1634), who believed it to have been the copy owned by Humphrey, Duke of Gloucester.

There is also extant another copy which tallies with the printed version, namely the English translation made by John Blount, a 'student in the universite of Oxforthe', in about 1500 (now Bodleian Library MS. Eng. Misc. D. 227), at the request of William Blount, Lord Mountjoy, K.G., the pupil and patron of Erasmus and friend of Sir Thomas More. Parts of it have been published by F. P. Barnard, with a most useful introduction and brief biographical particulars of John Blount, and he concludes that there are indications that the codex from which Blount translated, then in the possession of an unnamed nobleman, was not any of those consulted by Bysshe.[7] The racy style, rather reminiscent of Lord Berners's translation of Froissart, makes this copy a joy to read, but the translation is pretty free throughout and Blount did not hesitate to paraphrase or even skip portions when he felt like it.

The texts of all these copies follow the same sequence as the printed version:

Introduction and dedication to Humphrey, Duke of Gloucester.

Book I.   *De milicia et nobilitate*
Of nineteen chapters or sections. The first seven discuss war in general, knights and knighthood, discipline, and the rights of belli-

BOWND·TO·OBEY· AND·SERVE·

·REGINA· IANE·

Jn Amos ye thrid of nobill memorie yn fiele
dir lenfit to hnem hintie marreit ye Dowgt
of Denmark Dowghter fair ye Hnem
Dowgt Jamos ye ford to him sche bure

gerents. Chapters eight to twelve treat of couriers, pursuivants and heralds. The remainder deal with privileges and punishments and the duties of commanders and their lieges, while the last discusses 'to whom dessendyth nobilite'.

Book II.   *De bellis et actibus exercitus*
Of fourteen chapters, beginning with a consideration of just wars and the different kinds of war. Chapters three to eight concern duels and trial by battle, and the rest discuss safe-conducts.

Book III.   *De nobilitate colorum in armis depictorum*
Of sixteen chapters or sections, discussing in great detail the colours of heraldry, their relative nobility, precedence, and symbolism. Following John de Bado Aureo, Upton places the colours in the following sequence: white, black, gold, blue, red, purple and green; plus 'graye or russett coloure', 'leden or browne', 'asshen or cr[e]ame', 'eerthy or sandy', and 'fawny or salowe coloure' (the Latin is not much help, so one can sympathise with John Blount's difficulty in translation).

Book IV.   *De regulis et signis in armis*
Of some one hundred and ninety-five sections, beginning with a short introduction, after which it treats of the Lion in heraldry, and wanders off into a discussion of the arms of Scotland and the attributed arms of Uther Pendragon, King Arthur and Edward the Confessor, coming back to the Lions in the arms of England. This evidently reminded Upton of a poem relevant to the subject, which he quotes, commenting that 'by these forsaid verses yt ys evydent that the foresaid [King] Rycharde bore leons & no leopards'. This is followed by a dissertation on the Royal Arms, leading to a discussion of the rights of the Kings of England to quarter the Royal Arms of France.

The memory of those earlier, glorious campaigns in France under King Henry V leads Upton to disgress still further, and he includes a copy of the statutes of King Henry V regulating the conduct and discipline of the army on active service. These begin with the inviolability of churches, priests, and women ('spirituall men and . . . . women not to be ravysshed'), watch and ward, musters, lodgings, prisoners, safe-conducts and 'the avoydance and ridding away of common harlottes'. This part, consisting of some seventeen chapters or sections, ends with the remark that 'here nowe may you evidently see, by the chapter alledged here affore as touching prisoners, how that John the Frenche Kinge was trewe prisonier to Edward the iijd. Kinge of Englande'. Upton then returns abruptly to the Leopard in heraldry. (It was this part, interpolated between the Lion and the Leopard, which persuaded Professor E. J. Jones that the tidier and more logical sequence of the Baddesworth Version was the correct one, but I suggest that it is just as likely that this is a typical medieval digression, and that Sir Edward Bysshe can be absolved from the charge of carelessness in the collation of his source material. If this view is correct, then the printed version, and the copies which tally with it, most nearly represent Upton's original).

Having dealt with the Royal Beasts, the Lion and the Leopard, Upton then discusses the other beasts borne in heraldry, which are dealt with alphabetically by their Latin names, beginning with the Ram (*de ariete*), and which total thirty-one. In the medieval

King James III of Scotland and his wife Margaret, daughter of the King of Denmark. The fourth quarter of her skirt depicts the Dragon quartering in the arms of Denmark. (Coll. Arms ms. Hector le Breton, vol. ii, f. 13)

fashion, we find the Spider, the Bee, the Toad, the Ant or 'pysmer', the Griffin and the Unicorn included among the beasts. The birds borne in heraldry begin with the Eagle and Double-Eagle, being royal and imperial birds, and then continue alphabetically; among them we find the Harpy, the 'Merlion' or Martlet, and the Bat, with the Dragon tacked on at the end. Of the fishes borne in arms, only the Dolphin and the Pike or Luce are mentioned. The sections on the beasts, birds and fishes used in heraldry bear a close resemblance to similar passages in contemporary French heraldic treatises. Next come examples of Roses and Fleurs de Lys in arms, and then follow the Ordinaries and Subordinaries, beginning with twenty-eight different kinds of crosses. These take up some ninety-four sections of the book. Upton concludes with a consideration of the 'questione wych hathe bene often tymes movyd', whether arms given by a prince or lord are of greater authority than those self-assumed, and repeats the views expressed a century earlier by Bartolo di Sasso Ferrato.

DE STUDIO MILITARI (BADDESWORTH VERSION)

The Baddesworth Version of the *De Studio Militari* was compiled some eleven years after Nicholas Upton completed the original version, as appears from the copy now in the British Museum,[8] 'explicit libellus vocatus libellus de officio militari script per Baddesworth ao. dom. m.iiij.lviij' (i.e. 1458). This version has been discussed at length by Professor E. J. Jones, who has compared it in some detail with the Rede copy, so it is not necessary here to do more than mention its main characteristics. The principal difference is in the order of the four books which comprise the treatise; also, Baddesworth omits the passage containing the statutes of King Henry V from his Book II (Upton's Book IV), while there has been some rearrangement of the other books. As Professor Jones pointed out, the Baddesworth Version is in many ways more logical, but it is difficult to think of it as more than an attempt to tidy up the discursive original. It is not without significance that Upton died the year before Baddesworth produced his version. So far it has not been possible to identify Baddesworth, although the name is very uncommon.

Whoever its author, Baddesworth's Version was sufficiently popular for several copies to be made of it, possibly because of its very bold and lively illustrations, not only of the beasts and birds of heraldry, but also of the couriers, knights, pursuivants and heralds with which his fourth chapter (the larger part of Upton's Book I and all of his Book II) is concerned. The best and most notable copy is that made in 1572 by Robert Glover, Somerset Herald (College of Arms MS. Vincent 444), which reproduces most of the illustrations; these are more finely executed than those in the British Museum copy (Add. MS. 30946). At least two copies[9] of Baddesworth's Version contain an *explicit* (or conclusion) at the end of Book I, which is preceded by a cipher or monogram 'HL' and reads 'Lancaster Rex Heraldorum in partibus Borialibus'. The only Lancaster King of Arms of the North of England who was living at the right time was William Tyndale, who was created Lancaster King of Arms in 1450 and died shortly after 1460. Sir Thomas Holme was created Marshal of the North in 1462 and Norroy King of Arms in 1464, since which date Lancaster ceased to be King of Arms of the North.

JOHN'S TREATISE

Of the many works on armory which exist from this period, there is a group of English heraldic treatises which were compiled about the middle of the fifteenth century, and are important for the light they shed on armorial theory and practice at that time. Not only do they follow much the same sequence,

...in in ffyssellis goddes ... and ... ...

He beryth gold in ... chastlewis goddes. And he bere in

thys wyse ... thow most say he beryth sylu in lossengeor

verte. And if þ be many lossengeor than he beryth lossege

And if þ be many chastelewis pan he beryth maskle And

if he bere many ffussellis than he beryth ffusele. And all

man of brędis be membryd. And all man of bestes ben

armed save only the Grysto. to hym þe most say þ he is

bothe membryd And armed for he is halfe fowle halfe

best. fforthermore yhe shall knawe þ it is bothe pittyd

And delfed in armes And yf he bere thus He beryth

sylu A pitte sabyll And if he bere thus he beryth verte

a delfe sylu. Also they yo in armes Byllet And hedonuett

Of he bere thus he beryth sylu in Byllett goddes.

And if he bere thus he beryth Asure in hedonuett

goldis Also they is in endentyng of in armes one after the

seyow. And Anothyr after closidez. And if he bere thus

He beryth gold is goddes pty þ pale endentyd. And

if he bere thus he beryth sylu a goddes pty þ

pale closidy endendyng. Also þ ben thyndges in armez

that be yased as hedes and leggz as thus if he bere in

thys wyse he beryth sylu A lyouns hede yased

goddes. And if he bere thus he beryth

Asure And esses hedi yased gold. And if he bere

thus he beryth verte A lyonus leggz yased goddes

Also there be many armes that be overcrussy þ fielde

men knawez. As thus he beryth sylu a sabyll overruwy

And also they is in armez lenyy and belly of he

ber in thys wyse he beryth sylu and goddes lenyy

And if he bere in thus man of wyse

he beryth sylu and verte belly. j. et extey. j.

but their phraseology is remarkably similar. In some cases they may represent lectures given to law students at the Inns of Court; in others they are evidently notes made by students. A closer study of them might well give us some idea of the kind of curriculum which was followed in the law schools for teaching heraldry at that time.

The prototype seems to be John's Treatise.[10] There is, alas, no clue as to its author's identity, although Dallaway suggests he might be John Dade.[11] One can infer that John was probably a teacher of heraldry, as his opening remarks seem to indicate:

> Forasmoch as I, John, have late in this Worldes ende perceyued in saule many Gentilmen in armes blasying slomerously to slepe and dreme, them from their sompnolency, that besemes no gentill blode to which Armes belongen, to wakyn and their oppynions to socour and counceill, al curiositee sette opart, have existimate myself that me foloyng may have the more waker conyngsaunce in that partie of ciuylians conclusions, this litill tretis oute of latyn into englissh, suying [i.e. following] the fote steppes of the right nobill predecessour Fraunces de Foueys in his boke intitled *De Picturis Armorum,* have putte my vigilant penne.

It rather looks as if John may have been a lecturer in the law schools, because his reference to 'ciuylians conclusions' must refer to the civil law, which governed the laws of arms and still does.

John's Treatise, then, falls into the following parts or sections, most of which are accompanied by examples and small drawings of the charges discussed:

(i) A brief discussion of the origin of armory, beginning 'As herodes [i.e. heralds] recorden, the beginninge and grownde of Armes was at the sege of Troy . . . '. (This opening is found in all the treatises in the group).

(ii) The six cadency marks, still used in English heraldry, for differencing the children of an armiger, 'and if ther were any moo brederen then [i.e. than] VI then the fadir shuld giffe them what difference that shuld plese hym best'.

(iii) A brief treatment of the tinctures of heraldry: 'And ye shall undirstonde that in armes ar ij mctalls and V colours.'

(iv) The prinicipal Ordinaries: 'And ye shal knowe that ther be iiij thynges that breken armes, that is to sey, Bendes, Fecys, Cheuerons and Barres'.

(v) A description of the various roundels. 'Also ther be vij rounde thynges in Armes.'

(vi) 'Also ther be iiij thynges that partis colours in armes, that is to sey, Pales, Bendes, Cheuerons and Fecys.' Examples are given.

(vii) 'And ye shal undirstand that a bastard beres comonly in his armes a baston as thus.' Examples are given.

(viii) Further comments on the difference between a Bar and a Fess, also a Bend and a Baston.

(ix) 'Allso ye shall understande yt a man shall beare hysse fathers armes and hys mother quarterly, and hys own armes and hys wyves per paly'.

(x) Discussion of Frets, Fusils, Mascles and Lozenges in arms.

(xi) Discussion of the blazoning of birds and beasts.

(xii) 'Also ther is in armes both Pittes and Delfes.'

(xiii) Discussion of Billets and Humetts.

(xiv) 'Also ther is ij endentynges in armes, one after Paale and one after

THE
ART
OF
Making
DEVISES.

Done into English
by Tho: Blovnt
Gent:
1646.

Cloudes.' Examples are given.
- (xv) Discussion of Gyronny arms.
- (xvi) 'And also ye shall undirstand that ther been xv maners of lyons in armes.'
- (xvii) 'Also ther been xv maners of crosses in armes.'

Another version of John's Treatise, now in my possession and formerly in the Phillipps Collection, follows this text pretty closely, but it is on a loose sheet of paper and looks like a lecturer's notes.[12] Other versions of this treatise usually include further matter.

Strangways' Book

Another armorial manuscript which has affinities with this group is Strangways' Book, the first part of which appears to be notes of lectures based on John's Treatise, and taken down by Sir Richard Strangways when he was a law student at the Inner Temple, in about 1450. Both the writing and the drawings give the impression that they were roughly and hurriedly done. This treatise is discussed in considerable detail by the late Hugh Stanford London, Norfolk Herald of Arms Extraordinary.[13]

Somewhat similar is the Harleian Version of John's Treatise,[14] the Heralds' Version, the Ashmolean Version,[15] and Dethick's Version.[16] The Sloane Tract[17] also appears to fall within this group of treatises. It begins to look as if the general rolls of arms, of which many examples have survived from the Middle Ages – some mixed up with treatises on heraldry and some alone – were probably used for teaching purposes, while others may have been produced as 'masterpieces' by which pursuivants completed their apprenticeships before being created heralds.

With the advent of printing towards the end of the century, books on chivalry began to appear, like Ramón Lull's *Book of the Order of Chivalry* – first written some two hundred years earlier and included in several heraldic treatises since – which was printed by William Caxton in about 1484. This was followed in 1486 by *The Boke of St. Albans,* printed by the Schoolmaster of St. Albans. In this, the third and largest part concerns armory; much of it, particularly the sections on the different kinds of crosses and the Ordinaries and Subordinaries, is lifted from Upton's *De Studio Militari.*

The sixteenth and seventeenth century writers on heraldry were clearly influenced by their predecessors, as we may see by a glance at Gerard Legh's *The Accedens of Armory,* first published in 1562 and reprinted five times; or John Bossewell's *Workes of Armorie,* published in 1572; or *A Display of Heraldrie* by John Guillim, Rouge Croix Pursuivant, first published in 1611, which was so popular that it ran to six posthumous editions.

However 'slomerously' sleeping and dreaming the armigerous gentry may have been in the fifteenth century, it is clear from this necessarily superficial survey of the heraldic literature produced during the later Middle Ages that the lawyers and the heralds were diligently studying the art and science of armory and publishing the results of their labours, which were widely read by contemporary courtiers, lords, knights and also heralds. We can therefore take it that their views were generally accepted and, in the arms, crests, supporters and badges which were granted in the fifteenth and sixteenth centuries, we can see how the heraldic imagination made its contribution to the literary, social and military life of the period. In the chapters which follow, we shall see how this imaginative approach to an essentially stern and military art produced some of the most enchanting flights of fancy.

Part III
The Heraldic Imagination in Action

THE romances and poems of the Middle Ages show that armory was regarded as a gay and colourful part of life, and this is echoed by many of the heraldic treatises. Heraldry was fun, and at the same time packed with allegory and symbolism, embellishing with a wealth of colour houses, clothes and books, while serving at the same time the practical necessities of war and politics. Like most things in the Middle Ages there was a certain cheerful disorder about it, for only since the Tudors have writers on armory tried to turn it into a portentous and pedantic science.

As we have seen, it was not until the fifteenth century that the heralds began to cater for the more flamboyant armorial whims of their masters; and, with the rise of the Tudors, the sixteenth century kings of arms really embarked on extravagant flights of fancy, harnessing some odd chimerical creatures – although they had fairly respectable literary antecedents – and inventing some remarkably bizarre ones. They were, however, reflecting the spirit of their age and we should be curmudgeons to cavil at these flights of the heraldic imagination. We have been fortunate in having the fantastic beauty of heraldry to enrich our lives, and the tenacious traditions of Western Europe have kept it alive and vital to this day.

8
The Heavenly Host in Heraldry

T is not, perhaps, surprising that heralds have always been drawn towards Angels, for they are the ambassadors and messengers of God, (the Herald Angels of whom we sing at Christmas) and the normal duties of a medieval herald were very similar. A mere earthly herald can therefore discuss his more exalted professional colleagues with the respect due to their seniority. In the rigidly hierarchical world of our forefathers, it was natural that they should look for and find a similarly hierarchical order in heaven; but with such conflicting evidence from the Scriptures and the early Fathers of the Church, it is small wonder that there is some obscurity about the functions of the different ranks of Angels and a blurring of the lines of demarcation between them. It is not for a herald to venture into a theological discussion of these celestial beings, but only for him to discuss them in their heraldic context; nevertheless, to understand their heraldic significance and use one must touch briefly on their theological significance, imagery and iconography, for one led to the other and the last influenced the heraldic artist.[1]

There seems to be a little uncertainty regarding the precise sequence of the Orders, or ranks in the celestial hierarchy. Apart from the earlier references in the Bible to the Seraphim, Cherubim, Archangels and Angels, St Paul in the Epistle to the Colossians states: 'By him were all things created that are in heaven, and that are in earth, visible and invisible, whether they be thrones, or dominions, or principalities, or powers.'[2] This was taken by the early Fathers to refer to types of heavenly beings, and the Pseudo-Dionysius tidied them all up about the fifth century, attributing his work to Dionysius the Aeropagite, St Paul's Athenian convert, thus giving his thesis immediate respectability and providing succeeding generations with an order of battle of the heavenly host. St Gregory the Great, in the next century, produced a slightly revised list of the Orders and, on the testimony of Ezekiel, allocated to each certain jewels, by which they were distinguished. Between the triune God and mankind, the Pseudo-Dionysius deduced nine Orders in the celestial hierarchy, arranged in three triads. The first triad is nearest to the throne of glory and dedicated mainly to the ecstatic adoration of God, but it is employed on rare occasions on the most important business of the Lord.

The Orders consist of :

1. SERAPHIM, of whom there are said to be four, who surround the throne of glory, ceaselessly intoning the trisagion. They usually have six wings and are generally depicted as human in form with the upper pair of wings crossed behind their heads, the middle pair displayed, and the lower pair crossed in front of their legs. Sometimes they are depicted as boys' heads, wiht the six wings around them similarly positioned. Their jewel is the sard (red), emblematic of the fire of divine love, and, by the same token, they were frequently shown as standing in flames. They are exceedingly rare in heraldry.

2. CHERUBIM, who are the guardians of the throne and of the holy places and act from time to time as the terrible ministers of God. A more precise description of them follows under the appropriate head, but complete Cherubim generally have four wings. While by no means common, they are usually depicted in heraldry as boys' heads with two wings displayed on either side. Their jewel is the topaz (yellow) and, as repositories of divine wisdom and as keepers of the celestial records, the attribute most frequently given them in Christian iconography is the Book of Knowledge.

3. THRONES, a class of usually six-winged Super Angels. They are in close attendance on God, and help to reflect the divine effulgence outward to the next triad. Their stone is the jasper (green) and, as agents of divine justice, they are often depicted as holding scales. I have not found them specifically mentioned in heraldry.

The second triad also normally avoids direct contagion with mortal man, directing and largely working through the lowest triad. They are usually shown with four wings, although six-winged and two-winged varieties are known. They do not appear specifically in heraldry. They consist of :

4. DOMINATIONS, who represent the concept of divine sovereignty and manifest the majesty of God, as well as directing the duties of the lower Angels. They are usually depicted with royal crowns, robes and sceptres, and their jewel is the chrysolite (green and gold).

5. VIRTUES, whose principal task is to work miracles on earth and to bestow grace and valour on those worthy of it. Their stone is the sapphire (blue) and they are often shown holding a pyx.

6. POWERS, whose duty it is to frustrate the knavish tricks of those devils who are bent on overthrowing the world, and to combat the forces of evil. In consequence they are frequently shown embattled in armour, holding a drawn sword and, unlike most of the other Angels, are often shod. Their jewel is the beryl (white).

The third triad concern themselves directly with the affairs of mankind. In consequence they appear quite often in heraldry, sometimes as charges in a shield of arms or crest, but more often as supporters to it and frequently just as artistic adjuncts to a general heraldic composition. They are nearly always depicted with only two wings and consist of :

7. PRINCIPALITIES, who are essentially the Angels of the establishment, protecting religion and watching over the princes of the world and the leaders of peoples. They are, therefore, often depicted with princely crowns and drawn swords. Their jewel is the onyx (pink).

8. ARCHANGELS, of whom there are seven, 'who stand before God' and are his ambassadors plenipotentiary. They also hold positions of command in each of the higher Orders, and each has an emblem appropriate to him. The jewel worn by all of them is the carbuncle (red).

9. ANGELS. The name comes from the Greek *angelos*, a messenger, and confusion can arise because the name is loosely applied to those in all the other Orders also. The ordinary Angels are the private soldiers of the heavenly host and their duty is to deal directly with mankind, each also concerning himself with one particular individual: they are the Guardian Angels who look after each of us. The Bishop of Tusculum estimated in 1273, that after the Fallen Angels had been driven out there were left in heaven 266,613,336 Angels; so that unless their number has been subsequently augmented the population explosion on earth has outrun the supply of Angels per capita – although Randle Holme, writing in 1688, believed that 'there remained still in Heaven . . . . more Angels than there was, is, and shall be'.

However, we need not linger over the exact computation of the number of Angels in heaven: one more or less is not going to affect their employment as supporters to a coat of arms, or as charges in a shield or crest. What matters is how the various Angels should be depicted in heraldry, their significance, attributes and iconography. I shall be discussing these in more detail in the following pages, but there are certain broad considerations which apply generally to the several Orders.

During the Renaissance and the opulent days of the eighteenth century and on into the romantic revival of the nineteenth century and the irreligious twentieth century, Angels were frequently depicted as female, but such scriptural authority as there is points to their being either male or sexless. The Prophet Mohammed was quite clear on the point and in Sura 53 of the Koran states, 'It is they who believe not in the life to come, who name the Angels with the names of females.' Gustav Davidson, in his *Dictionary of Angels*,[3] has noted a number of female Angels, but in general they seem to be a later Jewish accretion and several of them are pretty disreputable, like the enthusiastic Lilith, one of the four Angels of Prostitution. A heraldic artist, would therefore, be well advised to avoid female Angels. [We must also be grateful to Mr Davidson for drawing our attention to the fact that the Talmudic name for an Angel of indeterminate sex is a 'Tumtum'.]

Because people find it difficult to imagine superior beings in other than their own image, or at any rate in some combination of the human and the fabulous, Angels of all sorts have usually been depicted as winged human forms. Guillim considered that

> albeit those heavenlie Spirits bee in their selfe nature void of all corporall or materiall substance, yet it is certaine, when it pleased God so to imploy them, they had assumpted bodies for the time, to the end they might the more effectuallie accomplish the service that God injoined them . . . . These bodies and the bodily faculties were given them to the end they might more familiarly converse and discourse with the godly, to whom they were sent, and the better performe the charge injoined them, insomuch as they did unfainedly eat and drinke, as Zanchius noteth; whereby they did the better conceale their proper nature, until such time as they should make knowen unto men what they were indeed. Heerupon it seemeth the Ancients of forepassed ages have usurped the bearing of Angels in Coat-armours, according to the bodily shapes and habits wherein they appeared unto men.[4]

As the ordinary Angels of the lowest Order act as the Guardian Angels of mankind, it would be appropriate to depict them as benevolent; but those in the higher Orders become increasingly terrible the closer they get to the throne of glory, and it would be more correct to show them as embattled, stern or minatory rather than as amiable. We must necessarily be dependent on medieval art for representations of the Angels of the several Orders and, although their iconography was interpreted pretty freely, there are certain guide-lines for us to follow.

We have seen that the Angels of each of the Orders have certain characteristics and that certain jewels and objects are especially associated with those in each Order. It is important, when depicting and blazoning heraldically an Angel in one of the higher Orders to specify what sort he is. An Angel *tout court,* for example, must be taken to be of the ninth Order and so depicted.

In medieval England Angels were usually depicted wearing a long white or sometimes gold garment, like an alb, reaching down to the feet and girded in at the waist, with apparels or borders, often of the colour of their jewel. They also wear either a scarf around the neck or an amice, with similar apparels. Throughout the Middle Ages, however, in most European countries we find them from the earliest times wearing garments of any of the symbolic colours used in Christian art, and in the later Middle Ages this was usually so in England as well. There are also examples of naked Angels. With the exception of the Powers and some of the Archangels they never wear shoes or sandals. In the fifteenth century the Angels of the first triad were often

Royal Arms of France with Angel supporters (drawn by G. Mussett)

depicted with their bodies and legs covered in red or golden feathers. Arch-angels and some in the higher Orders sometimes wear a cross-diadem, and all have haloes. Any or all can also be depicted as playing musical instruments symbolic of rejoicing. They are always depicted as young, clean-shaven and vigorous, ever ready to do the instant bidding of God. Unless blazoned other-wise, they are to be taken as standing, the Seraphim upon flames, while the rest can be free or standing upon clouds or anything suitable.

Towards the end of the Middle Ages the Kings of France dressed the Angels supporting their shield in tabards of the royal arms of France, a conceit which was later followed by several of the German princes. But it seems to be going a little too far to harness Angels to shields in a subservient capacity, because Angels are the heralds of God and not the retainers of mortal men, and their employment as supporters should really be in their capacity as Guardian Angels.

Angels' wings are usually shown as displayed, in the semi-open position, but they can be depicted fully open; if the latter, they should probably be so blazoned. Although they were earlier depicted with the outer wing-feathers gold and the inner of the colours appropriate to the Order, there are many examples in medieval art of Angels with wings of any of the symbolic colours and some where the feathers are of two different colours alternating. It would seem therefore that, within reason, a heraldic artist has some welcome latitude in painting Angels.

Randle Holme strikes a cautionary note on blazoning.[5]

> In the Blazoning of Angels, I do not use the term proper to the Face, Hands and Feet; for they are ever understood to be of the fleshy colour like to that of a man; except they be all of one entire Colour or Mettle, in which respect the naming of one colour serves for all parts of the Angel. Yet if the Blazoner please, he may use the term proper, but then he is tied, and of necessity he must add that he is clothed in a long robe, etc. of such a Colour, which in the leaving out the word proper, he needeth to say no more, than an Angel in such a posture, and of such a colour, naming only that of the Garment.

The nimbus, or halo of light, was originally reserved for representations of the deities and emperors of pagan Rome, as a symbol of rank and power; but with the rise of Christianity it was used, by a natural transference of associa-tion, for the persons of the Holy Trinity, the Angels of all the Orders, and later for the saints. Care should therefore be taken, when depicting them in heraldry, to ensure that the correct halo is given because, for instance, that appropriate to the Trinity is subtly different from that appropriate to an ordinary Angel. The mandorla, or glory, a kind of oval or almond-shaped halo entirely surrounding the body, is an attribute of divinity and also awarded to the Blessed Virgin Mary.

Although many of the saints have attributed arms, or have been used as charges on shields or banners, they do not fall within the ambit of this book, since they are but human beings elevated to their exalted state and not super-natural beings or creatures composed of incongruous elements. Nevertheless, I have included the Virgin Mary, as the kind of heraldic context in which she appears approximates to that of the Holy Trinity and of Jesus Christ.

THE HOLY TRINITY AND THE ARMS OF THE FAITH

The Athanasian Creed, that sonorous statement of faith, makes any exact pictorial representation of the Holy Trinity almost impossible. Nevertheless, the desire to represent abstractions in concrete form was very strong in the early Middle Ages and it was not long before our ingenious forefathers hit

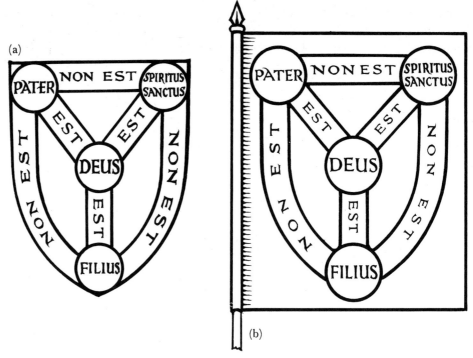

(a) Arms of the Faith
(b) Banner of the Faith
(drawn by G. Mussett)

upon a diagrammatic representation of the triune nature of the Holy Trinity. Because anthropomorphic representations of the subject were discouraged and frequently condemned by the Church at that period, this triune device achieved rapid popularity and became widely used in the decoration of churches and abbeys, as well as in theological manuscripts, and it is regularly found in many of the general rolls of arms.

As God, in his single and triune nature, is the supreme ruler of the universe, it was natural that when the triune device was represented on an armorial shield, the field should be of red, a colour early regarded as appropriate to kings and rulers and persons of noble birth and high rank. The device itself is depicted as white, with the lettering black. Sometimes the lettering is omitted because the triune device, generally known as the 'Scutum Fidei' or 'Arms of the Faith', and sometimes as 'Arms of the Trinity', was so well known that the explanatory words were unnecessary.

One of the earliest examples of the Arms of the Faith is in the *Chronica Majora,* written and illuminated with paintings of some eighty shields of arms by Matthew Paris, between 1250 and 1259, at St Albans, and presented by him to the Abbey.[6] This shows a slight variation in that a cross is inserted between the central and lowest roundels, labelled 'v'bu' caro f'm est', i.e., 'verbum caro factum est'. When the abbey church of St Albans, now the cathedral, was rebuilt in the early fifteenth century, the red shield of the Arms of the Faith was placed on the ceiling of the nave, in the series of thirty-two painted shields of arms.

Another early example is in the Lambeth Apocalypse, written and illuminated in the late thirteenth century, and depicts a young penitent woman warding off the attacks of the Devil with the Shield of the Faith. Above her head is a swarm of enormous flies representing evil thoughts, being brushed away by an Angel with a fly-swatter. It is a charming example of the predilection for allegory and symbolism, which is found throughout the Middle Ages, not least in heraldry.[7] The seal of Corpus Christi College, Cambridge, which was probably made in the late fourteenth century, includes the Arms of the Trinity and the Arms of Christ.[8] Other examples occur all through the Middle Ages and into Tudor times, but after the break with Rome its use in England virtually ceased.

A somewhat similar device to that of the Arms of the Faith was the 'Scutum

94

Anime', or 'Arms of the Soul'. The only armorial example I have come across is that depicted by Matthew Paris in his *Chronica Majora*, where a similar triune device is employed, but with the roundels differently labelled; that in the centre 'anima', the two uppermost 'memoria' to the dexter and 'voluntas' to the sinister, and that in base 'ratio'; the outer lines joining the corner roundels bear the word 'non', while the inner lines, joining the corners to the centre, are labelled 'est'.[9]

Another curious variation is that given in Randle Holme's Book, compiled about 1460. In this case the field is blue, but the triune device is similar, and the shield is labelled 'Sent Myhell armys', i.e. St Michael the Archangel.[10] I do not know why this was so attributed.

Although the Church in the early Middle Ages had constantly discouraged anthropomorphic pictures of the persons of the Trinity, with their tritheistic undertones, we find occasional representations of the subject during that time. By the fifteenth century these prohibitions were relaxed and pictures of the three persons of the Trinity in human form were one of the commonest subjects depicted.[11] The most frequent treatment of the group in English art represents the first person as an aged and bearded man, the 'ancient of days', with cross-nimb, seated on a throne and holding in front of his knees the figure of Christ Crucified, while a Dove, representing the third person, emerges from his mouth.

Banner of the Trinity, based on Peter le Neve's Book, but the original artist forgot the Dove (drawn by G. Mussett)

It was not long before such pictures of the Holy Trinity were painted on heraldic banners and carried in ceremonies of state, or at the funerals of kings, princes and the higher nobility, as well as at the great Feasts of the Church. Because the heralds were responsible then, as now, for organising and marshalling lay ceremonies, they naturally kept records of the designs of these banners of the Trinity in the rolls of arms which they compiled from time to time. A banner of the Trinity was borne beside Henry V at Agincourt.

Wrythe's Book, compiled about 1480 and still in the College of Arms,[12] gives us a vigorous and boldly painted example of just such a banner. This shows us a blue banner with the bearded figure of God the Father enthroned and holding, in front of his knees, the Cross by the extremities of its arms and on it the figure of Christ Crucified, both figures all gold. The Holy Ghost is, by some oversight of the artist, omitted. There is no inscription over this drawing, but Peter Le Neve's Book, compiled between 1480 and 1500, evidently by the same artist, has an identical painting and that is headed 'Sca Trinitas'.[13]

THE ARMS OF CHRIST

Gerard Legh, writing in the opening years of Elizabeth I's reign, described Our Lord as 'Jesus Christ, a gentleman of great lineage',[14] and this sentiment echoes that of the *Boke of St Albans,* which was printed in 1486:[15] 'Of the ofspryng of the gentilman Jafeth come Habraham, Moyses, Aron and the profettys, and also the kyng of ye right lyne of Mary, of whom that gentilman Jhesus was borne very god and man: after his manhode kyng of the lande of Judea of Jues, gentilman by is modre Mary, prynce of Cote armure', and it adds 'Christe was a gentilman of his moder behalve and bore cotarmure of aunseturis', that is, by descent from his ancestors. It is pretty certain that this view of Christ was also held at an earlier period.

Because all earthly lords – the kings and princes, earls, barons and knights, the commanders great and small of the feudal army, and those of gentle blood – were all armigerous by the end of the thirteenth century, it was natural that Christ, our heavenly overlord, should be assumed to be armigerous also. There is, however, no evidence that specifically personal arms were attributed to him in the early Middle Ages. Perhaps it was taken that, as the descendant of the royal line of David (who was already widely accepted in Europe as one of the Nine Worthies of the World), he would have inherited his arms, but normally the Cross alone was regarded as his emblem and the Crusaders enthusiastically adopted it.

By the early years of the thirteenth century the Mass of St Gregory had achieved widespread popularity throughout Europe, not least because of the numberless indulgences which could thereby be obtained, and this brought with it increasing veneration for the Instruments of the Passion, those symbols of Our Lord's suffering and death which had redeemed mankind. This coincided with the flowering of the romantic movement in Western Europe, and its impact on courtly life, chivalry and heraldry.

We soon find the Instruments of the Passion being depicted on armorial shields and it is evident that they were regarded as the especial emblems of Our Lord and personal to him in the same way as a coat of arms. There is early evidence that these 'Arma Christi', sometimes called the 'Scutum Salvationis' or Arms of Salvation, were held to be heraldic, for there is a Book of Hours of the early fourteenth century in the Bibliothèque de l'Arsenal, which describes them in heraldic terms.[16]

One of the earliest examples of the Arms of Christ is to be found in the seal of the Vice-Custos of the Grey Friars at Cambridge. This was one of the seven Custodies of the Minorites in England, having been founded in 1225, when they built their minute church in Cambridge in a few days. Important chapters of the Order were held there in 1240 and 1246, and the seal matrix

Arms of Christ, from the Seal of the Vice-Custos of the Grey Friars at Cambridge, c. 1240 (drawn by G. Mussett from British Museum Seals xxxvi, 243)

AVDI

TACE

VIDE

Arma Summi Pontificis

Arma Cesarie maiestat Imparat

(which is now in the British Museum) is believed to have been cut at about that time. It is one of the most beautiful examples of the Arms of Christ and was evidently drawn by someone with a real feeling for heraldic design. It depicts, in front of a ragged Passion Cross with the three Nails at its head and at the extremities of the arms, the Lance in bend enfiled at its head with the Crown of Thorns, and the Sponge upon the Reed in bend sinister, in base two Flagella triple thonged erect.[17]

In a late fourteenth century manuscript volume which includes a copy of Geoffrey of Monmouth's *Historia de Gestis Britonum* and other tracts,[18] there is a charming little poem about the Arms of Christ, which breathes the very spirit of the Middle Ages:

> A scheld of red, a crosse of grene,
> A crown ywrithe with thornes kene,
> A spere, a spounge, with nayles thre,
> A body ybounde to a tre,
> Who so this scheld in hert wyl take,
> Among hys enemyes thahre he not quake.

This poem is typical of the period when the emblems normally regarded as the Instruments of the Passion were the Cross, the Crown of Thorns, the Lance, the Sponge of Vinegar on the Reed, the Nails, the Pillar of Flagellation and the Flagella. These were usually grouped together on one shield but, by the beginning of the fifteenth century, the number of these emblems had increased and it became customary to place them on several shields, each charged with one or more of the Instruments of the Passion.[19]

An excellent and delightful example of the latter are the two paintings of the Arms of Christ in the 'Hyghalmen' Roll, which was probably compiled in the archdiocese of Cologne in Germany (hence its name) between 1447 and 1455. It is a general roll of arms, containing some six hundred and ninety-one shields, mostly with crests and all in colour, boldly and vigorously drawn. It begins with the armorial bearings of Christ, followed by the arms of the saints, the Nine Worthies of the World, bishops and sovereigns, and continuing with the arms of German nobles and knights.[20]

The Hyghalmen Roll evidently found its way to the English heralds soon after it was finished, because a few years later (probably between 1464 and 1480) Randle Holme's Book was completed.[21] The heraldic artist who painted the latter, which is also a general roll, mainly of English arms, included drawings in trick of some from the Hyghalmen Roll; most important of these were the Arms of Christ, to which he added a few interesting explanatory notes.

In the Hyghalmen Roll the two figures of Christ are facing each other on opposite pages. Above the figure on the left-hand page is written 'Arma Dni Jhesu Christi' (the Randle Holme version reading, 'The armys of oure lord Jesew cryst after the forme of the passyon'). The figure of Christ, half turned towards his left, is standing barefoot on a grassy mound, and is clad in a white alb reaching down to his toes and girt at the waist (on which is written, in the Randle Holme version, 'This is made for gods cote'). He is wearing a gold tilting-helm of a fifteenth century type. With his left hand, Christ is holding an azure shield charged with the Vernicle, commonly called Veronica's Veil, proper. Upon his helm is the Seamless Garment, serving for the mantling, and held in place by the crest-wreath of indeterminate colour; thereon rises the Cross, with the Nails at the extremities of the two arms and the Inscription at the head, between the Birch Rod to the dexter and the Scourge to the sinister. With his right hand he holds a staff with a square azure banner at its head, charged with the Agnus Dei proper, distilling drops

Opposite page
An Angel holding shields of arms of the Papacy and the Empire, from the Hyghalmen Roll. Painted about the mid-15th century, the arms and tiara of the Papacy were evidently scored through at the time of the break with Rome in the reign of King Henry VIII. (Coll. Arms ms. 1st M.5, f. 5b)

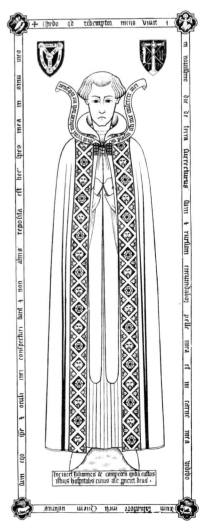

Brass of John de Campden, Warden of the Hospital of St Cross, Winchester, d. 1382, with the Arms of the Faith and the Arms of Christ (from *Monumental Brasses of England*, ed. C. Boutell)

of blood from its breast into the Chalice of gold by its forefeet. From the top edge of the banner there hangs a long red 'schwenkel', which, in German heraldry, was a mark of eminence. It is interesting to note that the schwenkel is omitted in Randle Holme's Book, which suggests that it was copied by an English artist, since the schwenkel is not used in English Heraldry.

On the opposite page there is a similar picture of Christ, half turned towards his right and thus facing the opposite figure, and also standing barefoot on a similar grassy mound and wearing a gold tilting-helm. There is no inscription over this figure in the Hyghalmen Roll, but the Randle Holme version has 'The armys of oure lorde oute of the passyon', and this is indexed as 'Tropheys of Christ's passion'. With his right hand he holds a shield of arms quarterly: (1) Argent, the Five Wounds, represented as points distilling drops of blood, (2) Azure, the three Jars of Ointment gold, (3) Gules, the two Rods in saltire gold, and (4) Gold, the Head of Judas Iscariot with the Bag of Money pendant from his neck. Upon his helm is the Seamless Garment held in place by the crest-wreath argent; thereon rises the Pillar of Flagellation surmounted by the Cock, between the Lance to the dexter and the Sponge upon a Reed to the sinister. With his left hand he holds a staff with a square banner at its head of the following quarterly arms: (1) Gules, the Head of a Jew spitting, (2) Azure the Three Dice, (3) Gold, a Hand grasping a lock of Hair, and (4) Argent, the Head of a King crowned (possibly King Herod). From the top edge of this banner there hangs a long white schwenkel, also omitted in Randle Holme's Book.

In a copy of the Passion Version of Prinsault's Treatise, compiled about 1489, the top half of the second page is occupied by a beautifully executed miniature painting of a shield of the Arms of Christ, followed by a ballade (which I believe has not, hitherto, been noticed) on His arms.[22]

Cy commance le blazon des armes de nostre Redemption.

Nous dieu d'amours createur Roy de gloire
Salut a tous vrays amans d'umble affaire
Com il sort vray que depuis la victoire
De nostre filz sur le mont de calvaire
Plusieurs par peu de congnoissance
De nos armes font au diable aliance.
Si vous faisons pour vostre bien mander
Le fai d'argent au chef d'or luysant cler
A ung playes que quant prescheurs et armes
Com vrays heraulx les vouldront blazonner
Loyaulx amans recongnoisses ces armes.

Divignite du chief d'or poves croire
Pure innocence est l'argent ou pourtraire
Vouldrent juifz lez playes et encores
Parfit longis l'ouvraige necessaire
Pour vraye amans delivrer de grevance
Et si donnons et octroyons puissance
A l'eglise militant de passer
A nos gaiges passer tous ceulx qui retourner
Vouldront a nous, mais qu'en pleurs et lermes
De cueur contritt en foy sans abuser
Loyaulx amans recongnoisses ses armes.

Besoing sera quen ayes la memoire
Au derrain jour que vous vouldres retraire
Dessus le val de Josaphat chose est voire
Pour condampner l'ancien adversaire

La monstrerons ces armes sans nuiance
Pour nostre gent remectre en ordonnance
Et la vouldront souldoyers delivrer
Lors comvendra le plus hardy trambler
Car ny vauldront espees ne guisarmes
Mais quant orres nos trompettes sonner
Loyaulx amans recongnoisses ces armes

Prince, pitie vous semont impetrer
Quant a Romme voulumes pierre poser
Pour recepvoir toutes bonnes gens d'armes
Dont se voules en nostre resgne entrer
Loyaulx amans recongnoisses ces armes.

In a fifteenth century Book of Hours, for the use of the Church of Toul in Lorraine,[23] there is an interesting example of the Arms of Christ, with some unusual features which I have not come across elsewhere. The single shield, rounded at the bottom, stands on two steps in front of a T-shaped Cross. The field is blue, with all the symbols of the Passion squeezed into it. The unusual features are in the crest and supporters. Above the shield is a gold affrontée barred helm, appropriate to royalty, upon which is the Crown of Thorns (serving as crest-wreath) and thereon a Lion couchant guardant to the sinister, both proper. The dexter supporter is a white Unicorn and the sinister supporter a white Lamb.

The use of the Crown of Thorns as a crest-wreath is an ingenious arrangement, while the Lion resting upon it alludes to the concept of Christ symbolising the Lion of Judah. The Lamb supporter is understandable as an allusion to the Lamb of God and the Paschal Lamb, but the Unicorn supporter is much more subtle. It alludes to the legend of the Holy Hunt and the symbolism of the Incarnation. A well-known form of this recondite allegory has the Unicorn being hunted out of heaven by the Archangel Gabriel and his four hounds, Veritas, Justitia, Pax and Misericordia, into the enclosure in which the Virgin sits, symbolising the descent of the Son of God into the Virgin's womb.

The compiler of the Cambridge Bestiary, in his homily on the Unicorn, observes that

> Our Lord Jesus Christ is also a Unicorn spiritually, about whom it is said : 'And he was beloved like the Son of the Unicorns' . . . .
> It says that he is swift because neither Principalities, nor Powers, nor Thrones, nor Dominations could keep up with him, nor could Hell contain him, nor could the most subtle Devil prevail to catch or comprehend him; but, by the sole will of the Father, he came down into the virgin womb for our salvation.[24]

The legend of the Unicorn was a favourite subject for illustrating the doctrine and mystery of the Incarnation during the Middle Ages. The belief that this exceedingly wild and fierce beast could be caught and tamed only by a virgin of pure and spotless life readily made the virgin identifiable as the Virgin Mary and the Unicorn as Christ; and the Holy Hunt was a popular subject of allegory in the late Middle Ages, when the code of chivalry readily accepted the notion of the softening influence of love upon the fiercest of men.

Many representations of the story are to be found carved or painted in churches all over Europe, as well as in many manuscripts. There is a charming picture in the Theodore Psalter, which was written in Greek and illuminated in the year 1066 by the monk Theodore of Caesarea.[25] This shows the Blessed Virgin Mary, dressed in a blue garment bordered with gold, and seated, with her right hand outstretched towards a Unicorn standing beside her, with its left forefoot resting on her knee.

An even more interesting and allegorical representation of the legend is to be found in a ninth century psalter in the Pantocrator on Mount Athos.[26] It illustrates the Psalm 'And he built his sanctuary as of Unicorns, in the land which he founded for ever', and the picture shows the Virgin Mary seated and giving her right breast to a Unicorn. In this case the beast has the paws of a lion, which serves to underline the allegory, while the legend accompanying the picture makes it clear that it is the Mother of God who is depicted, and specifically alludes to the legend of the Virgin Mary suckling the Son of God.

This takes us to the Syriac version of the bestiary by the author nicknamed 'the Physiologus', where we find a variant of the Unicorn legend which is somewhat similar. In this a virgin attracts the Unicorn, which begins to suck the breasts of the maiden and to conduct itself familiarly with her, whereupon she grasps its horn and the hunters rush in and capture it. An early Arabic version of this curious story tells us that the greedy Unicorn leaps onto the virgin's lap (it was, after all, 'a very small animal like a kid') and, having sucked its fill, falls in a drunken stupor at her feet, when the hunters capture it with ease.[27]

CHRIST AS A CHARGE IN ARMS

Towards the middle of the twelfth century, stories began to circulate in Europe of an immensely wealthy and powerful priest-king, with his capital in the fabulous and misty realms between India and Central Asia. This Presbyter John, as Prester John as the English called him, soon caught the imagination of Christendom, particularly when successive travellers' tales built him up as a victorious champion of Christianity against the embattled hosts of Islam and other terrifying heathens, diligent in good works and notable for his piety, and a descendant of the Magi.

About 1165 the Byzantine Emperor Manuel received a letter which purported to come from Prester John himself. This described in considerable detail, and in the most extravagant terms, the wonders of his empire, which was claimed to extend over the three Indies and stretched from the legendary lands of Farther India to the ruins of Babylon. Seventy-two kings were said to be his tributaries and the wealth of his dominions in gold and precious stones dazzled the minds of the simple knights of Western Europe. The letter was quickly copied and almost a hundred versions of it passed from hand to hand around Europe; it was widely hoped that the numberless armies of this Christian paladin could be brought to the aid of the crusaders fighting in the Holy Land.

The splendours and pageantry of the court of Constantinople were by now well known to the crusaders, so that the idea of a powerful potentate, who could write in such haughty terms to a brother emperor, gained instant credence and the forgery was swallowed whole. The fact that embassies and messengers from popes and kings failed to establish contact with the elusive Prester John only served to endow him with even more fabulous attributes in the credulous minds of the Middle Ages, and the legend persisted in full vigour for several centuries. About a hundred years later we find Matthew Paris referring to it, and, in the following century, that great gossip Sir John Mandeville, in his fantastic guide-book to the Holy Land and adjacent countries, discusses Prester John 'that is a great Emperour of Inde'.

It was, of course, unthinkable that so great and glorious an emperor should not have his own coat of arms, and the orderly heralds soon attributed an appropriately glorious coat to him. How soon this was we do not know, for the earliest remaining rolls of arms go back no earlier than the middle of the thirteenth century; but by then and in the following centuries we find the arms of Prester

100

John usually heading most of the general rolls of arms, along with the other emperors, kings, and saints of Christendom, and the Nine Worthies of the World.

It is some measure of the impression which Prester John made on the imaginations of Western Europeans that this legendary champion of Christendom had arms attributed to him of a blue shield charged with a representation of Christ Crucified upon the Cross. No secular emperor or king, not even the Pope himself, aspired to bear for their arms anything remotely approaching this. The field of the arms has its own significance, too, for Randle Holme tells us that 'this colour Blew doth represent the sky in a clear Sunshining day, when all Clouds are exiled . . . . and signifyeth Piety and Sincerity'.

The earliest reference to these arms is in the Herald's Roll, which was compiled between 1270 and 1280. The original, now in the College of Arms,[28] is evidently lacking certain shields and others have been misplaced when remounted, but the Fitzwilliam Version,[29] copied in the fifteenth century, begins with 'Prest Johan de ynde' and depicts his shield as *Azure, upon a Passion Cross gold the figure of Christ Crucified argent.*

Banner of the attributed arms of Prester John (drawn by G. Mussett from an early 17th century copy of Segar's Roll, c. 1282, Coll. Arms ms. L.14, part 1, f. 26)

The original of Segar's Roll, which was compiled about 1282, is now lost, but the College of Arms copy[30], made about 1600, depicts the arms of '[Prester] Johan' with a red field; but I think this may have been a copyist's error, because every other early roll of arms in which these appear gives them with an azure field. It is not until we come to Sir David Lindsay's 'Book and Register of Armes', compiled in 1542, that we find the tinctures reversed, with the Cross blue upon a gold field; but this is too late to carry weight. Very many of the general rolls, until the fifteenth century, begin with the arms of Prester John, but by this time he had begun to lose his glamour, and was becoming a kind of dynastic name attached to the Emperors of Ethiopia.

Randle Holme's Book, compiled about 1460, has a rather puzzling shield: *Per pale argent and sable the figure of Christ Crucified proper*, but without the Cross.[31] Above this is written, 'Seynt Bartholomew Spyttyll'. The famous arms of St Bartholomew's Hospital, in the City of London, *Per pale argent and sable a Chevron counterchanged*, were already in use by 1418, when Cok's Chartulary was compiled, and they appear in one of the illuminated capital letters.[32] The first seal of the Hospital to show their present arms was in use by 1423, and this has, above the shield of arms, a representation of Christ Crucified upon a Passion Cross.[33] It is just possible that the compiler of Randle Holme's Book may have telescoped these two in error.

As might be expected, the religious sentiments of the Middle Ages would only countenance the figure of Christ as a charge in arms, either Crucified upon the Cross or otherwise, for Prester John and, a little later, for a few bishops dioceses or abbeys of particular antiquity and eminence. Thus the seal of Richard de la Wich, Bishop of Chichester from 1245 to 1253, bore a representation of Christ enthroned, with the right hand uplifted in benediction.[34] It was not however until a century or so later that this became the basis of the armorial device of the Bishops of Chichester. We find then an interesting variation, the throne becomes simpler, while the Saviour usually holds an open book in his left hand, but sometimes an Orb, and a sword held fess-wise in his teeth, sometimes by the blade and sometimes by the hilt.[35]

Arms of St Bartholomew's Hospital, London (drawn by G. Mussett)

We now come to a sad lapse by Nicholas Narboon, Ulster King of Arms of Ireland in the time of Elizabeth I, who ought to have known better, since he had been an English herald from 1550 to 1566. In May 1583, Sir Theobald Butler persuaded Queen Elizabeth to revive the Barony of Caher in Tipperary in his favour, after it had become extinct on the death of his distant cousin. Not content with this, he then persuaded Ulster King of Arms to grant him a new coat of arms, in addition to the perfectly good arms he already bore.

By letters-patent, dated 30 November 1583, he was granted, as a first quartering to his arms, *Argent a Crosse graded* [*i.e. on three steps*] *gules with the Picture of Christ Crucified or,* which must have made all the medieval heralds turn in their graves. The flimsy reason given was that it was 'an augmentation attchieved by service in the holy land by the Ancestors of this Family (as by the constant relation is maintained)'.

Narboon's successor as Ulster, in the reign of James I, clearly had misgivings about it. When the new Lord Caher approached him in 1606 for a new Patent because 'by long continuance and evill keepinge the Patent above named is soe defaced as it cannot well be discerned', Ulster took the opportunity of removing this illustrious quartering and turning it into an honourable augmentation, saying tactfully, 'I have thought it better to place the same in a Canton with the Coats of the Familie, as best agreeing to the principles of this Aim.[36] The twelfth Baron was created Earl of Glengall in 1816, but the titles became extinct in 1858.

The Renaissance and the Industrial Revolution have put us all on nodding terms with the Almighty, but it still seems a little surprising to find the Lyon King of Arms in 1900 matriculating the arms *Gules our Lord upon the Cross proper* for the royal borough of Inverness. Thus it is that Prester John has fetched a circle round the earth, and, from the fabled Farther India, the aberrant form of his shield, as recorded in Segar's Roll, has come to roost with the City Fathers of Inverness.

The Arms of The Blessed Virgin Mary

We have seen how the Holy Trinity was identified by a heraldic device as early as the thirteenth century, and that by the following century the Instruments of the Passion were being depicted in a heraldic way as the arms of Christ. It was only natural, therefore, that the Virgin Mary, the Mother of God, should also be attributed arms by which she could be identified and honoured.

The medieval iconographers turned to the Holy Scriptures for their inspiration and, in St Luke's Gospel (ii, 34–5), they found the answer: 'Yea, a sword shall pierce through thy own soul also, that the thoughts of many hearts may be revealed'. As a result they produced one of the most beautiful coats of arms I know, which combines a dignified simplicity with a very vivid symbolism. The heart, winged in allusion to the Angel of the Annunciation, and transfixed by a sword with its hilt and cross-guard uppermost, echoing the form of the Passion Cross, on a blue shield signifying piety and sincerity, say everything neatly and concisely.

John Blount, in his translation of Nicholas Upton,[37] tells us that 'thys colowre ys callyd the hevenly colowre bycause ye ayre hathe moste dominion .... as hyt aperyth in saphyres, whych preciouse stoones resemble moste trewly thys azure or blew coloure. The Saphyre hys nature ys to take away envy, to expell fere, to make one hardy and victoriouse, to strength a man hys mynde in goodness and to make the berar meke, lowly and jentyll'. We can see now why blue was regarded as apt for the Virgin Mary.

This device is to be seen in many a church in Europe, usually depicted on a heraldic shield, but sometimes alone. In England examples will be found in the cathedrals of Bristol, Durham and Hereford. There is an excellent example of this attractive coat in a fifteenth century manuscript in the College of Arms,[38] which can be blazoned: *Azure, a Heart gules winged gold and transfixed with a Sword argent the hilt in chief gold;* and above it is written 'The Armes of the Virgin Mary'.

As in the case of Jesus Christ, the symbolism appropriate to the Virgin Mary was too profuse to be confined to one shield of arms, and we find different devices attributed to her by the early heralds. In Basynge's Book,[39]

102

FOUR VERSIONS OF THE ARMS OF THE BLESSED VIRGIN MARY

a roll of arms compiled about 1395, we find a painted shield: *Gules a Cross Botonny fitchy gold between two Wings expanded argent, on a Chief of the last the word AVE sable.* A somewhat similar coat is found in Randle Holme's Book (*c.* 1460),[40] which is in trick, but without the tinctures indicated, and shows a Crosslet fitchy set on a Winged Pedestal and a Chief with the words AUE GRACIA PLENA. The identification of these is made clear by the inscription which accompanies it: 'Owre Lady armys'.

There is yet another coat attributed to the Virgin Mary, which is equally famous: a blue shield and thereon a gold vase with a bunch of white Lilies, a flower most closely associated with her and her especial emblem. Sometimes the flower-vase is winged, but usually it is not. Examples occur in many churches in Europe.

The College of the Blessed Virgin Mary and Mother of Christ in Eton next to Windsor, more generally known as Eton College, was founded by King Henry VI and, on the 1st January 1448/9, it was granted arms by royal charter: *Sable, three Lilies slipped argent on a Chief per pale azure and gules a Lily of France (Francorum flore) and a Leopard (leopardo) gold,*[41] the Lilies being a clear reference to the patron saint of the College. Corpus Christi College in Cambridge was founded in 1351 by the two Guilds of Corpus Christi and the Blessed Virgin, and the arms confirmed to them at the Visitation of Cambridge in 1575 were a quarterly coat, first and fourth *Gules a*

Arms of Eton College (drawn by G. Mussett)

103

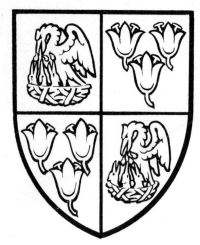

Arms of Corpus Christi College
(drawn by G. Mussett)

Banner of the Blessed Virgin Mary
(drawn by G. Mussett)

The attributed arms of King Arthur
(drawn by G. Mussett)

Pelican in her piety upon a Nest containing three young all argent, and second and third *Azure three Lilies argent.*[42] The royal burgh of Dundee, however, being under the patronage of the Blessed Virgin Mary, had a confirmation of the undifferenced arms of the Virgin, by Lyon King of Arms on the 30 July, 1673, which would seem to be flying a little high.[43]

THE VIRGIN MARY AS A CHARGE IN ARMS

As with the Holy Trinity and with Christ, one finds the Virgin Mary herself borne as a charge on banners and shields, and often as the common device of a Christian army – a practice no doubt borrowed from the Byzantine emperors, whose armies carried holy icons into battle. There is a lively example of this in an early medieval manuscript in the Escorial Library in Madrid, which shows a force of knights rallying under a red banner, on which is a representation of the Virgin enthroned and holding the Child; in the next picture, we see them charging into battle under the protection of the banner of the Blessed Virgin, while the banners of the individual commanders are carried as well, although they are much smaller.

A profusely ornamented missal of the beginning of the fourteenth century, with richly illuminated initials and borders, possibly compiled for the Monastery of Grasse in Languedoc,[44] has a spirited picture of a knight in chain-mail, wearing a red surcoat and riding a vigorously drawn horse. In his right hand he holds a gold banner with the Virgin Mary standing holding the Child; on his left arm he holds a gold shield painted with the head and shoulders of the Virgin holding the Child. A later example of a banner of the Virgin Mary is in Peter Le Neve's Book, compiled about 1480–1500, which gives a blue banner with the Virgin standing and holding the Child on her right arm and a Sceptre in her left hand, all gold.[45]

In the same way that Prester John, that fabled paladin of Christianity, had arms attributed to him of Christ Crucified, so that other hero of legend, King Arthur, one of the Nine Worthies of the World, had arms attributed to him by the medieval heralds: an argent cross upon a green shield and in the first quarter the Virgin holding the Child, all gold.[46]

There is, however, an exceptionally interesting example in Froissart's Chronicle of the use of a representation of the Virgin Mary as a personal device in time of war.[47] Sir John Froissart, who knew most of the leading men on both sides, tells us that when the French and English armies lay encamped opposite each other, on the Sunday before the Battle of Poitiers, Sir John Chandos, one of the English commanders, rode out to reconnoitre the French dispositions. At the same time, Lord Jean de Clermont, one of the French Marshals, also rode out to view the English army. As they were returning to their own posi-

tions, they met by chance, and both simultaneously noticed that 'eche of theym bare one maner of devyce: a blewe lady enbraudred in a sonne beame above on their apayrell'. This was clearly a figure of Our Lady, dressed in blue, within a golden mandorla, embroidered on their surcoats. The Lord of Clermont said peremptorily, 'Chandos, howe long have ye taken on you to bere my devyce?' To which Chandos replied, 'Nay, ye bere myne, for it is as well myne as yours.' 'I deny that', said Clermont, 'but an it were nat for the truse this day bytwene us, I should make it good on you incontynent that ye have no right to bere my devyce.' Chandos retorted, 'Ye shall fynde me tomorrow redy to defend you, and to prove by feate of armes that it is as well myne as yours'. The altercation ended by Clermont saying, 'Chandos, these be well the wordes of you Englysshmen, for ye can devyce nothyng of new, but all that ye se is good and fayre.' And so each returned crossly to their own side. In the Battle of Poitiers, the next day, Marshal Clermont was killed fighting valiantly.

Now the interesting thing about this is that Sir John Chandos had family arms of his own, the red pile on a gold shield, which he bore in many a famous battle and on his stall plate in the Chapel of the Order of the Garter, and yet we find him also bearing in a heraldic way on his surcoat a device of the Virgin Mary. The fact that Marshal Clermont also bore a similar device on his surcoat, and that a heated altercation ensued when they discovered it, indicates that these were regarded as personal devices. There is no evidence that these superseded their normal family heraldic arms, displayed on the banners under which their followers fought, and around which they would rally in the press of battle.

It is not without significance that the poem on the life and feats of arms of the Black Prince, the victor of Poitiers, was written by the herald of Sir John Chandos and, like its contemporary poem *Sir Gawain and the Green Knight*[48], illuminates the spirit of chivalry of our intensely pious forefathers. Indeed, Sir Gawain himself is said to have had the image of Our Lady painted 'in the inore half of his schelde', and it would be characteristic of Sir John Chandos to follow the romantic example of King Arthur who, Geoffrey of Monmouth tells us, had the image of the Virgin sewn on his armour at the Battle of Mount Badon. The romantic revival of the fourteenth century was in full flood by this time, and King Edward III and the Black Prince and their court were the leaders of this revival.

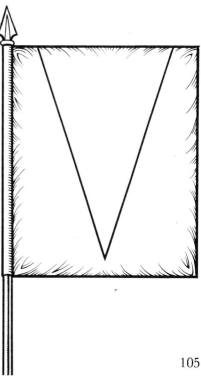

Banner of Sir John Chandos, and the device of Our Lady as probably worn by him at the Battle of Poitiers (drawn by G. Mussett)

In view of the great reverence in which the Blessed Virgin Mary was held in the Middle Ages, it is to be expected that representations of her would be used in the arms of several sees and abbeys, and this we find to be the case. There are many examples throughout Europe, but one or two will suffice.

The Benedictine Mitred Abbey of St Mary at Glastonbury in Somerset bore for arms: *Vert, a Cross Botonny argent, in the first quarter the figure of the Virgin Mary and Child standing argent, and in the other quarters three Crowns gold.*[49] This has a direct connection with the attributed arms of King Arthur, whom legend associated so closely with Glastonbury. Another version, of about the same period,[50] omits the crowns, and the inscription above the arms reads: 'Thabbey of Glastonbury in com. Wiltsher [*sic*] founded by a Jewe.' In the Visitation of Somerset in 1531, the arms are depicted without the crowns and with the Virgin and Child enthroned.[51]

The dean and chapter of Salisbury were using a seal with a representation of the Virgin Mary on it as early as 1239,[52] but it is not known when, precisely, this device was used heraldically on shields. However, it was certainly so used by the middle of the fifteenth century, as Ballard's Book (*c.* 1465–90) records a series of shields for the see, some of the bishops, and the dean and chapter.[53] Apart from Salisbury, the see of Sodor and Man also incorporate the Virgin in their arms, and there are further examples in other European countries.

The Worshipful Company of Mercers of the City of London is the most important of the present lay users of this illustrious charge in heraldry. Incorporated by royal charter in January 1393/4, their early seal depicted a female, full face, who was always assumed to represent the Blessed Virgin Mary; and in the records of the Visitations of London in 1568, 1634 and 1687, she is depicted in their arms. In 1911, when the Company was granted a crest, the position was clarified and the arms were blazoned as *Gules, issuant from a Bank of Clouds a figure of the Virgin couped at the shoulders proper, vested in a Crimson Robe adorned with gold, the neck encircled by a jewelled Necklace, crined or and wreathed about the temples with a Chaplet of Roses alternately argent and of the first, and Crowned with a Celestial Crown, the whole within a Bordure of Clouds also proper.* The crest is a similar figure of the Virgin.[54]

Arms of the Mercers Company (drawn by N. Manwaring)

THE SERAPHIM

To employ a Seraph as a charge in heraldry is rather like keeping a tiger in one's back garden, but it has been done. While it is unthinkable that any king of arms today would grant a Seraph as a charge in a shield or as a supporter to it, they have appeared in a heraldic context in the past, although mostly as incidental artistically to a heraldic composition. So for these reasons we must consider them here.

We have seen that the Seraphim are the first of all the Orders in the celestial hierarchy, the principal of all the ministers of God in constant attendance around the throne of glory. The Prophet Isaiah encountered them in the year that King Uzziah died, when he 'saw also the Lord sitting upon a throne . . . . Above it stood the Seraphims: each one had six wings; with twain he covered his face, and with twain he covered his feet, and with twain he did fly. And one cried unto another and said, Holy, holy, holy, is the Lord of hosts: the whole earth is full of his glory' . . . . Then flew one of the Seraphims unto me . . . . '[55] The Book of Enoch states that there are only four of them and they are equally rare in heraldry.

The *Mirouer historial abregie de France*, compiled probably between 1443 and 1461 at the behest of Charles of Anjou, Count of Maine, for his second wife Isabel of Luxembourg, is one of the few medieval manuscripts which illustrate the Seraphim in a heraldic context.[56] This remarkably beautiful manuscript book contains a brilliantly executed painting of a Holy Roman

106

emperor, haloed and with a triple crown, embracing a king of France, likewise haloed. It opens the chapter dealing with the match between the Capetian royal line and the descendant of Charlemagne.

Above the Emperor is a shield of the imperial arms, supported from below by a scarlet-winged Seraph's head very indistinctly depicted; but fortunately an earlier picture in the book shows us two flying Seraphim, with human-like bodies apparently covered in scarlet feathers all over, supporting the imperial crown. These however have only four wings, but their red colour leaves their identity in no doubt. The shield of the royal arms of France, above the king's head, is supported only by an Angel with two wings: an interesting example of Angelic protocol, and a timely reminder to us that the only lay mortal who could dare to aspire to a Seraph as a supporter was the Holy Roman Emperor.

Arms of Sir William Carruthers of Beckenham, Kent (drawn by G. Mussett)

The Most Noble Order of the Seraphim was traditionally founded by King Magnus of Sweden in about 1280, and appears to have been in existence around the middle of the next century, but the modern Order was reconstituted by King Frederick I in 1748. It is one of the most illustrious of the European Orders of Chivalry, restricted to thirty-two knights. The collar of the Order consists of gold six-winged Seraph heads alternating with blue-enamelled Patriarchial Crosses. The badge of the Order is in the shape of a white Maltese Cross with similar gold Seraph heads in the angles, while the star of the Order is similar but all of silver.

Nevertheless, there is one example in English heraldry of Seraphim as a charge in arms and that, as might be expected, is a modern one, in 1926. Sir William Carruthers of Beckenham in Kent was granted the following arms: *Gules, two Chevronels between in chief two Seraphim and in base a Fleur de Lys or;* and for crest: *Upon a Rock proper a Seraph as in the arms.* The Seraphim are here depicted as boys' heads with six wings about them.[57] A very pretty coat, but it is a far cry from the Holy Roman Emperor to a London banker, and one wonders why the then Garter and Clarenceux Kings of Arms passed such a grant; but perhaps they were influenced by the arms of Carruthers of Dormont, who had a Scottish grant in 1913 of a crest of *a Seraph volant proper.*

THE CHERUBIM

These curious creatures, the second of the Orders in the celestial hierarchy, excel in knowledge and are the archivists of heaven. They also have important guard duties to perform, as well as acting as the emissaries of God to the lower echelons of the heavenly host and sometimes to especially favoured mortals as well. Occasionally they are employed as celestial steeds upon which Jehovah rides when making his sudden sorties to intervene on rare occasions in the affairs of the universe.

The Cherubim have the distinction of being the first Angels to be mentioned by name in the Bible. After God had exiled Adam and Eve, 'he placed at the east end of the garden of Eden Cherubims, and a flaming sword which turned every way, to keep the way of the tree of life'.[58] This concept of Cherubim as guardians of the holy places and objects is carried a stage further when God gave Moses detailed instructions for the construction of the Ark and its accompanying furniture: two Cherubim of beaten gold were to be made and placed at either end of the Mercy Seat over the Ark, with their wings outstretched and covering it. The curtains of the tabernacle were also embroidered with Cherubim.[59] Later, King Solomon, no doubt inspired by this example, had two large Cherubim made of olive wood covered with gold, with their wings outstretched in the attitude of guardianship, and he placed them in the inner sanctum of the temple.

There is some conflict of opinion as to the correct form and shape of a

107

Cherub. Clearly it is wrong to depict the Cherubim as *amorini*, with Cupid's chubby body, underdeveloped wings and general air of naughtiness; for these terrible beings, devoted to the selfless service of God, have nothing whatever to do with the son of Venus, and are anything but cosy. How then should a herald depict a Cherub on a shield of arms?

Fortunately we have the testimony of the prophet Ezekiel, who claimed to have seen four of these alarming creatures and gave us a detailed description of them. The Cherubim appeared to him out of a whirlwind and an amber-coloured fiery cloud, and

> this was their appearance; they had the likeness of a man. And every one had four faces and every one had four wings. And their feet were straight feet; and the sole of their feet was like the sole of a calf's foot: and they sparkled like the colour of burnished brass. And they had the hands of a man under their wings on their four sides . . . . As for the likeness of their faces, they had the face of a man, and the face of a lion on the right side: and the face of an ox on the left side: they four also had the face of an eagle . . . . As for the likeness of the living creatures, their appearance was like burning coals of fire, and like the appearance of lamps.

Ezekiel further tells us that their whole bodies, backs, hands and wings were 'full of eyes round about', and each Cherub had beside him a wheel, which accompanied him wherever he went.[60]

I know of only one instance in English heraldry in which an entire Cherub has been employed, and that was in the grant of armorial bearings to the United Grand Lodge of Ancient Free and Accepted Masons of England, by royal warrant of King George V, dated 13 June 1919. Their crest was blazoned as a representation of an Ark supported on either side by a Cherub, while the supporters were blazoned as a Cherub on either side.[61] The Cherubim depicted on this grant are clearly inspired by those seen by Ezekiel, but they only have one pair of wings and no hands or arms, and lack the hundreds of sparkling eyes and the lion's, eagle's and bull's heads.

Nevertheless, in spite of Ezekiel's meticulous description, the heralds have never cared for these ungainly and disquieting creatures and, from the fifteenth century at least, have tended to think of a Cherub as a boy's face with one pair of wings sprouting from his neck and displayed open on either side of his head; and conceived like this they are, of course, much more attractive. These have usually been blazoned as a Cherub, Cherubs or Cherubim *tout court,* but it would seem better to blazon the winged head as a Cherub's head so as to distinguish it from the entire Cherub.

While there are many examples in fifteenth century manuscripts of Cherubim being depicted in association with shields of arms, these are in a purely artistic context. Possibly the earliest example of a Cherub in English heraldry was in a grant of arms and crest by John Wexworth, Guyenne King of Arms, dated 29 January 1460/1, to William Swayne of Somerset, where a Cherub's head was granted as a crest.[62]

Crest of William Swayne of Somerset (drawn by G. Mussett)

The Archangels

It seems to be generally accepted that there are seven Archangels, and most authorities agree that the first four are Michael, Gabriel, Raphael and Uriel; but there is considerable divergence of opinion among the early Fathers of the Church as to the identities of the last three. However, the last four are of no heraldic importance and, indeed, only Michael regularly appears in a heraldic context.

108

Michael is regarded as the chief of the Archangels in Jewish, Christian, and Moslem theology, as one 'who is as God', and the great general of the heavenly host who fights the battle of the faithful. In medieval art he is frequently depicted as fighting the Devil, in the form of a dragon. In consequence the Archangel Michael is normally shown as wearing full armour (usually of the period of the particular manuscript), sometimes with shoes and sometimes without, with a drawn sword or lance and a shield on his left arm, with the cognisance of a red cross on an argent field.

A fine example of this is in the early fourteenth century English Apocalypse,[63] in which the Archangel Michael is shown in armour, with a shield *Argent a Cross gules,* and assisted by three Angels. All four hold spears, with which they are transfixing a dragon, that 'old serpent, he that is called the Devil and Satan, the deceiver of the whole world'. It is a spirited picture. Another picture in the same manuscript portrays Michael as a knight in chain-mail with pot-helm, riding a white horse, and on his left arm a similar shield. Behind him follow a troop of Angels depicted as men at arms on horses, carrying four banners of the same arms.

It is not clear why or when these arms were transferred to St George, nor why he became more particularly regarded as the dragon slayer – at any rate in England, whose patron saint he became only in the time of King Edward III.

There are several families in Germany and France who bear a representation of St Michael (as the Archangel is often called) in their arms; and he is conventionally shown slaying a dragon.

THE ANGELS

While some of the Archangels and saints have attributed arms of their own, the Angels of the ninth Order have not. We sometimes see them carrying banners or, more rarely, shields of the arms of their immediate commander, such as the Archangel Michael, when they fight under his command against the Devil and the embattled forces of evil; but it would have been unthinkable to the medieval mind that they, as the rank and file of the heavenly host, should themselves have been armigerous, or indeed have any occasion to use arms of their own. Nevertheless the Angels have, from an early period, played an important and busy part in earthly heraldry.

A heraldic shield is nearly always colourful and frequently beautiful, but it tends to look a little lonely when by itself in a church, in the margin of a manuscript or upon a wax seal. The medieval artist sought, therefore, to unite it with the general decorative scheme, and often filled in the spaces around it with objects of one kind and another. Sometimes these were creatures, sometimes monsters such as Dragons, and frequently they were Angels. These had the advantage of being remarkably decorative and, because of their hands, could be depicted holding the shield; moreover they introduced the idea of the Guardian Angel and pointed the moral of the fallibility of mortal man and his need for divine guidance.

Supporters to a shield of arms, in the technical, heraldic sense of the term, did not become a recognised feature of heraldry until well into the fourteenth century. Before this time and, indeed, overlapping for a long time into it, the Angels holding shields of arms were there for purely decorative and symbolic reasons.

We have seen, in the fifteenth century *Mirouer historial abregie de France,* the nice distinction made between the Holy Roman Emperor and the king of France: how the shield of the former was supported by a Seraph, while that of the latter was supported by an Angel – and not a very senior Angel at that. From this and other medieval examples it is clear that the appropriate Angels for employment in a heraldic context are those of the ninth Order, and that those remote and exalted beings like the Seraphim and Cherubim should only be harnessed to a shield of arms on very rare and special occasions.

I have touched earlier in this chapter on the jewels and characteristics of the several sorts of Angels. The jewel appropriate to those of the ninth Order is the emerald, and this colour would be appropriate to them, although they have been painted from the earliest times in garments of every colour; this applies also to their wings, of which the ordinary Angels only have two. Unless blazoned otherwise, they were understood to be standing with their wings half open and their feet bare, for they are not earthly beings. Strictly speaking, they should be depicted with a golden halo, but in later medieval pictures this is not always included, so a heraldic artist would be excused for omitting it today, although it seems a pity not to observe the rules.

I know of two examples of naked Angels, and there may well be others. Although these two are separated by a hundred years, they both, by a coincidence, come from Naples. The first is in a portable ferial psalter, written in Naples about 1350, which contains a number of naked Angels in several of the marginal illustrations. One shows two such Angels, with pink wings and gold haloes, supporting an armorial shield which is now, alas, illegible.[64] The other example is in a copy of the *De Re Militari* of Vegetius, written in Naples between 1442 and 1458. This shows a shield of the arms of Aragon quartering Jerusalem, supported on either side by two naked Angels, with pink feathered wings and gold haloes.[65] According to these illustrations Angels are evidently sexless.

One of the most attractive examples of an Angel employed on heraldic duties is in the fifteenth century Hyghalmen Roll.[66] Here he is wearing the conventional long white garment girt at the waist, with gold wings and a gold halo. With his right hand he holds a shield of arms of the papacy (scored through, probably in the time of King Henry VIII, when the break with Rome occurred), and with his left hand he holds a shield of arms of the Holy Roman Empire.

A little earlier in the same century we get a splendid French illustration of the legend of the Fleur de Lys, in the Bedford Book of Hours,[67] compiled about 1423. When Clovis, King of the Franks from 481 to 511, was converted to Christianity in 496, together with some 3,000 of his followers, legends about him grew up in the following centuries. First we get the legend of the phial of Holy Oil, the 'Sainte Ampoule', which was brought down to him from heaven, by which the legitimate kings of France were henceforth to be anointed.

The Fleur de Lys occurs as a royal emblem in France at a very early period: Charlemagne's sceptre was tipped with it, as appears on his seal, while it also appears as the decoration around the rim of the crown of King Robert at the beginning of the eleventh century. But neither of these have any heraldic connotation, for it was before the days of heraldry in the true sense of the term. By the next century the Fleur de Lys was being regularly used as an emblem of the Kings of France. Louis VII had his son, Philip Augustus, dressed in blue powdered with Fleur de Lys when he was crowned, but the well-known shield semée of Fleur de Lys only makes its first appearance on the royal seal of Louis VIII in about 1223–6.

The legend of the Fleur de Lys arose, therefore, very much later than the reign of Clovis, but it is not known when it first gained currency. It was believed that the Virgin Mary sent from heaven a lily – from the earliest times her especial emblem – to King Clovis, as a mark of divine favour. The version of the legend in the Bedford Book of Hours has it that God himself sent this emblem to Clovis, and in the illustration we see God handing what appears to be a blue banner, charged with three Fleur de Lys, to an Angel. Below we see King Clovis being invested with the ritual of knighthood in his armour and spurs (the sword is still on the altar behind him), and being handed the famous shield: *Azure three Fleur de Lys or*. It will be noted that the armour and the version of the French royal arms are of the period of the book, as the semée shield was only reduced to three Fleur de Lys in 1376, to symbolise the Holy Trinity. By the fifteenth century we find the kings of France occasionally using Angels as supporters to their arms and, by the reign of Louis XIV, they become their principal supporters.

An English example of about the same date is in the letters-patent of the first Garter King of Arms, dated 10 March 1438/9, granting arms to the Worshipful Company of Drapers of the City of London.[68] It is, in fact, the earliest grant of arms by an English king of arms still surviving, and the original patent remains to this day with the Drapers' Company. This shows two kneeling Angels holding the shield of arms and, together with the illuminated capital letter, is a most beautiful example of the art of the period.

There are many fine specimens of late medieval English heraldic art in which Angels appear, such as the royal charter of 1441 founding King's College, Cambridge, but our next example is nearly a hundred years earlier. The psalter made for John de Grandison, Bishop of Exeter, in 1369, has a full-page illustration in ink and watercolour of an Angel standing and holding in front of him a shield of the arms of Bishop Grandison.[69]

As is to be expected, most of the popes also had Angels holding their shields, in one way or another, from the fourteenth century onwards, but here again the Angels were employed in an artistic and decorative capacity rather than as proper heraldic supporters. Indeed, supporters, in the heraldic sense, did not become hereditary and fixed adjuncts to a shield of arms until well into the fifteenth century, but from that time onwards we find many examples in European heraldry.

Not only did the kings of France use Angels as supporters, dressed in tabards of the royal arms, but the Romanoff emperors of Russia also employed an Angel as the sinister supporter, while the Prince of Lippe had two Angels dressed in tabards of his arms, and there were others.

Angels, or parts of them, as a charge in a shield of arms or a crest, are met with pretty frequently, but the majority of them are of late date, in English heraldry at any rate, and no particular purpose would be served in describing them. The *Dictionnaire des Figures Héraldiques* lists seven pages of families, in most of the European countries, who bear an Angel or part of an Angel as a charge.[70]

THE ARMS OF SATAN

It will be recalled that the Devil and his legions were originally Angels, 'so Lucifer with his cumpany may say all we be cummyn of hevyn'. There seems to be some doubt among the learned as to whether there were originally ten Orders in the celestial hierarchy, and whether Satan seceded with a complete echelon, or whether he seduced a tenth from each of the Orders. The Bishop of Tusculum, in 1273, computed their figure at 133,306,668, and I think we can be content with that, for St John (Revelation xii, 4) says a third fell from heaven.

As far as we are concerned, the point is that they were originally Angels, 'created in hevyn of gentill nature', and that Satan himself was at one time a prince among them. Indeed, he has been reliably reported to have been chief of the Seraphim, which is why he is sometimes depicted with six wings or more, and distinguished from other Seraphim by a crown. Clearly before his fall he was a gentleman, and an unfortunate gentleman does not cease to be armigerous just because he is cast into prison, even the prison of hell.

Apart from this, Satan remained the commanding general of the Fallen Angels and, as such, the medieval mind would naturally assume that he would have arms to identify himself in the heat of battle and a heraldic banner under which the forces of evil could battle against the forces of good.

Naturally, because men tried to avoid contact with him, there is some uncertainty as to the correct insignia to be assigned to him. Fortunately St John came to the rescue of our forefathers and, in the Book of Revelations, he tells us that he 'saw three unclean spirits like frogs come out of the mouth of the dragon, and out of the mouth of the beast, and out of the mouth of the false prophet. For they are the spirits of devils, working miracles, which go forth unto the kings of the earth and of the whole world, to gather them to the battle of the great day of God Almighty'.[71]

In the Douce Apocalypse,[72] written about 1280 or a few years later, we find two charming and lively illustrations of Revelations xx, 7–10: 'And when the thousand years are expired, Satan shall be loosed out of his prison, and shall go out to deceive the nations which are in the four quarters of the earth, Gog and Magog, to gather them together to battle . . . . And they . . . . compassed the camp of the saints about, and the beloved city: and fire came down from God out of heaven and devoured them . . . . And the devil . . . . was cast into the lake of fire and brimstone'.

The first of these pictures in the Douce Apocalypse shows us a manacled Satan being helped out of hell and then, on the opposite side of the picture, we see this hairy, cloven-footed monster wearing only a cuirass, leading a milling throng of his knights, fully armed, while Satan himself carries a shield on his left arm with the cognisance *Gules a Fess gold between three Frogs proper*. Behind him stands his esquire holding his square banner with the same device. The next picture shows us the siege of the beloved city and the defeat of the forces of evil, with Satan tumbling backwards into the lake of fire and brimstone, with his shield tumbled down with him. It is one of the most enchanting pictures of the Devil I know and it is as good a commentary on the medieval mind as any.

9

Human Monsters
in Heraldry

HILE the heraldic imagination found expression in every aspect of armory and heraldic design, its wilder and more exotic flights are more easily observed in the chimerical beings and in the fabulous and fanciful creatures of armory. Only those, therefore, which have been used as charges in heraldry, or mentioned in an early heraldic treatise, or as personal devices on seals, will be touched on in the following chapters. Those chimerical creatures which do not occur in any heraldic context, however deeply they may be embedded in European mythology and form part of the living traditions of the Western world, will find no place here.

We have seen how the medieval heralds and the writers of heraldic treatises were influenced by the Bible and the classical authors like Herodotus, Aristotle and Pliny, by Solinus and St. Ambrose, as well as by the Physiologus, Isidore of Seville, and the other early writers on the natural and fabulous creatures of the world.[1] There can be little doubt, however, that it was the contemporary writers of the Middle Ages, in their turn influenced by this earlier literature, who had the most immediate effect on the heralds, because their works were more readily available. In treatise after treatise one comes across ideas or phrases which were lifted straight out of the twelfth century bestiaries,[2] or from Alexander Neckham's *De Naturis Rerum*'[3] written about 1180, and especially from the *De Proprietatibus Rerum* of Bartholomew the Englishman, written about 1260 and translated into English in 1397 by John of Trevisa,[4] which was the standard encyclopedia for every civilised medieval gentleman.

In view of this it would be outside the scope of this work to do more than glance fleetingly at the mythological and classical origins of these creatures: in any case, this aspect of them has already been fully dealt with by many other writers. Instead we will turn mainly to the medieval bestiaries and encyclopedias to see what was the accepted symbolism and allegorical significance of the fabulous creatures which appealed to the heraldic imagination. At the same time we will have to take some notice of the sixteenth and seventeenth century writers on heraldry, for they were clearly influenced by the later medieval heraldic treatises and their views, however quaint they may seem to us today, will help to throw light on the earlier approach to armory and its symbolism.

It is the intention here not only to discuss the earliest ascertainable appea·rance in English heraldry of a particular creature, but also to touch on its development as a heraldic charge in subsequent periods. The illustrations, too, are of, or based on, both the earliest examples to be found and good or interesting examples in later centuries, with a few modern examples.

The first thing which strikes one is that throughout the Middle Ages these fabulous creatures were depicted in armory with great freedom and variety of interpretation. This is not surprising when one considers that the compilers of the bestiaries and encyclopedias had to grope their way through a tangled jungle of traditionary evidences, so that the medieval heraldic artist was often obliged to fill in the gaps with his own imagination. However, his imagination was kept in bounds by a natural respect for the early authorities; and for this reason he hesitated to employ many of those creatures which we find in later heraldry, for some of their properties, as depicted by the bestiarists, were both horrid and sanguinary. It was not until the fifteenth century that men's minds began to tame the chimerical beasts and they took courage to sport with the fabulous, and to adapt and soften their more revolting characteristics to the uses of heraldry.

T. H. White pointed out that 'it was the Elizabethans, the Euphuists, the metaphorsicians, the poeticals, who elaborated the Gorgons, Harpies, Lamias, Tritons and Nereids'.[5] It was not until Conrad Gesner and Ulysses Aldrovandus brought a more critical and modern approach to natural history, around the beginning of seventeenth century, followed by that demolisher of myths and pseudodoxies, Sir Thomas Browne, that the flamboyant abandon of the Tudor heralds was curbed and English heraldic art fell into the dull decline from which it is only now recovering.

It was commonly believed that every land creature had its counterpart in the sea and indeed in the air as well, Thus the Horse was matched by the Sea-Horse and the Pegasus, and even the Monk by the Monk-Fish, and so on. With the chimerical beings of human form – and here I have included all those with at least a human head in their make-up – we are on rather different ground, for most of these derive more immediately from classical sources, however transmuted they became in the hands of the bestiarists and writers of medieval encyclopedias. For convenience I have grouped the human monsters into the following categories :

1. Land beings
2. Beings of the sea
3. Beings of the air
4. Miscellaneous beings and charges

THE MANTYGER AND THE MANTICORE

This curious creature appears as a heraldic charge in the fifteenth century, but there has been considerable confusion as to its precise appearance and even its correct name. Many have held the Manticore (with some latitude over its spelling), the Mantyger, the Satyral and the Lampago to be one and the same creature; others have differentiated them.

The Cambridge Bestiary gives the Manticore an Indian origin and describes it as having a lion's body with the head and face of a man, with gleaming blood-red eyes and three rows of teeth meeting alternately, and its tail ending in a scorpion's sting. It had a shrill voice which resembled the notes of flutes; a remarkable agility, and a passion for human flesh. The accompanying picture shows the Manticore with a much more amiable, bearded man's head and face, wearing a small pointed hat and with no murderous teeth visible.[6] The bestiarist was evidently at a loss for something to say about it, as this is one of the few creatures whose symbolism and allegorical significance he fails to point out, and he draws no moral from it. Other bestiaries compiled during the thirteenth and fourteenth centuries have similar descriptions of this creature.[7]

Randle Holme, that indefatigable collector of heraldic minutiae, writing in 1688, differentiated the Manticore and the Mantyger.[8] The former he describes as having 'the face of a man, the mouth open to the ears with a treble row of teeth beneath and above; long neck, whose greatness, roughness, body and feet are like a Lyon: of a red colour, his tail like the tail of a Scorpion of the Earth, the end armed with a sting, casting forth sharp pointed quills'. This could be an exact description of the creature pictured by Edward Topsell in his *Historie of Foure-Footed Beastes (1607)*, which was still popular when Randle Holme was writing.

Manticore (from E. Topsell, *Historie of Foure-footed Beestes*)

Holme describes the Mantyger as having 'the face and ears of a man, the body of a Tyger, and whole footed like Goose or Dragon; yet others make it with feet like a Tyger'. He adds that some are horned and some are not.[9]

In view of this confusion about the creature we can only turn to such medieval examples as occur to see what the early heralds made of it. The earliest heraldic reference to it is in Mowbray's French Treatise, written before the middle of the fifteenth century, where there is a short paragraph about the Manticore among the beasts borne in arms. It is headed 'Quelle beste est mantitoire', and goes on to describe it as a beast with a face like a man, and as red in colour, with a body like a lion and the tail of a scorpion. It runs so swiftly that no beast can escape it, and it likes all sorts of food, including man. The author adds the curious information that 'il engendre en telle maniere que l'une foys le malle est desus et l'autre foys la femelle'.[10]

The attributed arms of Judas Maccabaeus, one of the traditional Nine Worthies of the World, were usually two ravens, but in the Hyghalmen Roll, compiled in the Rhineland about 1450, he is credited with a man-headed lion wearing a red hat.[11] The German heralds were, however, even more flamboyant and imaginative in their treatment of charges in arms than their English confrères, and happily invented a wide variety of chimerical creatures to suit every symbolic need, so it is difficult to say if this was intended for a Manticore or not.

The earliest example of the Manticore or Mantyger in English heraldry is the badge of Sir William Hastings, of Kirby in Leicestershire and Burton Hastings in Warwickshire. He was a staunch adherent and friend of King Edward IV during the Wars of the Roses, and was created Lord Hastings on 17 February 1461/2 and Knight of the Garter the following month. After the death of Edward IV he incurred the suspicion of Richard III and was beheaded in June 1483. His badge is depicted, in a lively ink-and-wash drawing, in Fenn's Book of Badges (compiled about 1470). The creature is shown with the body, legs, feet and tail of a lion, with a man's face, and with tusks like a boar in the lower jaw, hair and beard merging with the shaggy mane.[12]

When Lord Hastings mustered in the army assembled by King Edward IV for the expedition to France in 1475, he commanded a contingent of forty lances and three-hundred archers, and they wore as his badge the Bull's Head erased sable with golden horns and gorged with a gold coronet,[13] which was also his crest. It would seem, therefore, that his Mantyger badge was used in tournaments and for more peaceful and fanciful display, while the Bull's Head was his battle badge. His descendents continued to use the Mantyger, both as a badge and as supporters to their arms. In Prince Arthur's Book the banner of his grandson George, Lord Hastings, created Earl of Huntingdon in 1529, is supported by a Mantyger (without the tusks), but a few pages further on the same banner is supported by a Mantyger with two short horns.[14] The arms of Henry, Earl of Huntingdon (seventh in descent from the first Lord Hastings), are supported by two gold Mantygers.[15]

In the sixteenth century we find two other English families with the Mantyger or Manticore as a badge. Sir Robert Ratclyffe, or Radcliffe, K.G., created Earl of Sussex in 1529, had a Mantyger badge very similar to that of

Mantyger badge of Master Ratclyffe
(Coll. Arms ms. 1.2, f. 95)

Hastings, except that its body is purpure and it is wearing a gold hat. The feet are depicted like monkeys' hands.[16] The Book of Standards gives the badge of 'Mayster Ratleffe' (probably son of the Earl of Sussex) as a similar Mantyger; the body, tail and legs purpure; the paws drawn like a monkey's hands and feet; the man's face proper, with hair, beard and mane gold; and wearing a gold hat with the turned-up brim ermine. About his neck is a golden chain from which is suspended a padlock depending from a sun in splendour.[17]

The badge of the Ratclyffes was sometimes blazoned as 'a Babyon with a hatte upon hys hed', and the fact that the badge of Sir Anthony Babyngton was also a Mantyger purpure – the man's face proper, with hair and beard grey; and gorged with a gold collar, the chain flexed over its back[18] – gives us a further clue to the probable origin of the Mantyger, for the Babyngton beast was evidently intended also to be a Babyon, or Baboon, as a play upon his name, and it too is shown with monkey-like feet.

The thick and shaggy mane of the male baboon and its habit of walking on all fours, rather like a lion, together with its reputation for loyalty to its tribe and fierceness in the protection of its family, could easily have produced the heraldic Mantyger. Although its libidinous reputation was known in Western Europe (indeed Pope Alexander II related a curious story about this) it would not necessarily have been held against the creature, and it would have made a more acceptable emblem for armorial purposes than the Manticore of the bestiaries.

Nevertheless the English heralds continued to be confused about the beast until modern times. Not only could they not make up their minds about its correct name, but also there was much variation in the way they depicted it. In the trick of arms in the pedigree of Woodhull of Fryngford, and subsequently Mollington, in Oxfordshire, recorded at the heralds' Visitation of that county in 1566, the creature in their crest is drawn with cloven hooves and two short horns;[19] while the arms of the same family recorded at the Visitation of Oxfordshire in 1668–75 show it similarly horned but with lion's feet.[20] William Camden, Clarenceux King of Arms, in 1613 blazoned the crest of Lambert as a 'Mantichor', when it was in fact a Lamia, a creature of quite different origins. Sir William Pole, that great Devon antiquary, who died in 1635, blazoned the three Mantygers in the arms of Radford of Radford, in Plymstock, Devon, as 'Lampagols'.[21]

116

It is a pity that one of the most interesting of the chimerical creatures that can be differenced in a number of decorative ways should have been allowed to get into such a muddle in English heraldry. One cannot, obviously, rewrite the patents of the past, but we can be a little tidier about it in future, and the first step would be to separate the Manticore from the Mantyger, the former name being applied only to the creature described in the bestiaries and illustrated by Topsell. The Mantyger would then be the creature depicted by the late fifteenth and early sixteenth century heralds, which was inspired by the 'Babyon' or baboon of natural history.

THE LAMIA

The Lamia of heraldry has travelled a long way from the Lamia of Philostratus, of Burton and of Keats; that witch transformed by Hermes from a serpent 'of dazzling hue, vermilion-spotted, golden, green, and blue' into a beautiful maiden, 'a full-born beauty new and exquisite', whose happiness was wrecked by that pretentious old philosopher Apollonius, whereupon she vanished with a frightful scream. The serpent with a woman's face, of classical antiquity, was transformed in the course of the Middle Ages into a much cosier creature which bore little resemblance to it.

Randle Holme, whose descriptions of the chimerical creatures of heraldry appear to be drawn mainly from fifteenth and sixteenth century sources, describes the Lamia as

> a beast in the parts of Lybia, which hath a Woman's Face, and very large and comely shaped spots on her breasts, which cannot be counterfeited by Art; having an excellent colour in their fore parts; they hisse like Dragons. They are, as some write, scally all over; and the legs the same, to the feet; which foremost are like a Lyon, and the hinder a Goat, with a bushy tail like a Spaniel Dog, or an undockt Horse, his stones great and hanging down. Some term this a Phayrye Beast, because Lamyae is Latin for Phayries.

Others describe it as very swift, treacherous and cruel to men, whom it devours.[22]

Much as one can sympathise with the unfortunate creature of antiquity,

Lamia Crest of Lambert of Durham
(Coll. Arms ms. 2.D.5, f. 164)

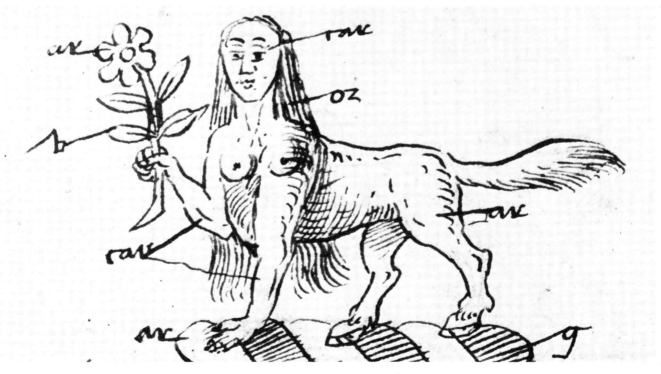

117

who was cheated of her love, the Lamia of the fifteenth century has even fewer allegorical or symbolic characteristics to commend it. Nevertheless it has been impressed on one occasion into the service of English armory, as the crest of a family of Lambert.

At the Visitation of Yorkshire in 1585 by Robert Glover, then Portcullis Pursuivant, was recorded the pedigree and arms of Lambert of Owton in County Durham, and subsequently of Calton in Craven, Yorkshire. The crest is drawn with a Lion's body, the hind legs with cloven hooves, a bushy tail like an undocked Spaniel, a woman's face, breasts and arms (instead of forelegs), holding in the right hand a red rose on a leaved stalk.[23]

When William Camden, Clarenceux, confirmed these arms to William Lambert in 1613, he blazoned the creature as a 'Mantichor'.[24] By chance the original letters-patent are also in the College of Arms and there the creature is painted with a woman's face and breasts, the hair gold, a Lion's body and legs, the forelegs ending in human hands, and a bushy tail. The creature is, of course, really a Lamia, being a play upon the name Lambert, (the family also bore three Lambs in their shield). It is surprising that the learned Master Camden, who was a notable antiquary, should have got into a muddle over it.

This is an interesting example of the increasing familiarity with the fabulous which men began to feel by the close of the Middle Ages, and their happy use in armory and the decoration of beings and creatures which former ages held in awe or horror. From being a female bogey, whose name was used by Greek mothers to frighten their children, the Lamia has been tamed into service as an elegant pun upon a name in an armorial achievement.

THE SPHINX

Although among the best known of the human monsters of classical antiquity, the Sphinx is not mentioned in the medieval heraldic treatises as a beast suitable to be borne in arms, and does not appear in English heraldry until the latter part of the sixteenth century. Even after that it was never a very popular charge; there was, moreover, some confusion as to the correct way to depict the creature.

In antiquity there were two quite distinct varieties of Sphinx, the Egyptian and the Greek. The Egyptian Sphinx can probably claim precedence in time, and its most famous example is to be found next to the Great Pyramid at Giza, near Cairo. In ancient Egyptian mythology the Sphinx was considered to be masculine, the body, legs and tail being that of a Lion, and the head that of a man, normally modelled on the reigning king, with the conventional head-dress and treatment of the beard. It was always depicted as couchant. The Greek Sphinx was usually shown as sejant, and was always winged, with the face and bust of a woman. Legend has it that this more tiresome variety established herself near Thebes, where she posed a riddle, on about a level with those found in Christmas crackers, to unsuspecting travellers passing her and, if they were unable to solve it she killed them. Oedipus was eventually persuaded to take her on and provided the correct answer, whereupon the Sphinx killed herself. Neither variety of Sphinx has much to offer armory in the way of allegory or symbolism, and its use as a charge in arms usually only indicates some connection with, or service in, the Near or Middle East.

A Greek Sphinx was granted in 1573 by Robert Cooke, Clarenceux King of Arms, to Robert Parris of Hitchin in Hertfordshire, as a crest.[25] At the Visitation of Leicestershire in 1681–3 it was also recorded as the crest of a family of Pochin, of Barkby in that county.[26]

With the grant of arms by Sir Isaac Heard, Garter, and George Harrison, Clarenceux, in 1815 to Colonel Sir Benjamin D'Urban, an outstanding soldier and colonial administrator, we get the first Egyptian Sphinx in English heraldry. His crest was *a Sphinx argent under a Palm Tree proper*.[27] It is not clear why he should have been granted an Egyptian Sphinx, since he never served in Egypt, but with the next grant the allusion is clear. In the following year the same two kings of arms granted to Henry Salt, British Consul-General in Egypt, who distinguished himself in a difficult mission to the Emperor of Ethiopia, arms and crest, incorporating an Egyptian Sphinx.[28] A recent grant of a badge, in 1921, to Philip Pandely Argenti makes the Egyptian Sphinx sejant.[29]

The *Dictionnaire des Figures Heraldiques* gives some fifteen European families as bearing a Sphinx of one sort or another as a charge in their arms, including Arrighi de Casanova, Dukes of Padua.[30]

It would avoid ambiguity if, in future, the female winged creature were blazoned as a Greek Sphinx, and the male wingless creature as an Egyptian Sphinx.

THE SAGITTARY

The Centaur without his bow is an almost unknown charge in English heraldry, although it has been borne in arms by a few Continental families; but the Sagittary drawing his bow has been borne by a few English and Scottish families as well as several Continental families. In heraldic art this most decorative of chimerical creatures is usually drawn with the body, legs and tail of a Horse, joined to the torso and upper parts of a man, drawing a bow and arrow, aiming sometimes ahead of him and sometimes backwards. Occasionally one finds the hooves depicted as cloven.

The Centaur Cheiron, famous for his knowledge of music, archery, and medicine, who taught mankind the use of medicinal herbs, and who after his death was immortalised among the constellations as Sagittarius, has many symbolic connotations in armory. He has been considered an appropriate emblem for those born between 22 November and 20 December under this ninth sign of the Zodiac, or for those to whom something notable happened at that time.

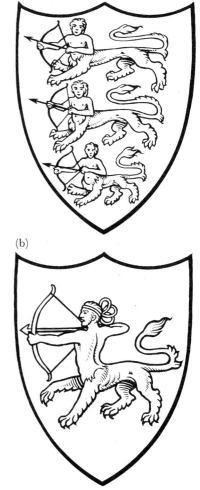

(a)

(b)

The most famous heraldic example is the attributed arms of King Stephen, *Gules three Sagittaries passant in pale or,* which were traditionally believed to refer to the fact that his invasion of England in 1135 to claim the throne was brought to a successful conclusion during the period when this sign of the Zodiac was in the ascendant and the battle was clinched by his archers. While ruling sovereigns and courts were beginning to use armorial devices at this time, there is no documentary evidence to support these arms, and we must conclude that they were thought up by later generations. Sometimes Stephen's Sagittaries were depicted with Lions' bodies instead of Horses'. Nicholas Upton, in *De Studio Militari,* gives Stephen's attributed arms as *Gules three Sagittaries passant guardant in pale, the Lions' bodies or, the men's bodies argent, and the bows gold.* Sometimes King Stephen is credited with only one such Sagittary.

The Sagittary is, however, a very rare charge in medieval English armory. One of the very few examples is the seal of John Wolverston of Kirketon, which is a Sagittary passant on a shield.[31] He features, at full gallop, on the crest of the Academy of the Muses Mansionary, granted about 1640. A red Sagittary upon an Escallop shell is said by Gerard Legh in 1597 to have been the badge of an esquire of England,[32] but I can find no other support for this.

The Sagittary has also been considered an appropriate emblem for those who have shown martial, and even sporting prowess, particularly where artillery or marksmanship is implied. Moreover this sagacious creature has obvious symbolic properties where medicine is concerned. It is, therefore, strange that greater use has not been made of him in armory.

(a) Attributed arms of King Stephen
(b) Another version of King Stephen's arms
(drawn by G. Mussett)

119

THE SATYR

The Cambridge Bestiary described the Satyr as a kind of Ape, with a quite agreeable figure but with movements of ceaseless pantomime,[33] a view echoed by Bartholomew Anglicus, who said that it was 'plesynge in face wyth mery meuynges and playenges'. He also said, however, that they 'benne stern and cruelle with bestyalle appetite: and such bestes be full lecherous, in so moche that they slee women in the dede of lechery, if they take them walkynge in wodes, and benne called Satiri, for they may not have inoughe of lechery, as Isydore [of Seville] saith'. Batholomew continues his account of the creature in increasing confusion, muddling it up with a whole covey of mythical monsters,[34] but this was, no doubt, as Topsell said, because 'Satyres are very seldom seene, and taken with great difficulty'. As so often, the last word on the subject rests with Randle Holme, who said the 'Poets and Painters do decipher the Satyr thus: a Man in the upper parts of his Body, with long Ass-like Ears, and from the middle to the feet a Goat, with a sharp-pointed prick. Some draw him with Horns and a short tail like a Buck'.[35]

The Satyr is not found in medieval heraldry – in England at any rate – doubtless because his libidinous reputation made it difficult to see what decently symbolic purpose he could serve as a charge in arms. While the Renaissance turned men's minds to the classical authors, and the Greek pantheon was ransacked to provide polished and civilised charges for the new coats of arms being designed by the Tudor and Stuart heralds, it comes as something of a surprise to find the Satyr harnessed to a shield of arms.

In June 1636 King Charles I wrote to the Lord Mayor and Court of Aldermen of London, requesting them to solicit contributions from the citizens

Armorial bearings of the Academy of the Muses Mansionary (Coll. Arms ms. Misc. Grants iv, f. 4)

towards the establishment of an academy or school for the education of the young nobility and gentry in the practice of arms and the arts. Almost a year later the King had to write again, rather sharply, to complain about the City's delay and requesting a speedy answer in writing as to what had been done already and what was intended to be done in the matter.[36] The King's solicitude for the education of the young gentlemen led shortly afterwards to the founding of the Academy of the Muses Mansionary at Covent Garden, a little way outside the walls of the City of London. An establishment for such worthy purposes, under royal patronage, needed a coat of arms to enhance its dignity, and Sir John Borough, Garter King of Arms, duly granted them an armorial achievement.[37] The arms were: *Argent two Bars wavy azure, on a Chief azure two Swords, the blades argent and the hilts or, crossed in saltire with the points uppermost, in base an open Book, the cover or.* The crest was a Sagittary courant proper. The supporters were: *Dexter a Mermaid with two tails, the upper parts and the tails argent and sinister a Satyr proper.*

The symbolism of the arms seems fairly straightforward: the barry wavy field referred to the river Thames, which then flowed nearby, while the book symbolised learning, and the crossed swords the practice of arms – and also no doubt a compliment to the City, since the arms of the See of London contained crossed swords. The Sagittary crest, too, has (as we have seen)

Armorial bearings of the Merchant Adventurers of Bristol (Coll. Arms ms. C.17, f. 16)

121

a worthy symbolism not inappropriate for such an academy. It is anybody's guess what symbolism was intended by the supporters. Unless music formed part of the curriculum, it is difficult to see what symbolic purpose the Mermaid served, while the obviously earthy Satyr is perhaps a curious reference to the studies of the young gentlemen. It is just possible that, because the City of London was dilatory in supporting the school, the King turned elsewhere for funds, and he may have tapped the wealthy merchants of Bristol, since the Academy's supporters bear some resemblance to those of the Merchant Adventurers of that town.

The Company and Fellowship of the Merchant Adventurers of Bristol have a long and illustrious history going back at least to the fifteenth century, and by the following century their influence was so great that they controlled the foreign trade of the town, and played a leading part in promoting and financing many of the great voyages of discovery to the Americas and Africa. Their first royal charter of incorporation was in 1552 and their arms and supporters were probably granted then or shortly afterwards;[38] their full armorial achievement was recorded at the heralds' Visitation of Gloucestershire in 1623.[39] The dexter supporter is a Mermaid proper, girdled about the hips or, holding in her exterior hand an Anchor gold, and standing on waves. Here one can see the point of a Mermaid, because she was one of the occupational hazards of overseas trade, and she is here because she has been tamed and overcome. The sinister supporter – a winged Satyr proper, the wings or and hair grey but without horns, standing on a grassy mound and holding in his exterior hand a Scythe, the shaft or and the blade downwards proper – appears to give him some of the attributes of Father Time, and makes his symbolism rather an enigma. Or was he, too, another occupational hazard of overseas trade and exploration, one of the many temptations to be found in foreign ports?

THE MERMAID AND THE MELUSINE

One of the best known of all the chimerical creatures of human form, the Mermaid has a long armorial history, stretching back to the early Middle Ages; but the elegant, sexy sea nymph, who is to be found admiring herself on many a shield and crest, has a very mongrel pedigree. Partly she comes to us from the misty beginnings of European folk-lore, and was known to the ancient Celts, the Teutonic tribes, the Vikings and the early English. To them she was more a fairy of the lakes than a creature of the sea, with the ability to foretell the future and impart supernatural powers to mortal men, and she was generally friendly rather than mischievous. At times she was equated with the Sirens of ancient Greece, whose melodious songs lured mariners to destruction; at others with the Harpies, those fell snatchers of men's souls. For instance, Lawrens Andrewe, writing around 1527, described the Mermaid as 'a deadly beast that bringeth a man gladly to death. From the navel up she is like a woman, with a dreadful face, long slimy hair, a great body, and is like the Eagle in the nether part, having feet and talons to tear asunder such as she getteth. Her tail is scaled like a Fish and she singeth a manner of sweet song, and therewith deceiveth many a good mariner . . . . .'[40]

Indeed, the Mermaid's reputation throughout the Middle Ages left much to be desired. Bartholomew Anglicus, writing around 1230, tells us that 'the Mermayden, hyghte Sirena, is a see beaste wonderly shape, and draweth shypmen to peryll by swetenes of songe'. He goes on to say:

> Phisiologus speaketh of Sirena and saythe it is a beaste of the see,
> wonderly shape as a mayde from the navelle upwarde and a fyshe
> from the navell donnewarde, and this wonderful beaste is gladde

and merye in tempeste and sadde and hevye in fayre wether. With swetenes of songe this beaste maketh shypmen to slepe, and when she seeth that they ben aslepe she gooth into the shyppe and ravysheth whiche she may take with her, and bryngeth hym into a drye place, and maketh hym fyrste lye by her and do the dede of lechery, and if he wolle not or may not, then she sleeth hym and eatheth his fleshe.[41]

Lawrens Andrewe, however, knew how to deal with this nautical hazard, and said that 'the wise mariners stop their ears when they see her, for when she playeth on the water all they be in fear, and then they cast out an empty tun to let her play with it till they be past her'.

The Angers Tapestry, made in the late fourteenth century, has one scene depicting the Angel introducing St John to the Great Whore, who is seated upon a mound in much the same attitude as that in which Mermaids were usually depicted, holding in her left hand a looking-glass and combing her hair with her right hand. To the medieval mind the Mermaid was a kind of nautical prostitute and, while laymen could regard her with indulgence, she provided a handy allegorical moral for the righteous; we therefore find her depicted, possibly more often than any other creature, upon misericords and elsewhere in churches. For example, the fourteenth century *Bestiare d'amour* of Richard de Fournivall has a picture of two Mermaids pulling a man out of a ship, with the smug comment, 'So is the woman guilty if she lulls a man with sweet words and then betrays him'. In spite of her fearful reputation the Mermaid has always been represented in heraldic art as a beautiful and seductive woman, with an elegant fish tail from the naval downwards, usually holding a looking-glass in one hand and a comb in the other, and her symbolism echoes the more kindly Western European aspects of her character and activities.

The Mermaid is borne as a charge in the arms or crests of more than three dozen English families, and Renesse lists some one-hundred and forty-four families who bear her.[42] One of the earliest English examples is the seal of William Banastre, of Sulhampstead, in Berkshire, dating from about 1230–40, which has a Mermaid with a long tail enclosing a horse,[43] but this may not have been truly heraldic. The Chronica Majora, which was written and illustrated by Matthew Paris shortly after 1250, depicts a scene from the Battle of Stamford Bridge in 1066, when King Harold defeated a Viking army, showing the principal figure on the English side holding a blue shield on which is a Mermaid proper, while his horse trappers are semée of Mermaids and stars.[44] Unfortunately it is not clear who is indicated by these attributed arms. Two well-known English families who bear Mermaids in their arms are the Berkeleys of Berkeley Castle, whose Mermaid supporters go back to the early fourteenth century, and the Byrons, whose Mermaid crest is of comparable antiquity.

The Mermaid can, of course, be depicted holding any suitable object, so long as it is specifically blazoned, for a Mermaid proper would be shown with her comb and mirror. An English family of Lanye have a Mermaid holding a hawk's bell in the right hand. An amphibious Mermaid is depicted in a fifteenth century copy of Froissart's Chronicle, where she is shown with four short legs beneath her fishy tail; and she is running along the ground holding aloft a banner of arms.[45]

Lawrens Andrewe, who wrote so confidently about the Mermaid, says 'they bear their young in their arms and give them sucke of their paps, which be very great, hanging at their breasts'. Two thirteenth century manuscripts,[46] the Tenison Psalter and the Amesbury Psalter, have charming illustrations of a mother Mermaid suckling her baby.

While the Mermaid is normally, and correctly, shown with one tail, there

123

is a variety which has two fishy tails. In English heraldry this one is blazoned as a 'Mermaid with two tails', or as a 'Mermaid double-queued', but she is fairly rare. In German armory, however, she is met with quite frequently; here, she is commonly called a Melusine, and usually shown without comb or mirror, holding instead the upward curving ends of her tails with each hand; she also usually wears a coronet.

It is not clear why the double-tailed creature is called a Melusine, for she bears litle resemblance to the fabled ancestress of the house of Lusignan. There are various versions of this legend of the fairy, the discovery of whose secret ends her life on earth – a story not unlike that of Lamia. Perhaps the best-known version of the legend is the *Chronique de la princesse*, written in 1387 by Jean d'Arras,[47] which was very popular in the later Middle Ages – as was another version, *The Romans of Partenay, or of Lusignan; otherwise known as The Tale of Melusine*.[48] Briefly, Count Raymond of Poitou encountered Melusine in the woods one day, beside a fountain, and was so enchanted by her beauty that he begged her to marry him. She consented to do so on condition that he never attempted to see her on a Saturday. The marriage was ideally happy and she made Raymond wealthy and powerful, presenting him with several sons, through one of whom the powerful family of Lusignan claimed descent and through the Lusignans, many of the noble families of Europe can, to this day, claim her as an ancestress. For very many years Raymond kept his promise, but at length curiosity overcome him and, through a hole he had bored in the door, he watched her one Saturday splashing in her bath and was horrified to see :

> Fro the hed ado[w]n unto the navell
> A full fair and gent[le] woman there was she;

Armorial bearings of the Worshipful Company of Fishmongers of London (drawn by G. Mussett)

AL·WORSHIP·BE·TO·GOD·ONLY·

124

> But under was a serpent of verite,
> A taill burled had of silver and asure.

So overcome with shame was Raymond at having spied on her that Melusine was prepared to forgive him; but the thought of being married to a kind of Mermaid, even though her tail was in the livery colours of his house, vexed him to such a degree that he uttered the fatal words 'Ha! Serpent!' Thereupon Melusine flew out of the window, uttering a loud cry of anguish.

All the medieval authorities agree that from the navel downwards Melusine was a snake and not a fish and, indeed, was a kind of flying serpent. It seems odd, therefore, that the woman with double fish tails should be blazoned a Melusine in German heraldry, but there is, no doubt, a reason for it. As Melusine was in all other respects an admirable creature, kind, considerate, generous and a good mother, her memory should be preserved by the heralds, and we could do well in future to call the double-tailed Mermaid after her.

THE MERMAN OR TRITON

The Merman, like the Mermaid, appears in the early folk-lore of Western Europe, but was never as popular, and is even rarer as a charge in heraldry. Apart from his masculine and usually bearded face and fishy tail, he has no special equipment and can be depicted holding any suitable object. When holding a trident and blowing on a conch horn he becomes the heraldic Triton, whose gusty breath conjures up the raging storm. In whatever capacity, he is alarming rather than amiable and provides no very satisfactory symbolism for armorial purposes.

The earliest example in English heraldry makes his appearance in 1575, in the grant of arms by Robert Cooke, Clarenceux King of Arms, to the Worshipful Company of Fishmongers of London, where he serves as the dexter supporter, wearing a cuirass and holding a falchion in his right hand.

In 1958 Sir George Bellew, Garter, and A. J. Toppin, Noroy and Ulster, granted arrms to John Samuel Mayer, of Manchester, which included, in base, a Merman double-queued proper grasping a tail finned gold in each hand. This is the only example in English heraldry of such a Merman.

THE HARPY AND THE FRAUENADLER

Harpies, those malevolent spirits of the storm winds with the faces of hideous hags, wild hair and drooping breasts, and the bodies of birds of prey, those hirelings of the gods whose duty it is to snatch away the souls of mortal men, do not appear in English heraldry before the fifteenth century. John Guillim, writing in 1610, says that 'of this kind of bird (or rather Monster) Virgil writeth in this manner':

> Of Monsters all, most monstrous this; no greater wrath
> God sends 'mongst men; it comes from depths of pitchy Hell:
> And Virgin's face, but wombe like gulfe insatiate hath,
> Her hands are griping clawes, her colour pale and fell.

It might seem odd that such a thoroughly nasty creature should be borne as a charge in armory, but by the fifteenth century the Harpy had begun to be credited with one redeeming feature and this made her, in certain circumstances, a suitably symbolic charge in arms. The earliest heraldic treatise in which she is mentioned is the *De Studio Militari* of Nicholas Upton, where he includes the Harpy among the birds used as charges in arms, and tells us why. The passage is headed, 'Of a byrd callyd in laten Harpia', and proceeds:

125

Seal of Thomas Hoo the younger (Coll. Arms ms. Vinc. 225, f. 35)

Harpia is a byrd . . . . being in the farther partes of the worlde in wyldernes rempant nere unto the see callyd Ionian. Thys byrde is marvelouse ravenouse . . . . Thys byrde hath a man's visage, but no parten of a man in hym . . . . Thys byrde, they say, will sley the fyrst man that he seeth in wyldernes. And then [he goes] to the water to drynke afterwardes and seeth his own visage like unto the manne's whom he slewe, then he is very sory therefore . . . . that he absteyneth from mete ontyll he dys.

Upton adds that the Harpy should be borne as a charge in arms by such as have committed manslaughter, to the end that by the often view of their ensigns they might be moved to lament their misdeed.[49]

Now it is significant that at the time when Nicholas Upton was writing we find the first Harpies used in English heraldry, and used by two men who would have been known personally to him. One was Thomas Hoo, younger half-brother of Sir Thomas Hoo, K.G., Lord Hoo and Hastings, a famous soldier and military governor during the French wars at about the time that Upton was serving in France under the Earl of Salisbury. Thomas Hoo, the younger, was lord of the manor of Ockley in Surrey and held considerable property in Sussex and elsewhere. He was Member of Parliament for the county of Sussex in 1446 and 1448 and for the borough of Horsham in 1472. He supported the Yorkist cause in the Wars of the Roses and played an important part in the end of the Second Battle of St Albans, in negotiating the surrender. He died in October 1486. There are three remaining examples of his seal, appended to documents in 1446, 1475 and 1480. These show his arms, Hoo and St Omer quarterly with St Leger in pretence; his crest, a Griffin sejant; and his supporters, two Harpies with wings expanded.[50] The fact that his brother, Sir Thomas Hoo, never bore the Harpies, although their arms and crests were the same, lends some colour to the suggestion that Thomas Hoo, the younger, may have borne them in expiation of some manslaughter committed during these turbulent times.

The other man who used the Harpy was Sir John Astley, an accomplished knight and famous jouster, who was regarded in his time as a great authority on the subject of single combats. On 29 August 1438 he jousted at Paris against Pierre de Masse, whom he smote 'thorwe the hede wt a spere' and killed him. It could well be that remorse over this accident moved him to adopt as his crest a white Harpy with wings expanded and gorged with a

Crest of Sir John Astley, K.C., from his Carter Stall Plate (drawn by Miss A. Urwick)

Coronet and chain of gold, standing upon a bed of reeds within a golden crest-coronet. The spirited picture in the Hastings Treatise of Sir John Astley, tilting against an opponent in the lists, shows him with this crest. On 30 January 1441/2, at Smithfield in London, he fought a famous single combat on foot with axes against Philip Boyle, a Knight of the King of Aragon and Sicily, who had travelled throughout France without finding anyone hardy enough to accept his challenge. Afterwards Astley 'was made knyght in the felde for his wele doyuge' by the King. In 1446 he was appointed to supervise the duel between the London armourer William Catur and his apprentice John David; unfortunately Catur had been so plied with drink by his friends that he was slain. David, who was clearly a pretty unruly character, was hanged at Tyburn some time later for a felony.[52]

In 1461 Sir John Astley was elected a Knight of the Garter, when his stall-plate was put in St George's Chapel at Windsor. In 1463 King Edward IV appointed him, 'the knight that fought so manly in Smithfield with an alien that challenged', captain of Alnwick castle, but he was taken prisoner by the Lancastrians shortly after. The next year the King granted 500 marks towards his ransom and a further 500 marks the following year, for his speedy deliverance from the dire prisons in which he had long been and was still remaining. This had the desired effect and in 1467 we find him one of Lord Scale's 'counsell', or seconds, when he fought the Bastard of Burgundy, a most famous contest. Astley was present at the funeral of Edward IV in 1483, when he was one of the four knights who bore the Cloth of Estate, and in 1485 was granted a substantial pension by the King; but by November 1486 he was dead.

There are two other examples of the Harpy borne in arms in English heraldry, in the middle years of the fifteenth century. Fenwick's Roll gives a shield, *Azure a Harpy wings expanded argent*, but does not name the bearer; and Randle Holme's Book gives the arms of William Tenterden as *Argent on a Bend gules three Harpies of the first*.[53]

It may be wondered why such eminent and illustrious men should bear such a revolting creature as the Harpy as a heraldic charge, and one is brought to the conclusion that Nicholas Upton's observations on the significance and symbolism of the creature may well have more force than has hitherto been accepted, and we would do well to take him more seriously. The importance of symbolism in the Middle Ages cannot be over-emphasised – and if moralising could be included, so much the better. When we add to this the romantic revival of chivalry in the fifteenth century, with its nostalgic regard for the courtly conventions of knighthood, it does not seem so surprising to find a Harpy used in arms, if we accept Upton's statement. It would be typical of the greatest jouster of his age, Sir John Astley, who was the very model of the chivalrous knight, to do something rather quixotic like adopting a Harpy for his crest, to signify his remorse at accidentally killing a gallant opponent.

As for the elusive William Tenterden, of whom nothing more can be discovered, we can only speculate. Maybe he was a tiresome and bloody-minded petitioner for arms, who thought he knew better than the heralds, and, in exasperation, the Kings of Arms slipped him a covey of Harpies to teach him a lesson. John de Bado Aureo, it will be recalled, mentioned that Kings of Arms in his day devised armorial charges for much more slender symbolic reasons, and Nicholas Upton's account of the Partridge in arms parallels the Harpy, so this surmise may not be so very wide of the mark.

It is not so easy to discern why the family of Ashley, originally of Ashley Place in Wiltshire, and subsequently of Winborne St Giles in Dorset (from whom were descended the family of Ashley-Cooper, Earls of Shaftesbury), bore for crest *a gold Harpy statant with wings close, the legs belled or*. As

Crest of Sir Harry Asheley, of Wimborne St Giles, Dorset (drawn by G. Mussett from Coll. Arms ms. 2.L.6, f. 10)

Arms of William Tenterden (drawn by G. Mussett from Coll. Arms ms. L.8, f. 45)

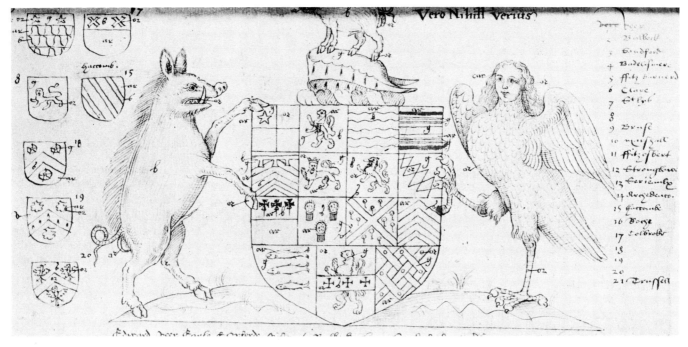

Arms and supporters of de Vere (Coll. Arms ms. Vinc. 172, f. 19)

Opposite page
Top
Satan (on the right of the picture) leading his army in the attack on the Holy City, bearing a shield of his arms, Gules a Fess or between three Frogs proper, with his standard-bearer behind him holding a banner on his arms.
Bottom
The defeat of Satan and his army, who are shown falling into an opening in the earth before a stylised representation of the Holy City, Satan's shield being shown tumbled down on top of him.
(Bodleian Library ms. Douce 180, pp. 87 and 88)

Crest of Pochin of Barkby (drawn by G. Mussett from Coll. Arms ms. K.2, f. 102)

they do not seem to have borne this crest much before Tudor times, it is possible that it was granted to them in the mistaken belief that they were connected with Sir John Astley; but his was a Leicestershire family with whom there was, in fact, no relationship. Several families of Moody also bore Harpies in their arms, but there is no solid evidence that they were all related; these, it seems, were cases of granting somewhat similar arms to families of the same name, just in case there was a remote connection, a post-medieval practice which has now been curbed. Once the Harpy was borne by such very eminent families as Hoo and Astley, people got used to seeing it around and in time forgot its symbolism; so that Harpies granted after the fifteenth century may well have little significance. Indeed, even her correct form was sometimes forgotten and she was depicted with a long snaky tail, as in the crest of Pochin, of Barkby in Leicestershire.

One of the most illustrious of all English families, that of de Vere, Earls of Oxford, were using during the Wars of the Roses, if not earlier, a creature which is usually blazoned as a Harpy, but which they themselves evidently did not appear to regard as such. Prince Arthur's Book, compiled around 1500, has an excellent painting of the banner of Sir John de Vere, Earl of Oxford, supported by this creature. An adherent of the Lancastrian faction, Sir John took an active part in the Wars of the Roses. After the Battle of Barnet he took to piracy on the high seas, but was finally captured and imprisoned at Hammes in Picardy. In 1484 he persuaded the constable of the castle to change sides and help him escape, and he accompanied Henry of Richmond to England, where he fought with distinction at the battle of Bosworth as Captain-General of the army, being rewarded by Henry VII who made him Constable of the Tower of London and Lord Chamberlain. He was later appointed High Steward and Lord High Admiral, and died in 1513. In his will (proved P.C.C. 20 May 1513) he bequeathed a jewel to Our Lady of Walsingham, which is described in the inventory as 'a splayed Egle of gold wt an angell face wt vj dyamoundes and xj perles wt iiij rubies' valued at £30. It may, however, have been intended for a Siren (often then equated with the Harpy), which is related to the Mermaid, thus alluding to his naval career.

The Frauenadler, or Jungfrauadler, of German heraldry is usually translated into English as the Harpy, to whom she does indeed bear a passing resemblance; but her pedigree and symbolism would seem to be somewhat different. She is usually depicted as a fairly attractive woman down to the

128

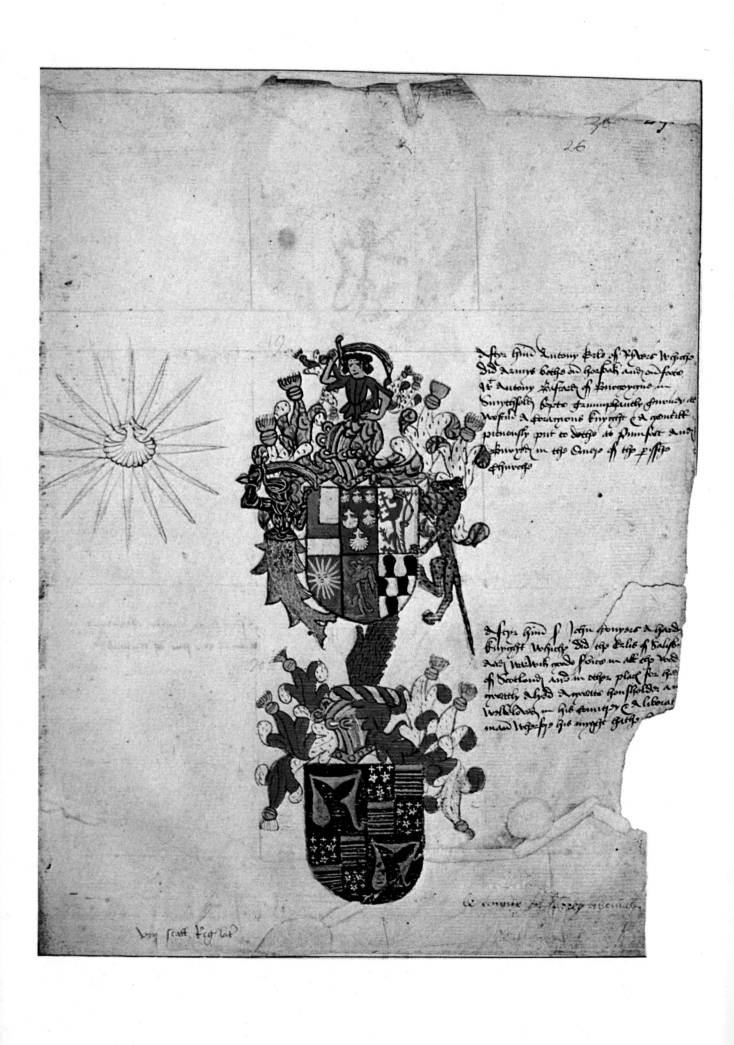

navel, wearing a coronet on her head, and with the displayed wings, tail and legs of an eagle. The register (now in the College of Arms) of the Knights of the Order of the Golden Fleece, compiled for Hector le Breton, Sieur de la Doineterie, Montjoye Roy d'Armes of France (1615–53), gives the arms of Messire Jehan de Rietberg, Comte de Ostfrise, as *Sable a Frauenadler displayed argent crowned and membered or between four Estoiles also gold*. The fourth quartering in the arms of the Princes of Liechtenstein is also a Frauenadler, but with the tinctures reversed. Possibly the best known are the arms of the old imperial city of Nurnberg, *Azure a Frauenadler displayed and crowned or*. Albrecht Durer's woodcut of the arms of the Empire and the city of Nurnberg, which is a splendid example of the early sixteenth century approach to heraldry, includes these arms.

Opposite page
Merman, with the body clad in armour, as the dexter supporter of the arms of Sir Richard Wydville, Earl Rivers, K.G. (died 1469). (Buccleuch ms. Wrythe Garter, Book, f. 54)

THE MANDRAKE

A mildly poisonous plant, the Mandrake grows widely all over the Mediterranean region and elsewhere in Europe. Its narcotic and emetic properties were much esteemed in the Middle Ages and it was also credited with aphrodisiac properties. The thick, knobbly and usually forked root has a curious resemblance to the human figure and, when dug up from the ground, was believed to utter a shriek so rending and piercing that it drove those who heard it mad. The Mandrake is not, of course, a monster or chimerical creature in the strict sense of the term, but in heraldic art it has acquired such anthropomorphic characteristics that it can be rated as one of the more fanciful of the fabulous creatures of heraldry, and a splendid example of the heraldic imagination in action.

The Mandrake is a very rare charge indeed and Renesse cites only one French family as bearing it, de Camps, of Nivernais, *Azure five Mandrakes argent a Canton ermine,* together with a branch of this family, de Camps de Ste Leger de Brechart, who bore it quarterly. The only English family on record is Bodyam, or Bodyham, of Essex, whose arms, *Gyronny of eight gules and sable three male Demi-Mandrakes argent, the hair, leaves and apples or, within a Bordure or charged with eight Cross Crosslets fitchy azure,* and crest, *a 'shee Mandrake' argent, the hair, leaves and apples proper, charged on the breast with a Cross Crosslet fitchy sable,* were confirmed by Christopher Barker, Garter King of Arms, between 1536 and 1547. The indications are that these arms were originally granted in the reign of King Henry VII. Unfortunately the christian name of the grantee is not recorded, nor is anything further known about the family, so it is impossible to hazard a guess as to the symbolism of the creature in this case, or why the Mandrakes are of both sexes.[54] In view of its medicinal properties one would expect the Mandrake to be a suitable charge for a physician.

Arms of the City of Nurnberg (drawn by N. Manwaring)

SOME FANCIFUL HUMAN CHARGES

While not – strictly speaking – heraldic monsters, there are a few fanciful charges, based on the human form, which have been used in English armory and which – as a glance at a couple of them will show – are instances of the more bizarre flights of the heraldic imagination.

Thomas Coram, who was born in Dorset in 1668, began life as a seaman and rose to become master mariner and captain of a merchantman. For several years he settled in Massachusetts, where he was a successful boatbuilder, but he returned to England in 1703. He was appalled by the miserable condition of the destitute children in the East End of London, and was inspired to provide a refuge for such abandoned children as had no homes. After seventeen years of tireless exertions he at last obtained a royal charter in 1739 authorising the establishment of the Hospital for the Main-

Serpent-Woman crest of Sir Walter Bonham (drawn by Miss A. Urwick from Coll. Arms ms. M.9, f. 50)

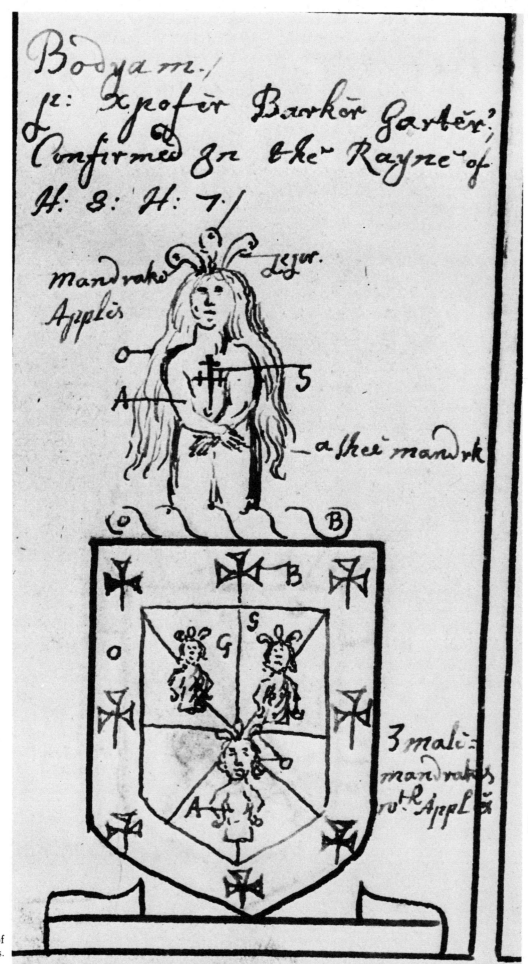

Mandrake arms and crest of Bodyam (Coll. Arms ms. EDN.56, f. 57ᵛ)

tenance and Education of Exposed and Deserted Young Children, since known more generally as the Foundling Hospital. On 27 March 1747, Coram obtained from John Anstis, Garter, and Stephen Martin Leake, Clarenceux, a grant of armorial bearings for his hospital, the blazon for which reads as follows:[55] Arms: *Party per fess azure and vert, a young Child lying naked and exposed, extending its right hand proper, in chief a Crescent argent between two Mullets of six points or.* Crest: *A Lamb argent holding in its mouth a sprig of Thyme proper.* Supporters: *Dexter, a terminal figure of a Woman full of nipples proper [eight are depicted] with a Mantle vert the Term argent, being the Emblem of Nature: Sinister, the Emblem of Liberty represented by Britannia holding in her right hand upon a Staff a Cap argent, and habited in a Vest azure girt with a Belt or, the undergarment gules.* Motto: *'Help.'*

This is a charming example of the civilised and cultured imagination of two of the more remarkable and interesting of the eighteenth century English heralds. Thomas Coram spent all his private means on the Foundling Hospital and other charities, and himself became destitute in his old age, so that an annuity of £170 was raised for him by public subscription.

We have already seen examples of the medieval propensity for punning arms and we shall end this chapter with a curious example. The Visitation of Surrey in 1531 records the arms and crest of Dodge and recites a patent of arms alleged to have been granted on 8 April 1306 by Jacques Hedingley, 'dict Guyen Roy d'armes', to Peter Dodge of Stopford in Cheshire, whose loyalty and valiant service against the king's 'graund Enemy & Rebell' John de Baliol, King of Scotland, and also at the sieges of Berwick and Dunbar, were rewarded by King Edward I with the grant of certain seignories, Guyenne King of Arms also assigned arms to Peter Dodge and his heirs in recognition of this, namely *Barry of six or and sable, on a Pale gules a Woman's Breast distilling drops of milk proper.* The crest was *a Demi-Seadog sable collared or.*[56] John Guillim gives us the clue to the symbolism of this unusual coat, for he blazons the breast as a 'Woman's Dugge', which was, of course, a somewhat tenuous play on the name Dodge and may indicate its pronun-

ciation at that time. Guillim also points out that 'by the Teates sometimes are meant the plentifull fields wherewith men are nourished', and the symbolism thus also refers to the King's bounty in endowing Peter Dodge with lands and lordships to nourish him and his descendants. A pretty conceit and one very typical of medieval heraldry, and possibly one of the earliest examples of an augmentation of honour.

10
Lions and
Kindred Creatures

F ALL heraldic creatures the Lion and the Eagle have the most ancient armorial pedigrees. The Lion in particular has a remarkably wide range of symbolism which covers most of the allegorical spectrum, providing emblems for knights who were rashly valiant and for those who were prudent tacticians, while monkish clerks could use him as symbolic of Christ and, on occasion, of the Devil.

The fourteenth and fifteenth century treatises on heraldry closely followed the description of the king of beasts given by Bartholomew the Englishman and emphasised his princely qualities of boldness and magnanimity. 'In perill the lion is moste gentell and noble, for whanne he is pursewed with houndes and with hunters, the lyon lurketh not nor hideth himselfe, and arayeth hymselfe to defence, and ronneth out of wode and coverte with swyfte rennynge and course, as thoughe he wolde acounte vile shame to lurke and to hyde himself.' On the other hand 'it is the kynde of lyons not to be wrothe with man, but if they be greved or hurte. Also theyr mercy is knowe by many and oft ensamples, for they spare theym that lie on the grounde, and suffre them to pas homewarde that ben presoners and comen out of thraldome, and eate not a man nor slee hym but in great hunger'. It was these aspects of his character which most appealed to the imagination of the medieval knights and to heralds at all times.

For this reason he was adopted as an armorial device by the kings and greater barons and knights. An analysis of French seals and enamels between 1127 and 1300 shows the Lion as by far the most popular charge in heraldry after the ordinaries, with two hundred and twenty different examples of the Lion rampant and forty of the Lion passant (although many of these may have been meant to be Leopards).[1] The earliest example is the blue shield with six little gold Lions rampant which Henry I gave to Geoffrey of Anjou in 1127, and there is reason to think that Henry himself may have used one or more Lions as his emblem. John de Bado Aureo, writing some two centuries later, repeats the story of the Lion's characteristics and adds 'wherefore beware who so evyr bere Lyons or a Lyon in armys, that he do not apen the nature and kynde of a Lyon'.

The Lion, as Bartolo di Sasso Ferrato tells us, was depicted in heraldry as nobly and vigorously as possible: normally as rampant, with gnashing teeth

Le Counte Daryn dell porte de goules oue bn leon rampant dor

e Counte de Lincolne port dor a bn leon rampant de purpre.   Hertouled

e Counte de Northfolk mouss Roffer Bygod porte parte dor ede sert a bn leon rampat

e Counte de Cornebaille port arthet a bn leon ramp de goules coronee dor a bn bordo
                                                                                   besau

Symon Mouffort conte de Leicestre porte de goules a bn leon rampat durset a la colle fourchee

e conte de Deuenschire port dor a bn leon rampat azure   Le Sire Pey port les mesnes

atrik conte de Dimbure port de goules a bn leon rampat durset a la bordo daryt pouduree de ...

lan Sire de Galebray port azure a bn leon ramp de argent coronee dor

Mouss Piers Bruys de Skelton port argent a bn leon ramp azure   Lauconbeys port mesme

uss Roffer Moubray port de goules a bn leon rampant de argent

e Sire de Segraue port de sable a bn leon rampant dargent coronee dor.

e Sire de Welles port dor a bn leon rampant de sable la colle fourchee.

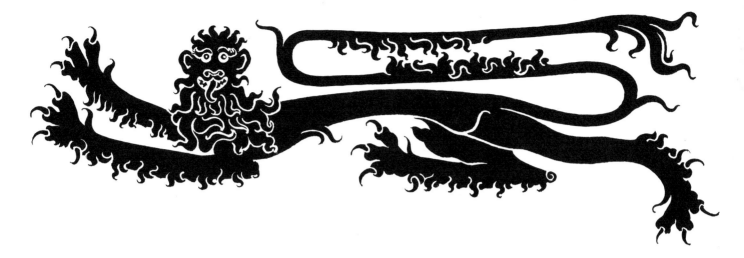

and clawing feet, like the two combatant Lions borne by King Richard the Lion Heart during the Third Crusade.

The clerics, however, basing themselves on the Physiologus – the principal source-book for the twelfth century bestiaries – discerned quite different qualities in the beast and drew appropriate morals from them. The Lion was held to have three further characteristics:

First, when he perceives that the hunters are pursuing him, he erases his footprints with his tail so that he cannot be traced to his lair. In like manner our Saviour, the Lion of the Tribe of Judah, concealed all traces of His Godhead when He descended to the earth and entered into the womb of the Virgin Mary. Secondly, the Lion always sleeps with his eyes open; so our Lord slept with His body on the Cross, but awoke at the right hand of the Father. Thirdly, the lioness brings forth her whelps dead and watches over them until, after three days, the Lion comes and howls over them and vivifies them by his breath; so the Almighty Father recalled to life His only-begotten Son, our Lord Jesus Christ, who on the third day was thus raised from the dead and will likewise raise us all up to eternal life.[2]

It was Sir Thomas Browne, with his inquisitive Renaissance eye, who brought the heralds down to earth with a curious observation about the Lion.

We are unwilling to question the Royal Supporters of England, that is, the approved descriptions of the Lion and the Unicorn. Although, if in the Lion, the position of the pizel be proper, and that the natural situation, it will be hard to make out their retrocopulation, or their coupling and pissing backward, according to the determination of Aristotle; All that urine backward do copulate aversely, as Lions, Hares, Linxes.[3]

The heraldic Leopard, which we now blazon as a Lion passant guardant, was the offspring of the adulterous union of a Lioness and a Pard, or a Lion and a female Pard. Nicholas Upton said that the 'Leopard ys a most cruell beeste engendered wilfully of a Lion and a beeste called a Parde, lyk unto a Catt of the moutaine.' He also says that 'a Leopard ought to be painted wt his whole face shewed abroad openly to the lookers on', a point made in the *Tractatus de Armis,* by John de Bado Aureo, who adds that to bear a Leopard in arms is a token that the first bearer of the arms was begotten in adultery. It will be recalled that when Richard the Lion Heart altered his arms in about 1195, after losing his Great Seal during his captivity, he changed them to three gold Leopards on a red field, and this may have been

A Leopard of England, based on a heraldic embroidery of c. 1330, in the Musée de Cluny, Paris (drawn by N. Manwaring)

Opposite page
An ordinary of Lions from Thomas Jenyn's Book, c. 1410 (British Museum Add. ms. 40851, f. 6)

135

The fielde Or, a Lion Sa-
lyaunt, his tayle forked,
Verte. L. Is this difference
enoughe from the other
Lyon, if the fieldes & Lyons were both of one co-
lour? G. Yea, a lesse thinge
then this were difference
enoughe, to beare a cote
vnchallenged.

He beareth Argent, a Lion
Salyaunt, his Taile forke
nowed Geules.

Lions Queue Fourchee, as drawn by Gerard Legh (*Accedence of Armorie*, p. 43ᵛ)

in allusion to his famous great-grandfather William the Bastard, the conqueror of England.

THE LION QUEUE FOURCHEE

The double-tailed Lion makes his appearance in heraldry in the late twelfth
century and was probably invented as a way of differencing Lions borne by
different members of the same family. In some instances it may have been an
allusion to the creature's fierceness, 'for when the Lion is wroth, first he
beateth the earth with his taile, and afterwards as the wroth encreaseth, he
smiteth and beateth his owne backe'. For this reason the Lion's tail is usually
depicted in armory as waving vigorously over his back. One of the best-known
examples of the creature is the arms of William the Marshal, Earl of Pembroke, *Party per pale or and vert, a Lion rampant queue fourchée gules.*[4]

THE TWO-HEADED LION

The double-headed Lion, which is usually depicted as rampant, is a latecomer
to armory. Here again, it was probably invented as a method of differencing
new arms from old, although Gerard Legh said, 'this betokeneth him that
beareth the beast, to be homager to two such princes as do both bear the
Lions, which both are his heads'.

THE LION BICORPORATE

The Lion with one head and two bodies is a fairly rare charge in English
heraldry; only some half-dozen examples are known. One of the earliest

Lion queue fourchee from the brass of John Kyngeston of Childrey, d. 1514 (drawn by N. Manwaring)

136

He beareth Sable, a Lyon with two bodies, Argent. L. I thinke this ſhoulde be ſome monſter. G. Not ſo. But the reaſon therof you ſhal vnderſtand. whē there be two gentlemen, that in fielde do meete together, eche enemy to the other, in the Prices quarell, both bearing a Lyon after one ſorte, althoughe diuers in coulours. He that vanquiſheth the other in fielde, or driueth hym from his ſtanderd, becauſe the lawe of Armes will not ſuffer the vanquiſher to beare the vāquiſhed cote, all wholy as his aduerſarye did, for that they be both Chriſtians, the Herehaught ſhall haue a conſideration thereof, and ſhall put both the bodies of the ſame Lyons, vnder one headde as a perpetuall memory, to him that ſerued his Prince ſo well, & this is very good armory.

Lion Bicorporate, as drawn by Gerard Legh (*op. cit.*, p. 47ᵛ)

occurs in Strangway's Book, compiled about 1450, but the bearer is not identified.[5] Perhaps the best-known example is that on the arms of John of Northampton, Mayor of London in 1381–3, *Azure a Lion Bicorporate sejant guardant crowned or, the tails cowed and erect*.[6] The tinctures are sometimes given differently, and the beasts sometimes depicted as more or less rampant.

The reason for this charge is not known and it was probably just a flight of heraldic fancy, but the explanation adduced by my learned brother herald, Mr C. W. Scott-Giles, Fitzalan Pursuivant of Arms, is just as plausible :

> Lions bi-corporate, rampant and crowned,
> Even in arms are not frequently found.
> I can recall but a single example;
> That, if you're prone to night terrors, is ample.
> How did it happen? The tale is in sooth
> Like one you probably heard in your youth :
>
> Two lions rampant, one nebuly night,
> Started a quarrel, which grew to a fight.
> One had a crown, and the other had none
> (Which is the way many wars have begun).
>
> 'I'll have that crown,' said the sinister lion.
> 'That,' said the dexter, ''s a rascally try-on.'
> 'I will have that crown, or I'll tear you tronconne.'
> 'You shan't have this crown. You're no lion couronne.'

137

Lion Tricorporate (drawn by N. Manwaring)

In combatant postures, enraged and incensed,
Their talons they bared, and their muscles they tensed;
Then, hurtling together in head-long collision,
They ran their two heads into one, with precision.

All the king's heralds, for all of their art,
Never could prise the two lions apart,
So they called the beasts locked in this grim tête-à-tête,
One lion rampant and bi-corporate.[7]

THE LION TRICORPORATE

This unusual and attractive charge can be depicted in several ways. Usually three bodies are shown as issuing from the three corners of the shield, united to the single head in the middle, or fess point, the two upper bodies with their feet downward and the lower body rampant. Sometimes they are all three shown walking in a clockwise direction, and sometimes they are depicted with the head in the dexter chief corner of the shield, with the upper body passant, the middle in bend, and the lower rampant. It is, of course, essential that the positions should be blazoned.

The earliest example is in the first seal of Edmund Crouchback, Earl of Lancaster, second son of King Henry III, which was in use in 1273 and continued to be used until 1290. This device was clearly based on the three Leopards in the royal arms, but it may have been more in the nature of a badge, because the Earl also used the royal arms differenced with a Label of three points, each charged with a Fleur de Lys.[8] Another equally early example is in the seal of Nicholas de Carew, on a deed dated 1283 at Exminster

Seal of Edmund, Earl of Lancaster, c. 1273, with another version of the Lion Tricorporate (Coll. Arms ms. Vinc. 88, f. 96)

138

in Devon. Here again, the connection with the well-known Carew coat, *Or three Lions passant sable,* is obvious and it may have been a way of differencing the coat of a cadet branch of the family.[9]

Gerard Legh's comment on the Lion Tricorporate is worth quoting:

Le : 'Is this good armory?'
Ge : 'I say to you, it is verie antient and lawful, and borne to a good meaning. As it might be, the agreement of so many, and thereupon to use one consent.'
Le : 'That were to be marveled at, to see three Lions of one consent.'

Winged Lion of St Mark (drawn by N. Manwaring)

In short, this would appear to be a suitable emblem for a committee or corporate body.

THE LION QUADRICORPORATE

This ungainly and monstrous creature makes but one appearance, on the seal of Cicilie de Heworthia, in the thirteenth century,[10] and we can put it from our minds. There is no evidence that it was regarded as the family arms.

THE WINGED LION

The Winged Lion, symbolic of the Resurrection, has been associated with St Mark from very early Christian times, and when the relics of the Evangelist were transferred to Venice in the ninth century it became the emblem of that city state. It is a rare charge in English armory. The earliest example is in the seal of John Hoo of Norfolk, made in the latter part of the thirteenth century, where it is shown with its tail cowed (that is, drooped between the hind legs). John Norwich, the son of John of Norwich, in Norfolk, possibly a descendant of John Hoo (for surnames were still fluid at that time), also used a Winged Lion sejant in his seal in 1403.[11]

To John Bossewell, writing in 1597, the symbolism of the Winged Lion with tail cowed had moved a long way from the Evangelists.[12]

This Lyon cannot well abide the field. Wherefore? Because ye woulde take him to be a coward. Not so : in that he is simple, gentle, and meeke of nature, he hath therefore more neede of wings to flye. Yet the bearing of such an ensigne is noble, and conteineth in itselfe an hyghe mistery. A prince given to vertue and godliness can seldome escape th'assaults or malignities of his owne vassals and subjects, wherefore such his innocencie flyeth unto the heavens and there purchaseth an immortal Crowne, for the earthly which would have perished, to the confusion of his enemies, and th'advancement of the glorie of the high God.

THE SEA LION

It seemed reasonable to the medieval mind that, if there were creatures on earth, they should have their counterparts in the sea, and thus the Lion was balanced by the Sea-Lion. It was a creature quite different from the Sea-Lion of the natural world, although the Seal, imperfectly observed, may have prompted the analogy. The Sea-Lion of heraldry is depicted with a Lion's head and mane, with the forelegs ending in webbed paws; from the waist downwards, it consists of a scaly fish with a finny tail. Like all heraldic creatures, it can be of any colour. Only the natural animal, depicted in its true colouring, should be blazoned as a Sea-Lion proper and, to avoid confusion, it would be better to blazon it as *a Sea-Lion* [followed by its scientific name in brackets] *proper.*

It is not, however, until the sixteenth century that the Sea-Lion makes his appearance in English armory. Then, our seafaring ancestors, exploring undreamt-of lands and building the foundations of our overseas trade, needed

Sea Lion (drawn by N. Manwaring)

139

IMHOFF

Sea Lion, as depicted by Otto Hupp
(Münchener Kalendar 1919)

Opposite page
Winged Sea Lion supporting the
banner of Hercules, Duke of Ferrara,
in the Book of Standards (Coll.
Arms ms. I.2, f: 10)

140

The duc of ferrare hercules knyght of the garter

Gamelyon from the arms of Gardner, of South Brent, Somerset (drawn by Miss A. Urwick from Coll. Arms ms. Vinc. 163, f. 157)

Lion Umbrated, arms of Trazeguies (drawn by Miss A. Urwick)

suitably symbolic creatures to epitomise their activities; and what could be better than a Sea-Lion, with its simultaneous allusion to the Royal Lions of England and the high adventure of the seas?

THE WINGED SEA-LION
An early Tudor manuscript in the College of Arms shows this creature supporting a banner of the arms of Hercules, Duke of Ferrara, K.G.

In recent times two Winged Sea-Lions were granted as supporters for the arms of the Bank of Bermuda.

THE GAMELYON
This odd creature makes but one appearance in armory and was evidently conjured up in the mind of Sir William Dethick, Garter King of Arms, who granted to Thomas Gardner of South Brent in Somerset, in July 1557, the following arms: *Quarterly gules and azure on a Bend cotised or between two 'Gamelyons rampant and volant supporting in their forefoote a Ring or with a Garnett proper' or a Lion's-head caboshed of the first with a Buckle in his mouth silver between two Fleur de Lys sable.*[13] In the Queen's College version the beasts are depicted in trick with a lion's body, legs, feet and tail, indeterminate head with slightly turned up snout, and Dragon's wings. In two College of Arms manuscripts they are depicted like Dragons rampant, while another depicts them like Griffins segreant. Clearly Sir William Dethick had his contemporaries guessing; but as he was considered the most skilful herald of his day, and a member of the original Society of Antiquaries, it is likely that he had some reason for creating this creature.

THE LION UMBRATED
The first heraldic treatise to mention the shadow or ghost in armory is the *De Studio Militari* of Nicholas Upton, but the Lion Umbrated can be found in the thirteenth century in the Low Countries. There it was used by a family of Trazegnies, who imposed the outline of a Lion on their bendy shield, and their descendants still bear it to this day.[14]

Upton considered that the outline or umbra of any object could be borne as a charge in heraldry, and we certainly know of the Peacock Umbrated and Fish Umbrated, as well as the Crosses Umbrated illustrated by Upton; but the Lion Umbrated has been more widely used. A well-known English example is the Leopard Umbrated borne on the golden bend in an azure field by Sir Henry Scrope, 3rd Lord Scrope of Masham, K.G., who was executed for treason in 1415 on the Agincourt expedition. It is thought that

Lion Umbrated, as depicted by Gerard Legh (*op. cit.*, p. 43b)

He beareth Or, a Lion Saliaunt vmbrated. This is as much to say, as the shadow of a Lion, and yet the Armorye is good. Here maye neuer be blazed ani colour becaufe hee is but traced with a pēcell, vpō the field. So that the fielde sheweth through him, & therfore is of no more effect, then the shadow of a mā in armory.

he assumed it on his second marriage to Joan Holland, who bore England within a silver bordure.

THE LEOPARD'S FACE JESSANT DE LYS

This is one of the prettiest of heraldic charges and seems first to have been adopted by Sir Nicholas de Cauntelo, or Cantilupe, about the middle of the thirteenth century, to distinguish his arms from those of his elder brother William de Cauntelo (d. 1254), which were *Gules three Fleur de Lys or*.[15] Some members of this family further differenced these famous arms by showing the Leopards' Faces upside down. A few other English families also bore three Leopards' Faces Jessant de Lys, in various tinctures and combinations, and a few bore a single Leopard's Face Jessant de Lys.

(a)

THE PANTHER INCENSED

The heraldic Panther Incensed is depicted rather like the natural animal, but covered with spots of various colours and with flames issuing from its mouth and ears: it is, in fact, a rather muddled version of the Panther of the bestiaries.

> There is an animal called a Panther which has a truly variegated colour, and it is most beautiful and excessively kind. Physiologus says that the only animal which it considers an enemy is the Dragon. When a Panther has dined and is full up, it hides away in its own den and goes to sleep. After three days it wakes up again and emits a loud belch, and there comes a very sweet smell from its mouth, like the smell of allspice. When the other animals have heard the noise, they follow wherever it goes, because of the sweetness of this smell. But the Dragon only, hearing the sound, flees into the caves of the earth, being smitten with fear. Thus, unable to bear the smell, it becomes torpid and half asleep, and remains motionless, as if dead.[16]

It is clear, therefore, that the flames which are depicted in heraldry as issuing from the mouth and ears of the Panther are, in fact, its savoury belch, exciting and attractive to all other creatures but repellent, terrifying and soporific to Dragons. This kind, amiable and very decorative beast has rarely been employed in English armory. Its earliest mention is by John de Bado Aureo, in the *Tractatus de Armis*, (c. 1394), and Nicholas Upton has rather more to say about it some fifty years later. A manuscript in the College of Arms, of later date, gives a Panther as the badge of King Henry VI, who bore 'for his supporters a lyon Crowned and a Panther wch beast belonged

(b)

(a) Leopard's Face Jessant de Lys
(b) The same, upside down version
(drawn by N. Manwaring)

Panther Incensed badge of Sir Charles Somerset, Lord Herbert and later Earl of Worcester, from the Book of Standards (drawn by N. Manwaring from Coll. Arms ms. I.2, f. 83)

143

to the house of Lancaster wherof he was then chief and was borne by him to shewe that a Kinge should have so many excellent and severall vertues as there are diversities of spottes and most beautifull Coullors in this Beast, and then his People will love and followe him for his vertues as all other Beastes love and follow the Panther for his sweete smell and glorious coullors'.[17]

The Earls of Somerset, as descendants of John of Gaunt, Duke of Lancaster, also bore a Panther Incensed as their badge, and their descendants, the Dukes of Beaufort, bore it as a supporter. A number of continental families also bear one or more Panthers in their arms.

THE TYGER

Bartholomew the Englishman described the Tiger as a beast of dreadful swiftness, and the medieval bestiarists concur in crediting both the male and female Tiger with remarkable ferocity and perseverance in the pursuit of the hunter who has taken its whelps. Its celerity is such that one cannot easily escape the beast, even on the swiftest horse, and the only ruse is to throw down mirrors behind one, 'and the moder foloweth and fyndeth the mirrours in the waye, and loketh on theym and seeth her owne shadowe and ymage therin, and weneth that she seeth her children therin; and is longe occupied therfore to delyver her chyldren oute of the glasse; and so the hunter hath tyme and space for to scape'.

Tigers were believed to inhabit Hyrcania, a region of Persia by the Caspian Sea, and to be speckled rather than striped. But in late medieval haraldry they seem to have been regarded as red in colour, for that is the more usual tincture.

The Tiger was not used as a charge in English armory before the fifteenth century, when Nicholas Upton mentions it in the *De Studio Militari*, but he omits to attribute any particular symbolism to it. One would have thought that bravery and implacable perseverance, coupled with tender care and devotion to its offspring, would be the characteristics most suitable to associate with it.

The only actual examples in English heraldry date from the sixteenth century, the most colourful being the arms of the family of Sybell of Eynsford in Kent, namely *Argent a Tyger statant tail cowed gules, gazing at its reflection in a Hand-mirror, frame and handle or, by its feet; and for crest a Hand-mirror erect, frame and handle or, reflecting the Head of a Tyger gules.*[18] The heraldic Tyger is often depicted with a curiously pointed snout and tusks in its lower jaw, as in the arms and crest of Lutwich, in Shropshire.

Modern English heraldry also recognises the natural Tiger, which is depicted in the normal way and blazoned as a Bengal Tiger proper, presumably because the tigers of India were better known to the wealthy merchants and soldiers of the East India Company and to the kings of arms who confirmed their gentility with a grant of arms.

11
Some Fabulous Beasts
in Heraldry

OST people tend to think of the fabulous and chimerical creatures of armory as typical creations of the medieval heralds, but we have seen that very few of them indeed were employed on shields, or harnessed as badges or crests before the fourteenth century. The majority, in England at least, were adopted or concocted during the following century.

Bouly de Lesdain's analysis of early French seals and enamels of the twelfth and thirteenth centuries shows that some seventeen different real beasts were used on two hundred and ninety three different seals, but only one fabulous creature, the Chimera, was employed in a more or less armorial way, in the later thirteenth century. The earliest English heraldic treatise, *De Heraudie*, (*c.* 1300), mentions no fabulous beasts at all. Even Bado Aureo, writing in England some ninety years later, mentions only eight real beasts (if we include the Pard) and no fabulous beasts at all.

Mowbray's French Treatise, written in the early fifteenth century, gives some thirteen real beasts as borne in arms, and produces three fabulous beasts, the Leucrota, Parandrus and Unicorn; while Banyster's French Treatise, roughly contemporary, mentions only the Unicorn and adds the Winged Antelope and Winged Stag. Nicholas Upton's *De Studio Militari* (1446) mentions twenty-seven real beasts, if we include the Tyger and the Panther; but the Unicorn is the only fabulous beast that Upton mentions as borne in arms. It would seem, therefore, that the fashion for using chimerical creatures in heraldry started in France, and probably also Germany, and spread to England as a by-product of the French wars.

The passion for pageantry, which was such a marked feature of society in the fifteenth and sixteenth centuries, particularly among the nobility and gentry, and the masques and mummeries which took place after the jousting was over, undoubtedly encouraged the use of increasingly bizarre creatures in heraldic display. If the bestiaries sometimes proved inadequate, the heralds did not hesitate to conjure up suitable creatures from their imaginations.

It is not without interest that about this time two of the ablest and most active Garter Kings of Arms were concentrating particularly on the armorial aspects of heraldry. John Wrythe was already Falcon Herald under King Edward IV, probably by 1473, and was appointed Norroy King of Arms in 1477 and Garter King of Arms in 1478. He was reappointed on the succession of Henry VII, and after his death in 1504, was succeeded by his son,

The arms and crest of Thomas Sybell of Aynsford, Kent, from the Visitation of that county in 1531. In spite of its colour the beast is obviously a Tyger, because it is gazing at its reflection in a looking-glass. (Coll. Arms ms. D.13, f. 2)

145

The Alce (drawn by N. Manwaring, based on James Bossewell, *Works of Armorie*, p. 111ᵇ)

Sir Thomas Wrythe, alias Wriothesley, who held the office of Garter until his death in 1534. Several important armorial manuscripts, compiled by or under the direction of John Wrythe, still remain and testify to his close and competent interest in the subject. The many remaining manuscript books, rolls of arms and the like, compiled under his son's direction and beautifully executed and painted, such as Prince Arthur's Book and The Book of Standards, show that Sir Thomas Wriothesley too played an important part in the development of English armory during the formative years of the sixteenth century. It is to these two that we must attribute the introduction of many of the more fanciful creatures of English heraldry.

THE ALCE

John Bossewell, writing at the end of the sixteenth century, mentioned the Alce as a charge in armory, describing it as 'a wilde Beaste in the woods of Germany, in fashion and skinne like to a fallowe Deere, but greater, and hath no joints in his legges'. His woodcut of the armorial achievement in which it appears, shows it leaning against an oak tree, but he gives no clue to its bearer and it cannot be found in the English ordinaries of arms.[1] The Alce was, in fact, a kind of elk and not really a chimerical creature, but the curious fable about its jointless legs makes it worthy of inclusion here. Julius Caesar first mentioned it, and the story about it recalls the similar medieval notion that the Elephant could be caught by sawing halfway through its favourite tree: when it comes to lean against the tree it falls down and, by reason of its stiff legs, cannot get up again and is slain by the hunters.

THE ALLOCAMELLUS

Sometimes called the Ass-camel, this quaint creature consists of a camel with the head of an ass, and is said to have formed the crest of the Eastland Company, which was established in Elizabethan times to exploit the English trade with Lithuania – or Elbing, as it was usually then called, after its principal port. Unfortunately the arms of the Eastland Company were never recorded in the official registers of the College of Arms, so it is not possible to say with certainty what they were, but contemporary writers regarded the beast as a kind of elk. The trade of the Company with Lithuania was short-lived and we can also bury the memory of this ungainly and unsymbolic beast without compunction, for it is clearly an unworthy interloper in the heraldic bestiary.

Alphyn badge of Richard (West), Lord de la Warr (Coll. Arms ms. I.2, f. 82)

THE ALPHYN

This strange creature, which bears an erratic resemblance to the heraldic Tyger, is sometimes depicted with the clawed forefeet of an Eagle, sometimes

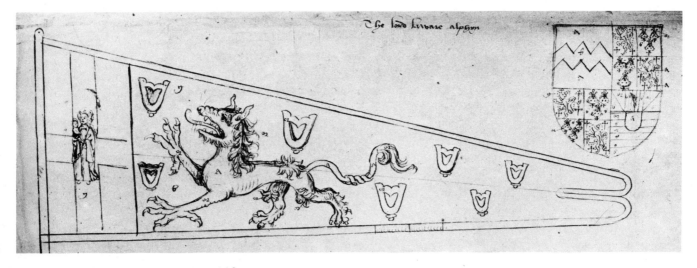

146

with the forelegs ending in cloven hooves, and sometimes with paws on all feet. Its origin is obscure, for it does not appear among the creatures normally described in the medieval bestiaries, or in the early heraldic treatises. The name, sometimes spelt Alfin, is thought to derive from Old French and thence through the Moors of Spain from the Arabic *al fil*, the elephant, the former name of the bishop in chess, but the Alphyn of armory bears not the slightest resemblance to that beast.

The earliest appearance of the armorial version of this creature in heraldry, or indeed in European literature, is in Fenn's Book of Badges, where it is shown as the badge of Richard (West), seventh Lord de la Warr, and is drawn with cloven forefeet and a fairly straight, tufted tail.[2] The seventh Lord de la Warr (*d*. 1476) was active on the Lancastrian side during the Wars of the Roses, being rewarded with a royal pension. His grandson Thomas (West), ninth Lord de la Warr (*d*. 1554), was a more colourful character, being dubbed a Knight of the Bath on the creation of Prince Arthur as Prince of Wales in 1489, promoted Knight Banneret in 1513 and created Knight of the Garter in 1549. He was very active in Sussex affairs and was appointed Lord Lieutenant of that county in 1551. He died in 1554. Thomas was the kind of man who at that time would have used a heraldic badge, and we do indeed find his ancestral Alphyn badge depicted in the Book of Standards; but here the beast is shown with the forelegs and feet of an Eagle and with a knotted tail.[3]

Sir William Chamberlain, of East Harling in Norfolk, who was active in the French wars, was created a Knight of the Garter in 1461, and the crest on his Garter stall-plate has been thought to be a Mule's head, or an Onager's head; however, in Wrythe's Garter Armorial it is clearly described as an 'Alfyn'.[4]

The Antelope (Sensu Antiquo)

This creature probably derives from the Antalops of the medieval bestiaries, being a confusion of the real antelope and other similar animals. It used its long, serrated horns to saw down the largest of trees and its remarkable celerity enabled it to escape the hunter; but these horns frequently proved the antelope's undoing. It lived beside the river Euphrates where, coming down to drink, it finds the Herecine shrub fatally attractive and gets its horns caught in the twigs, whereat the hunters, hearing its bellows, come and kill it. The bestiarist drew an appropriate moral from this unhappy event, adding, 'but beware, O Man of God, of the shrub Booze, and do not be entangled in the Herecine pleasure of Lust, so as not to be slain by the Devil. Wine and Women are great turners-away from God'.[5]

With its reputation for ferocity the Antelope undoubtedly appealed to the medieval heralds and their warlike masters. (Spencer writes of 'the Antelope and wolfe both fiers and fell'). Henry of Bolingbroke, afterwards King Henry IV, who was distinguished for his knightly prowess and went on crusade with the Teutonic Knights to Lithuania and subsequently visited the Holy Land, bore as his badge a white Antelope with golden horns and tusks, gold hooves, mane and tufts on the tail; about his neck he is gorged with a gold coronet and therefrom a gold chain flexed over his back. There is some doubt as to the origin of the Antelope as a royal badge. Some authorities consider that it was a badge of the family of de Bohun, and that Henry acquired it on marriage to one of the co-heiresses of Humphrey de Bohun, Earl of Hereford; others, that it was a badge of the Dukes of Lancaster and came to Henry through his mother, Blanche of Lancaster, heiress to the duchy, who married John of Gaunt. The Antelope badge was widely used by King Henry V and can be seen on his tomb in Westminster Abbey. It was also used by King Henry VI.

Edward (Stafford), Duke of Buckingham, Knight of the Garter and Lord

The duc of Buc
kyngham Edward
erll of hereford
staford: northm
buryngt of the mu
for the howse of
forthe

148

High Constable of England, also bore a similar white Antelope, which gives some colour to the view that it was originally a Bohun badge, for Stafford was descended from another co-heiress. Stafford entertained pretensions to the Crown and his flamboyant use of the royal Antelope may well have been one of those things which irritated King Henry VIII, who eventually had him executed for high treason in 1521.

Antelopes, both passant and rampant, have been borne by very few English families, but a somewhat larger number have borne Antelopes' heads in their arms and crests. The beast is even rarer as a charge in Continental heraldry, and Renesse, in the *Dictionnaire des Figures Héraldiques,* gives only one example: the family of Windeg, of Switzerland, who bear a black Antelope rampant on a gold field.

The Winged Antelope is mentioned in Banyster's French Treatise (early fifteenth century) as a charge borne in arms, but no further useful heraldic information is given about it.

The Kings of Arms of England have recently ruled that, in order to avoid confusion between the Antelope of the medieval heralds and the creature known to modern zoologists, the former shall in future be blazoned as an Antelope (*sensu antiquo*), while the latter shall be blazoned as an Antelope of a specific kind followed by its scientific name in parentheses.

THE APRES

This enigmatic beast, with the head, body and legs of a bull, but with a bear's tail, is sometimes called the Apre, and makes only one appearance in English armory – as the sinister supporter of the arms of the Worshipful Company and Fellowship of the Merchant Adventurers trading to Muscovia, commonly known as the Company of Muscovy, or Russian Merchants.[6] They traded cloth of all sorts to Russia and also 'much defective Wines and Fruits, not fit to be spent in this Kingdom [of England]', together with all sorts of English commodities. In return they imported skins, fish, caviar, potash, isinglass and much else besides. It looks as if they got much the better of the bargain, but it does not explain the Apres, which must have been a Tudor concept of some Russian beast.

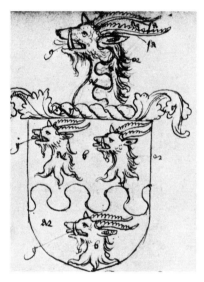

Antelope arms and crest of Snowe of Chicksands (Coll. Arms ms. 2.H.5, f. 46)

Apres supporter of the Muscovy Company (Coll. Arms ms. Vinc. 183, f. 90)

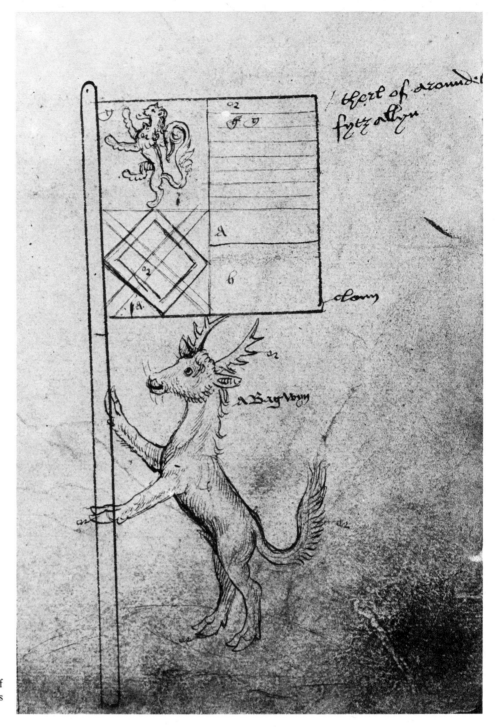

Bagwyn supporting the banner of William, Earl of Arundel (Coll. Arms ms. I.2, f. 11)

THE BAGWYN

This is another of that flock of curious and chimerical creatures which the lively minds of the late fifteenth and early sixteenth century heralds conjured up. Its first appearance in English armory is in Prince Arthur's Book (*c.* 1539), where it is depicted supporting the banner of William (Fitzalan), eleventh Earl of Arundel. The body, head, legs and upper part of the tail are black, and the horns, hooves and long hairs on the tail are gold, and beside the beast its name is clearly written.[7]

William's son, Henry, Earl of Arundel, K.G., a godson of King Henry VIII and active in government and politics, also bore a Bagwyn as the sinister supporter of his arms, as may be seen on his Garter stall-plate. The dexter supporter of the arms of the seventeenth century Lords Hunsdon was thought to be a Bagwyn, but it was, in fact a Yale, as the late Hugh Stanford London pointed out.[8] The origin of this creature is obscure.

150

THE BEAVER

Although the heraldic Beaver is really only a garbled version of the real animal, its appearance and habits are sufficiently remarkable to merit its inclusion here. Its earliest appearance in armory is in Mowbray's French Treatise (early fifteenth century), while Nicholas Upton included it in the *De Studio Militari.*

The Beaver, once common in Europe and England, was well known to the ancients, who considered the substance contained in two pear-shaped glands, situated near its organs of reproduction, to be a most valuable medicine, curing all manner of diseases, including convulsions (once regarded as a sign of diabolical possession). Our ancestors were not, however, very acute observers of nature and mistakenly believed these glands to be the creature's testicles. By the time the Physiologus and the bestiarists had dealt with it, the wise and gentle Beaver was credited with making the supreme sacrifice in order to escape capture. James Bossewell, whose *Workes of Armorie* was printed in 1597, tells us that 'he geldeth himselfe, when he perceiveth that he is pursued of the hunter, and biting off his stones, which are marveilously good in medicines, layeth them in the sight of the hunter, knowing by nature that he is hunted for the same, and so he escapeth death'. Sir Thomas Browne devotes a chapter to the Beaver, in which he discusses this tradition, concluding that 'the original of the conceit was probably Hieroglyphical, which after became Mythological unto the Greeks, and so set down by Aesop; and by process of tradition, stole into a total verity, which was but partially true, that is in its covert sense and morality'.[9]

Be that as it may, the Beaver has been used as a charge in arms or as a crest by a number of English and Continental families. This wise and useful creature would seem a suitable and appropriate charge for a physician or a pharmacist.

THE BONACON

It is difficult to think what allegorical or symbolic significance can be attributed to the Bonacon or Bonasus, other than that it commemorates a gallant rearguard action, such as holding the pass at Ronçevalles. This creature, which somewhat resembles a Bull, but with very convoluted horns, a horse's mane and a rather

Beaver, as depicted by Robert Glover in his copy of Baddesworth's version of *De Studio Militari* (drawn by N. Manwaring from Coll. Arms ms. Vinc. 444, f. 117)

ole,

side
tish

Museum Add. ms. Ch.

151

Boreyne badge of Sir Thomas Burgh (drawn by A. Colin Cole from British Museum Add. ms. 40742, f. 12)

'a Bonacon's Head coppe (couped) sable, horned and maned silver' as a crest to Richard Candelor, of Walsingham in Norfolk. The next year he granted 'a Bonacons hedd rased [erased] gules, horned and mayned and aboute the necke a coronett or' to Hugh Hollynside alias Hollenshed, of Bosley in Cheshire.[11] It is odd that these two grants should have been so close together and to two quite different families. One can only suppose that this was a private reference to some event which happened about that time.

THE BOREYNE

This is another of those curious creatures which suddenly appear in the armory of the later fifteenth and early sixteenth centuries and then vanish again into the confused mists from which they sprang. There appears to be no clue whatever to its origin, symbolism, or significance, and one cannot even hazard a guess, for it only occurs once in English heraldry. Fenn's Book of Badges gives it as the badge of Sir Thomas Borough, or Burgh,[12] who was created a Knight of the Garter by Richard III and two years later was summoned to Parliament as a Baron by Henry VII. It may be that this creature was adopted by him as a slight and fanciful play on his name.

THE WINGED BULL

Writers on armory have tried to derive the heraldic Winged Bull from the pre-Christian winged bull of Assyria, but there are no grounds for any such assumption. It first appears in Prince Arthur's Book as the beast of Lord Cromwell. This was probably Gregory Cromwell, son and heir of the notorious Thomas Cromwell, Earl of Essex, who was beheaded in 1540. Although his father's honours were forfeited, Gregory managed to keep in royal favour and was created Baron Cromwell five months later. He died in 1551. His descendant, Thomas, Lord Cromwell, used as his supporters in 1617 two red Winged Bulls armed, membered, tufted and winged gold.[13] This is a typical example of a beast badge turning into supporters by the seventeenth century.

Winged Bull supporters of Thomas, Lord Cromwell (Coll. Arms ms. Vinc. 172, f. 69)

THE CALOPUS OR CATWOLF

This is another of those chimerical creatures which first make their appearance in English armory in the early sixteenth century, and is borne by only one English family. On 9 June 1513 Thomas Wriothesley, Garter King of Arms, and John Young, Norroy King of Arms, granted to Godfrey Foljambe of Walton in Derbyshire, *'ung Calopus aultrement dit Chatloup d'or de sable esquartele, les cornes aussi esquarteles'*, as a badge or 'cognoisence pour son estandart'. In the Book of Standards, compiled shortly afterwards and still in the College of Arms, we find the standard of Sir Godfrey Foljambe drawn in trick with his badge upon it. Here it is described as a 'Caleps, Chatloup, a Catwolfe' and depicted with a wolf-like body, feet and tail, and a cat-like face with two serrated horns.[14]

Calopus badge of Sir Godfrey Foljambe (drawn by N. Manwaring from Coll. Arms mss. I.2, f. 60, and Vinc. 88, f. 21)

THE CALYGREYHOUND

Although this beast is not mentioned either in the bestiaries or in any dictionary, it has a respectable fifteenth century origin in English armory. Its earliest appearance is on the seal of John de Vere, twelfth Earl of Oxford, who was executed in 1462 on a charge of planning a Lancastrian uprising.[15] His son, another John de Vere, the thirteenth Earl, was the unruly Lancastrian noble whom we encountered earlier in connection with the Harpy. He died in 1513, and in his will he mentions 'ij censors of silver with the Caligreyhoundes'. The inventory is even more interesting for it mentions 'an hanging staynid wt Calygreyhaunds', a 'Celer and a tester of crymsyn blue and white satteyn embroderid wt a parke powdrid wt boores, moletts and Calygreyhondes', also 'ij newe sensors of silver wt ij Calygreyhondes uppon the toppes of them', and a 'vestyment crymsyn Sarcenet th'orfreys blue cloth of gold embroderid wt moletts and Calygreyhondes', as well as altar-cloths similarly embroidered and a 'long Cussheon of purple Damaske embroderid wt Calygreyhondes'.[16] It is evident that this was as favourite a badge as his Blue Boar.

Calygreyhound badge of the de Vere Earls of Oxford (drawn by A. Colin Cole from their contemporary seals)

THE CARETYNE

Sir Francis Bacon – Tudor courtier, soldier, sailor, diplomat and poet, with a remarkable facility for keeping on his feet in the tangled politics of the age – is the only Englishman to have borne a Caretyne as his badge. It is depicted on his standard as white with gold spots all over it, and the cloven hooves, horns, tusks, mane and tufts are also gold; flames issue from its mouth and one ear. The origin of this creature is not known and it must be regarded as another Tudor whim.[17]

THE CASTER

This strange creature has nothing whatever to do with the Beaver, resembling rather a Panther and likewise spotted, with a single horn, like that of a Unicorn,

Caretyne badge of Sir Francis Bryan (Coll. Arms ms. I. 2, f. 134)

Chimaera (drawn by N. Manwaring)

Cony Trijunct arms of Wells (drawn by N. Manwaring from Coll. Arms ms. L.8, f. 41)

Arms of Hopwell (drawn by N. Manwaring from Coll. Arms ms. C.7, f. 114)

rising from its forehead. Its only appearance in English heraldry is in a sixteenth century manuscript in the College of Arms. Above the picture, which is among half a page of beasts and birds drawn in trick, is written 'Caster with owt horne but eares'. There is no indication of the bearer of this device and it must be regarded as a somewhat doubtful creature.[18]

THE CHIMAERA

The eponymous ancestor of all chimerical creatures, the Chimaera makes its debut in armory in 1264, on the seal of Hugues Rostaing,[19] but in spite of its early use it has always been a very rare charge in heraldry. It is essentially a creature of Greek mythology, the offspring of Typhon and Echidna, two singularly unattractive monsters, and is generally depicted with the body and head of a lion, 'armed with flame', the head and neck of a goat issuing from its back, and its tail terminating in a serpent's head. John Bossewell, however, depicts an example with the head and neck of a dragon also issuing from its back.[20]

Renesse gives only four Continental families who bear Chimaeras in their arms: Chimera, of Italy, where it is an obvious play upon the name; Fada, of Verona; Friss, of Carniola; and Renaud, of Lorraine, who bear both a Chimaera and a Dragon respectant.

THE CONY TRIJUNCT

This interesting heraldic conceit consists of three Conies (the medieval name for the rabbit), of which two issue from the two top corners of the shield and one from the bottom, with their heads to the centre and joined together by their ears. It is an ancient coat, which first appears in Randle Holme's Book; here it is tricked and described as the arms of Harry Well, about whom nothing more is known.[21]

While on the subject of Conies, one is reminded of the charming medieval coat of the family of Hopwell, of Hopwell in Derbyshire, *Argent three Conies gules each playing the bagpipes*, which is quartered by the Sacheverells of

154

Morley, in that county.[22] This coat is also borne by the family of Fitz Ercald of Derbyshire, so there may well have been a family connection with the Hopwells.[23]

THE WINGED HARE

A modern example of a chimerical creature is the gold Hare courant with white wings, which was granted in 1923 to Arthur James Hare, of Fieldhead in the parish of Thorne, Yorkshire.[24] Apart from the play upon the name, there is no indication as to why the wings were added to the fleeting Hare.

THE SEA-DOG

John de Bado Aurea said that 'to bere a dogge in armys betokenyth a trewe werryour, the which purposeth nevyr to forsake his lord nouther in lyf nor in dethe', and this is echoed half a century later by Nicholas Upton.[25] One assumes that the Sea-Dog, which is an invention of the early Tudor heralds, must partake of these sterling qualities in a more nautical context, and would thus appeal to the medieval mind; but it is a rare charge in English armory.

Sea Hound Arms and crest of Thomas Harry of Rescrow, Cornwall (Coll. Arms ms. 2.H.5, f. 51)

The earliest example is in the Book of Standards, where the crest of John Flemyng, of Southampton, is given as a *Demi-Sea-Dog sable scaled argent and finned or*, with webbed forefeet.[26] The badge of John Brydges, Lord Chandos of Sudeley (d. 1559) was a Sea-Dog, with all its feet webbed,[27] but Clarenceux Hawley's grant of armorial bearings to Thomas Harry (or Harris) in 1547 depicts his three 'See Hownds' courant with normal dogs' paws, the crest being a *'demy Hownde of the See'* gules, eared, and finned or.[28]

Edward Stourton, Lord Stourton (c. 1555–1633) also used two black Sea-Dogs, with gold ears and fins, as supporters to his arms.

THE EGRENTYNE

This creature, which is not mentioned in the dictionaries and textbooks of heraldry, makes its only appearance in English armory in a College of Arms manuscript of pedigrees compiled in the sixteenth century. There it is shown as

Egrentyne supporter of the Arms of Fastolfe

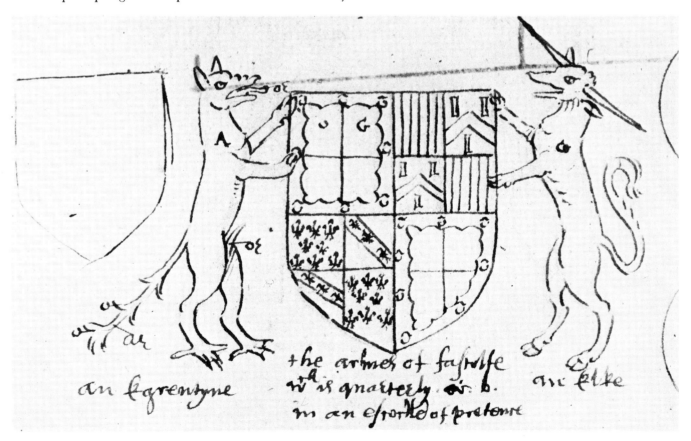

155

Enfield (drawn by N. Manwaring)

the dexter supporter of the arms of a branch of the family of Fastolf and is depicted as a beast with a white, dog-like body and head, langued and tufted gold, with the forefeet cloven and the hindfeet webbed. Underneath is written 'an Egrentyne'.[29]

The most famous member of this family was Sir John Fastolf, of Caister Castle in Suffolk, who died in 1459. He was a well-known soldier and active in the French wars, distinguishing himself at the Battles of Agincourt and Verneuil; later he was employed as military governor in the captured territories, and in 1426 was created Knight of the Garter. He is the kind of man who would have used a badge, and it is probable that the Egrentyne of the Fastolfs dates from his time, but this particular record should be regarded with some reserve.

THE ENFIELD

This fanciful beast with the head and ears of a fox, the body, hind-legs and tail of a wolf, and forelegs of an eagle, is a rare charge in heraldry, and a relative latecomer to the scene. Its best-known modern example is as the principal charge in the arms of the London Borough of Enfield, granted in 1966: *Or on a Fess wavy vert a Bar wavy argent charged with a Barrulet wavy azure, over all an Enfield rampant gules.*[30]

THE WINGED GOAT

Winged Goat supporters of the arms of Lord Sandys (Coll. Arms ms. Vinc. 172, f. 63)

The badge of Sir William Sandys, First Lord Sandys, of the Vyne, who had a distinguished military career, and was created Knight of the Garter in 1518, is given in Prince Arthur's Book as a white Winged Goat, the horns, wings and hooves gold. This is also recorded as his badge in another contemporary manuscript in the College of Arms,[31] but there is no indication as to why he adopted it. His great-grandson, William, Lord Sandys, bore two such Winged Goats as supporters to his arms and a Demi-Winged Goat for his crest.

THE SEA-HOG

This most curious of chimerical creatures is depicted in the Book of Standards as the crest of Sir William Smythe of Elford in Staffordshire, evidently one of the new men brought to the top when Henry VII won the throne, who consolidated his position by two well-connected marriages with the daughters of ancient noble families. He died in 1525 and was buried in a grand alabaster tomb in Elford Church. On his standard the Demi-Sea-Hog is drawn with a hog's head argent, tusks gold, the forelegs those of an eagle with the claws azure, and the body scaled argent and gules alternately.[32] There is insufficient information about the career of Sir William Smythe to suggest why he was granted this beast, and it may only be the offspring of the lively imagination of a Tudor king of arms. The Sea-Hog (if that is indeed its correct name) is borne by no other English family.

THE PEGASUS

The winged horse of Greek mythology, which sprang from the blood of Medusa when Perseus cut off her head, and was later Bellerophon's mount when he slew the Chimaera, subsequently became the steed of the Muses and thence was harnessed to the service of heraldry. The use of the Pegasus as an emblem goes back to pre-Christian times; it was then the device of the ancient Greek city-state of Corinth, but was little used in European armory until the Renaissance.

A Pegasus forms the principal charge in 'the armes apperteynynge and belonginge to the followshippe and corporacon of the burgesses and Marchant Adventurers, Clothiers and Weavers, Drapers and Taylers and others usinge anye arte or facultie within the Towne and Boroughe of the Devyzes', which were ratified and confirmed by William Hervy, Clarenceux King of Arms, at the Visitation of Wiltshire in 1565.[33] From the wording it would seem that these arms were already in use by the confraternity, so they may be of earlier origin. Two such creatures form the supporters to the arms of the City of Exeter and are equally ancient.

Anthony Cavalier, an Italian merchant resident in London, was naturalised by King Henry VIII and granted arms in 1544: *Azure a Pegasus rampant wings addorsed or, on the shoulder a Rose gules, within a Bordure compony argent and vert.*[34] The arms used by the Honourable Society of the Inner Temple, but still without proper authority, *Azure a Pegasus rampant or*, were probably assumed by them in the later sixteenth century and may have been based on a misunderstanding of the seal used by the Knights Templar, a horse walking with two poor knights riding it – a reference to the origins of the Order.

Several other English families bear a Pegasus as a charge in their arms, but its symbolism in the later Middle Ages and in Tudor times may well have been derived from the symbolism of the horse given in several medieval treatises. 'A horse borne in arms signifies a man who is willing and prepared to fight with little cause, for at the faint sound of the clarion is the horse provoked to battle. It also signifies a well-formed man who has four attributes which are found in the horse, namely form, beauty, prowess and colour.'[35] If to this is added a pair of wings the result is something unusual and very beautiful as well.

THE SEA-HORSE

The steeds of Poseidon, which have become one of the more decorative of heraldic charges, must not be confused with the elegant little Sea-Horse of the natural world, which should always be blazoned as a Sea-Horse proper, followed by its full scientific name, The chimerical Sea-Horse of armory is compounded of the head, neck, and foreparts of a horse, with webbed forefeet, and instead of a mane a scalloped fin; its hindparts consist of a fish's scaly tail embellished

Sea Hog crest of Sir William Smythe of Elford (drawn by N. Manwaring from Coll. Arms ms. I.2, f. 58)

Pegasus arms of the Merchant Adventurers of Devizes (drawn by N. Manwaring from Coll. Arms ms. G.8, f. 40ᵛ)

Sea Horse supporter of the arms of the Merchants Trafficking into Spain (drawn by N. Manwaring from Coll. Arms ms. Vinc. 183, f. 90)

157

Winged Sea Unicorn supporter of the arms of the Overseas League (drawn by Miss A. Urwick)

with fins. Like all armorial creatures, it can be of any colour or combination of colours.

Although the Sea-Horse is a late fifteenth century recruit to heraldry, its happy and obvious symbolism has made it a popular charge, and it is borne by many corporate bodies and families. With others, Sea-Horses formed the supporters of the arms of 'The Merchants trafficking into Spain', who were incorporated by charter of Queen Elizabeth I.[36]

THE WINGED SEA-HORSE OR SEA-PEGASUS, AND WINGED SEA-UNICORN

This very chimerical creature is depicted like a Sea-Horse, but with wings elevated. It should not be confused with the Sea-Pegasus, which is similar but has horse's hooves on its forelegs. There is also a Winged Sea-Unicorn, which resembles the Sea-Horse but has a Unicorn's horn. All these decorative creatures have sprung from the imaginations of modern heralds and express most happily the added element of flight which takes us across the oceans to meet the exigencies of the modern world. A Sea-Pegasus was granted in 1969 by the English Kings of Arms as the sinister supporter of the arms of the Town of St George, Bermuda; while a Winged Sea-Unicorn had been granted in 1960 to the Overseas League as the dexter supporter of their arms.[37]

THE LEUCROTA

This fabulous beast has been thought by some early writers to be identical with the Manticore, but there seems little doubt that they are different creatures, and the Cambridge Bestiarist's description of it makes this clear. 'A beast gets born in India called the Leucrota, and it exceeds in velocity all the wild animals there are. It has the size of a donkey, the haunches of a stag, the breast and shins of a lion, the head of a horse, a cloven hoof, and a mouth opening as far as its ears. Instead of teeth there is one continuous bone: but this is only as to shape, for in voice it comes near to the sounds of people talking.'[38]

Mowbray's French Treatise is the only medieval heraldic treatise to mention the Leucrota as an armorial creature. The short passage on it begins 'Quelle beste est lucrete', and goes on to describe it more or less as given in the Bestiary, but it gives no hint as to why the beast might be considered a suitable charge in armory. We must, therefore, view it with reserve.[39]

THE MUSIMON

This is another of those Tudor creatures which are evidently the product of muddled natural history. John Guillim, who was created Rouge Croix Pursuivant of Arms in 1613, describes it as 'a Bigenerous beast of unkindly pro-creation (like as the Mule) and is ingendered betweene a Goat and a Ramme, like as the Tityrus is ingendered between a Sheepe and a Bucke Goat, as Upton noteth'.[40] It is usualy depicted in armory with the body, legs and tail of a goat, with a ram's head and horns, together with the horns of a goat. It is, however, almost certainly derived from the moufflon, the wild sheep of southern Europe.

THE NEBEK

This odd beast makes its sole incursion into heraldry in the Book of Standards, when it is given as the badge of William Fitzwilliam, Earl of Southampton. An intimate friend of King Henry VIII, Fitzwilliam saw much military service both on land and at sea, being Lord High Admiral. He held several other important offices and was created Knight of the Garter in 1526; he died on active service in 1542. His Nebek is black, with white mane and tufts of fur on its back, breast, legs and tail, on its shoulder a pierced mullet and about its neck a gold coronet with chain; beside it is written its name, so that there shall be no mistaking what it is.[41] On his Garter stall-plate the beasts become his supporters.

THE PANTHEON

The late Hugh Stanford London, Norfolk Herald Extraordinary, devoted a long article to this more decorative of the curious creatures conjured up by the lively imaginations of the Tudor heralds.[42] As with so many of the fabulous beasts of the period, there is some variety in the way it is depicted, but basically it has a head like a hind and a body like a rather stocky hind, cloven hooves and a bushy tail like a fox; its body is powdered with stars.

A grant of arms and crest was made by Sir Gilbert Dethick, Garter, in 1556, to Henry Northey of Bocking in Essex: *Gold, on a fess azure between three 'Pantheons in their proper colours' a Wild Pansy between two Lilies argent.* Here the Pantheon is shown as red, powdered with silver stars, and black hooves.[43]

The crest of Sir Christopher Baynham, as depicted in the Book of Standards and at the Visitation of Gloucestershire in 1531, was *a Pantheon statant sable powdered with gold estoiles, the ears and legs gules.*[44]

THE PARANDRUS

Mowbray's French Treatise is again the only authority for the use of this curious creature in heraldry, and the description of it is clearly taken from the medieval bestiaries; but nothing is said about its armorial symbolism, so it must be regarded as a rather insubstantial recruit to heraldry.[45] The Cambridge bestiarist knew of it and said that 'Ethiopia produces an animal called a

The Northey Pantheon (drawn by A. Colin Cole, from Coll. Arms ms. Misc. Grants iv, f. 37ᵛ)

Pantheon supporters of the arms of the Marquess of Winchester (Coll. Arms ms. Vinc. 172, f. 17).

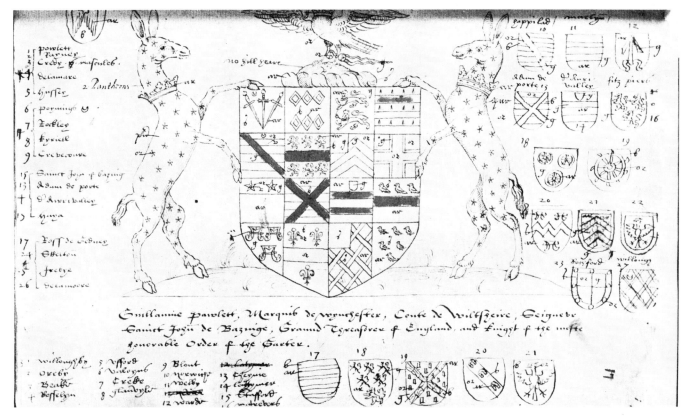

The armes of the
realme of france

160

Parandrus, which has the slot of an ibex, branching horns, the head of a stag, the colour of a bear and like a bear, it has a deep shaggy coat. People say that this Parandrus runs away when it is frightened and, when it hides somewhere, it gets changed into the likeness of whatever it is close to – either white against stone or green against a bush, or in any other way it likes'.[46]

THE POLYGER

While there is no record that this beast has ever been in actual use as a badge, supporter or charge in arms, it must be mentioned here since it appears in a sixteenth century heraldic manuscript in the College of Arms. This book deals mainly with the officers of arms and their duties, creations of nobility and the fees payable to the officers on such occasions, but halfway through is half a page of beasts and birds roughly drawn in trick. Among them is a beast resembling a Lion passant but with long horns like an Antelope or Yale, and above it is written 'polyger'.[47] It does not appear in the O.E.D. and its etymology is a mystery.

THE WINGED STAG

King Charles VI of France (d. 1422) used as his device a Winged Stag with a crown about his neck, and his son King Charles VII (d. 1461) used the Winged Stags as supporters of his arms. The latter's son, Louis XI, at first used Winged Stags as his supporters, but changed them later to two gold Eagles, and finally adopted as supporters, dexter, a gold Eagle crowned, and, sinister, the figure of St Michael wearing a tabard of the royal arms of France and holding in his exterior hand a lance with a banner of the arms of France.[48] Charles VII had also borne this saint on a banner, following the appearance of St Michael who helped to defend the bridge of Orleans against the English.

In Prince Arthur's Book the banner of 'The armes of the Realme of France' is supported by a white Winged Stag, the underside of his elevated blue wings powdered with gold Fleurs de Lys and about his neck a gold crown.[49]

THE THEOW, THOYE OR THOS

Originally a natural beast, imperfectly observed and garbled in the recounting, this became a mildly chimerical creature in the hands of the fifteenth and sixteenth century heralds. It was known to Pliny, who described it as a species of wolf, differing from the common kind in having a larger body and very short legs. The Cambridge Bestiary echoes Pliny and adds a little more: 'Ethiopia produces a kind of wolf which is maned on the neck and so variegated that no colour is missing, they say. It is a characteristic of Ethopian wolves that they are as able as a bird in leaping, so that they do not cover more ground by running than by flying. But they never attack man. They are hairy at the winter solstice, naked in the summer. The Ethiopians call them Theas.'[50] In fact this beast was probably based on the jackal, which has a thickish mane, and the modern sub-genus *thous* embraces the lupine forms of the *canidae*.

What makes the heraldic Thos interesting is that it has acquired cloven hooves and thus a chimerical characteristic. It is a very rare creature in English armory and was unknown to the Continental heralds. The late Hugh Stanford London was the first to notice the Theow, or Thos, and to unravel the tangle created by the sixteenth, seventeenth and eighteenth century writings on it.[51]

The earliest appearance of the creature is in Prince Arthur's book, where it is holding the banner of Sir Thomas Cheyney, K.G. It is depicted with a wolf-like body, with a head rather like that of a jackal, and a long tail; it is green, with gold cloven hooves and a gold collar and chain; and it is clearly described in the margin as a 'Theow'.[52]

Sir Thomas Cheyney was another of those supple Tudor courtiers who served Henry VII, Henry VIII, Queen Mary and Queen Elizabeth with equal

Opposite page
Winged Stag supporting the banner of France (Coll. Arms ms. I.2, f. 9)

Theow or Thos supporter of the banner of Sir Thomas Cheyney, K.G., (drawn by A. Colin Cole from Coll. Arms ms. Vinc. 152, f. 107)

assiduity and consistent profit. A Knight of the Shire for Kent on six occasions, employed on several diplomatic missions, Treasurer of the Household and Warden of the Cinque Ports, he was created Knight of the Garter in 1539 and died in 1558. There is nothing in his career to suggest why he should have adopted this lupine emblem. It was used by his son Henry, Lord Cheyney of Todington, both as supporters and crest, but in his case it is named a 'Thoye' and, while shown as green with gold hooves, collar and chain, its body is powdered with red and gold roundels.[53]

THE TROGODICE

On 14 July 1549 Thomas Hawley, Clarenceux King of Arms, granted armorial bearings to Robert Knyght, of Bromley in Kent. The arms were blazoned as *Silver a Chevron engrailed azure fretted gold between three Trogodices heads erased gules and tongue apparant azure;* and the crest, *betw   two Hawthorn trees proper upon a mount vert a Trogodice statant gules horne. and unguled gold and on his side three dropps of the same.* The beast is depicted like a stag but with reindeer-like antlers sweeping downwards and forwards.[54] This is another of those beasts which were evidently plucked by the Tudor heralds from the wastelands of Eastern Europe and, in the process, became a little muddled. It was very probably intended to represent the natural reindeer.

Unicorn supporters of the arms of The Heraldry Society (by courtesy of the Editor of *The Coat of Arms*)

The Heraldry Society.

The Unicorn

This most beautiful and decorative of all the fabulous creatures which have been harnessed to the uses of heraldry is properly depicted with the body, head and mane of a horse, but with a beard like a goat's on its chin, the legs and cloven hooves of a hart, the tail of a lion and, of course, the long and delicately spiralled single horn arising from its forehead. Its normal colour is white – for it is the purest of all creatures – with the horn, hooves, mane and tufts on the tail and elsewhere gold. It can, however, like all heraldic creatures, be of any of the recognised armorial tinctures; and it can be depicted as rampant, saliant, courant, statant or couchant.

So much has been written about the Unicorn by so many that there is no point in ploughing once more a well-tilled field; we will therefore glance only briefly at the medieval notions of this creature and then consider it in its heraldic context.

The rhyming bestiary, written in Old Norman French by Guillaume le Clerc in 1210 or 1211, gives us the typical medieval view of this elegant beast, which one finds described in much the same terms in bestiary after bestiary. Guillaume's bestiary was translated in recent years by the late G. C. Druce, F.S.A.[55]

> Now I will tell you of the Unicorn,
> A beast which has but one horn
> Set in the middle of its forehead.
> This beast is so daring,
> So pugnacious and so bold,
> That it picks quarrels with the elephant.

Royal Arms of England with the Unicorn supporter to the sinister (drawn by F. Booth)

163

It is the fiercast beast in the world
Of all those which are in it.
It fights with the elephant and wins.
. . . .
This beast has such strength
That it fears no hunter
They that would ensnare it
Go there first to spy
When it has gone to disport itself
Either on mountain or in valley.
When they have found its haunt
And have well marked its footprints,
They go for a young girl,
Whom they know well to be virgin.
Then they make her sit and wait
At its lair, for to capture the beast.
When the Unicorn is come back
And has seen the damsel,
Straight to her it comes at once;
In her lap is crouches down
And the girl clasps it
Like one submitting to her.
With the girl it sports so much
That in her lap it falls asleep
Those who are spying at once rush out :
There they take it and bind it.
Then they drive it before the king
By force and despite its struggles.

Guillaume then goes on to the appropriate moral from this most symbolic of all creatures. (We have already touched on this, in Chapter 8 above, in connection with the heraldic symbolism of the Arms of Christ.) The religious symbolism of the Unicorn naturally made it a suitable subject in ecclesiastical architecture and in furnishings of a religious nature.

The fierce and dainty Unicorn was also very popular with the European aristocracy; it was brought into romantic literature, and was the subject of such beautiful works of art as the Unicorn Tapestry, now in the Metropolitan Museum of Art, New York. Even the medieval erotic poets drew on the Unicorn for inspiration, some praying their mistresses to let them lay their heads in their laps and be enslaved by their charms; while others, like the Swabian knight and minnesinger, Burkhart von Hohenfels, likens himself to the Unicorn because a fair lady has lured him to destruction. Thibault 'le chansonnier', Count of Champagne and King of Navarre (1201–54), troubadour and crusader, describes in one of his lyrics the treachery of the hunters, who catch and kill the Unicorn while it lies faint and languishing in the virgin's lap, and adds :

Unicorn's arms and crest of J. P. Brooke-Little, Richmond Herald

Thus love and my lady have done to me,
And my heart can never again be free.[56]

There has been much learned discussion about the size of Unicorns. Some hold them to be about the size of polo ponies; others believe they are much smaller. As the Unicorn's method of killing elephants is to rip their bellies open with its sharp pointed horn, one assumes it must be small enough to charge underneath them. The Physiologus describes it as 'a small animal, but exceeding strong and fleet', while the author of the Cambridge Bestiary says that it is 'a very small animal like a kid', and that on seeing the seated virgin 'he soon leaps into her lap . . . . and embraces her and hence he gets caught'.[57] This description is met with in many medieval authorities, and one must conclude that this

164

wild, untameable beast must be pretty small; for even the most long-suffering virgin, with unswerving devotion to duty, might find a polo pony in her lap rather too much of a good thing. However, in armory, size is not significant; one could, if one wished, have an elephant and a mouse as supporters to a shield and they would be drawn the same size.

A beast which has such wide ranging symbolism, from the sacred to the profane, might be thought to be a splendid subject for heraldry; but its high religious symbolism was so overwhelmingly important that it was evidently regarded throughout most of the Middle Ages as too sacred to be used as a charge on a banner or shield. John de Bado Aureo (1394) does not include the Unicorn among the beasts borne in arms, and it is not until we come to Mowbray's French Treatise, written in the early fifteenth century, that we find it mentioned. Thereafter we find Unicorns, or their heads, in increasing numbers in the rolls of arms, ordinaries and heraldic treatises of the fifteenth century. Thomas Jenyn's Book (*c.* 1410), which is an ordinary of arms, gives a Unicorn's Head,[58] while Nicholas Upton mentions the Unicorn as a beast borne in arms, and in the Rede copy the arms of Robert James of Boarstall are given as *Per chevron gules and argent three Unicorn's Heads couped counterchanged.*[59]

The Unicorn does not make its appearance as a royal beast in Scotland before the reign of King James I. His coinage showed a single Unicorn supporting his arms, though two Lions support his arms on his Privy Seal. A single Unicorn appears from time to time in subsequent reigns, but it is not until the reign of James III, towards the end of the fifteenth century, that two Unicorns are used as supporters. Mary, Queen of Scots, used two Unicorns as supporters on her Great Seal but two Lions as supporters on her Privy Seal. It was King James VI of Scotland and I of England who adopted the well-known supporters of the United Kingdom: a crowned Lion to the dexter and a Unicorn with a crown about his neck to the sinister.[60]

Sea Wolf badge of Busschy of Houghton (Coll. Arms ms. I.2, f. 34)

THE SEA-WOLF

The crest of Sir Myles Busschy, as recorded in the Book of Standards, was a Sea-Wolf argent, tail nowed, and charged on the body with three barrulets sable. It is the sort of creature one finds in German heraldry, and it may be that Sir Myles got the idea from close acquaintance with the heraldry of that country and persuaded the English Kings of Arms to grant him a crest of this kind.[61]

THE YALE

This creature was known to Pliny and the medieval bestiarists and is probably a garbled version of a real animal. The Yale has intrigued many writers on heraldry and the late Hugh Stanford London wrote a most interesting article on it a few years ago.[62] The Yale first appears in heraldry as one of the supporters of the arms of Henry IV's third son, John, Duke of Bedford. Created a Knight of the Garter and Constable of England by the age of fourteen, and Duke of Bedford and Earl of Kendal in 1414, he was one of the great magnates of his time. A successful general, both on land and sea, he was Protector of the Kingdom of England during the military expeditions of Henry V in France and, on the death of that king in 1422, was made Regent of France, and commanded the English and Burgundian armies at Verneuil. While he was Regent, the officers of arms on duty in France would have come under his authority, and there is reason to think that he took an informed interest in armory. He was a great patron of the arts, and died in 1435. His arms, supported by an Eagle and a Yale, are to be seen in the magnificent Bedford Book of Hours, which was produced during his Regency and is now in the British Museum.[63]

The Bedford Yale. Its tusks distinguish it from the "Elke" of Fastolf (drawn by A. Colin Cole from the Carter Stall Plate of Sir John Beaufort, Earl of Kendal and Duke of Somerset, d. 1444)

165

The Beaufort Yale (drawn by A. Colin Cole from the Garter Stall Plate of John Beaufort, Duke of Somerset)

The great Duke died childless, and in 1443 Sir John Beaufort, K.G., Earl of Somerset (John of Gaunt's grandson) was created Duke of Somerset and Earl of Kendal. With the earldom, he adopted the Bedford supporters, the Eagle and the Yale, and these are to be seen on his beautifully enamelled Garter stall-plate; but here the Yale has been slightly altered and has become rather more ram-like, with curved horns and a short tail.

Beaufort died in 1444, without male issue, and his daughter and heiress Margaret married Edmund Tudor, Earl of Richmond, and became the mother of King Henry VII. Although she used the Eagle and Yale supporters of her father, she more frequently used two Yales of the Beaufort pattern, and these are to be seen above the gateway of her foundation, St John's College, Cambridge, as well as above the gateway of Christ's College, which was greatly enriched from her estate.

The Bedford Yale is more the build of an antelope with a lion's tail and is black or very dark brown in colour; but it has, of course, the fierce tushes in the lower jaw and the swivelling horns, which are its distinguishing feature, though in this case they are long and straight. The Beaufort Yale is white, powdered with gold bezants, and has gold horns, tushes, hooves, and tufts; one of the ram-like horns is swivelled forwards. Through Lady Margaret the Yale descended to her son, Henry VII, and her grandson, Henry VIII, and it remains a royal badge. In 1525 Henry Fitzroy, the bastard son of Henry VIII, was created Duke of Richmond and Somerset, and was granted a Beaufort-type Yale as one of his supporters, differenced with a gold coronet about its neck, with a gold chain; it was stated to be for his Dukedom of Somerset. In 1559 Queen Elizabeth created her cousin Sir Henry Cary, Lord Hunsdon, and he was granted a Yale as a supporter, but differenced by being powdered with roundels of many colours.

THE YPOTRYLL

This curious, fierce, camel-like creature is only known to us from Fenn's Book of Badges, where it is depicted with two hairy humps on its back, a head and tushes rather like a boar, ox-like legs with cloven hooves, and a long, smooth, tapering tail. The beast is white and the fur on its head and humps is gold, as are its tushes and hooves. It is clearly labelled 'ypotryll', with the name 'Worcester' beside it. A modern hand has added that this was John Tiptoft, Earl of Worcester.[64] John Tiptoft was not created Earl of Worcester until 1449. He held many high offices, including that of Constable of England (1462–7 and 1470), when he would have had the heralds under his command. An active Yorkist, he was noted for his brutality, being known to his contemporaries as 'the butcher of England' but he was equally famous for his scholarship. He was executed by the Lancastrians in 1470.

Ypotryll badge of John, Earl of Worcester (drawn by A. Colin Cole from Fenn's Book of Badges, British Museum Add. ms. 40742, f. 10)

Two Curious Creatures

There are two very odd creatures in the records of the College of Arms which appear to be incognito. For the first, which I will call the West Beast, there are three manuscript references: the earliest is in a Visitation of Suffolk in 1561, the others are of the sixteenth and seventeenth centuries. All three claim to be verbatim copies of a confirmation of arms by Roger Legh, Clarenceux King of Arms, on 23 July 1446, of an earlier confirmation of arms by Roger Durroit, Lancaster King of Arms, in 1386, to Ralph West of Sudbury in Suffolk. There was also a confirmation of these arms in 1447 by John Wrexworth, Guyenne King of Arms.[65] The arms themselves are quite straightforward, *Sable a Lion rampant or collared argent;* but the crest, which is not blazoned, shows a beast rather resembling a heraldic Tyger salient gold, but instead of forelegs it has three straight tapering spikes protruding forwards from its breast, each spike wreathed with alternate bands of sable and gold.

The other odd creature is the Audley Beast. Its only appearance is in a manuscript in the College of Arms, compiled in the early seventeenth century. This depicts the two supporters of the arms of Thomas Audley, who was created Baron Audley of Walden, Essex in 1538, and Knight of the Garter in 1540 and who held the office of Lord Chancellor from 1532 until his death in 1544. Each supporter is drawn somewhat like a Lion with a Lion's tail, but with more slender legs, and the head of a dog; each has three long, straight, smooth gold horns (rather like those of a Unicorn) arising from the forehead; and each is collared gold with a line pendant and flexed over the back.[66] In neither case is there any clue as to the significance of the beast.

Crest of West of Sudbury (drawn by Miss A. Urwick from Coll. Arms ms. Grants ii, f. 639)

167

12

Eagles and Fabulous Birds

DOMESTICATED animals and the beasts of the chase were naturally well known to our medieval ancestors and therefore made their appearance at an early date as charges in arms, if their symbolism was appropriate. Birds, however, seem to have been less well observed and to have attracted fewer symbolic properties, which made them of less significance as armorial charges. In consequence we find only a few real birds and even fewer fabulous birds in the heraldry of the twelfth and thirteenth centuries. It is not until the fifteenth century that we get a more extended list of various wild and domestic birds used as charges in shields, but, even so, the number of fabulous birds continued small.

Bouly de Lesdain, in his analysis of the early French seals and enamels, dated between 1127 and 1300, notes forty-eight examples of the Eagle, but only one each of the Cock, Duck, Crow and Magpie. There were, however, eighty examples of the Martlet, five Double-Eagles, one Alerion, and one Griffin.[1] The three earliest English rolls of arms (Matthew Paris, Glover's Roll, and Walford's Roll, compiled between about 1244 and 1275) show that the most popular charges were Eagles (ten) and Martlets (ten), with three Popinjays, six Double-Eagles, and one each of the Cock, Crow, Heron and Sparrowhawk.[2] The Parliamentary Roll (c. 1312) adds the Barnacle, that curiously fabulous bird, while John de Bado Aureo (c. 1394) includes the Goshawk, Chough, Owl and Swan. Mowbray's French Treatise (early fifteenth century) gives some twenty real birds, and three fabulous birds, the Alerion, Caladrius and Phoenix.[3]

With Nicholas Upton's *De Studio Militari* (1446) the gates of the aviary are opened and a wide variety of birds escape on to coats of arms. His list of thirty-six real birds begins with the Eagle and includes the Bird of Paradise, Goldfinch, Seagull, Crane, Jay, Pheasant, Kingfisher, Golden Oriole, Partridge, Peacock, Woodpecker, Nightingale and Lapwing; but the fabulous birds borne in arms consist only of the Griffin, Caladrius and Martlet.[4]

From this it will be seen that the birds of heraldry, like the armorial beasts, were rather restricted during the early Middle Ages; it was only during the flamboyant years of the fifteenth century that the heralds scoured the woods, fields and bestiaries for additional charges to place on the surcoats, pennons and banners of the many new knights being created during the later French Wars and the Wars of the Roses.

DER NEUE REICHS ADLER

THE EAGLE

From the earliest times the Eagle has caught the imagination of men, not only by reason of its size, strength and unique ability to outstare the sun, but also because its majestic, measured flight and haughty, aristocratic appearance mark it as a king among birds; while the wild and craggy mountains among which it lives add an awesome remoteness. In consequence representations of the Eagle are found in the most ancient of civilisations, from Babylonia to the Indus, while pre-Christian representations of it have also been found in Asia Minor. In origin it was mainly a solar symbol, and in Greek mythology the Eagle was associated with Zeus and, indeed, is the only bird of divine character. In certain cults it was shown grasping a snake, an allegory of good and evil.

By Roman times the Eagle had acquired a military and political significance and was the special emblem of the legions, representing the power and majesty of the Empire. Being borne by the Romans to every corner of the western world, the legionary Eagle would have impressed itself on the minds of their subject peoples, and the fact that it was the special bird of Jupiter, and was held to bear the spirits of deceased Emperors to heaven, gave it the sanction of religion.

Eagle of the first German Republic, after 1919 (drawn by Otto Hupp for the Münchener Kalendar, 1921)

169

Armorial bearings of Gultlingen (drawn by Otto Hupp for the Münchenchener Kalendar, 1928)

Christianity, which evolved partly among the solar cults of Syria, was naturally influenced by the symbolism of the Eagle. In the Revelations of St John the Divine we are told that one of the four beasts in perpetual attendance on the Throne of God was like a flying Eagle, and before long the Eagle came to be regarded as the special emblem of St John. In consequence it has played an important part in Christian allegory since the Dark Ages, being symbolic of salvation, redemption and resurrection. It was believed that when the Eagle grew old and its eyes dimmed, it flew up towards the sun until it scorched and purged away the film from its eyes and rid itself of its worn-out feathers; it then plunged down into a fountain clear and pure, thus recovering its sight and renewing its youth. The moral drawn from this was that when we have grown old in the sinful love of this wicked world, we should seek the day-star of the divine word and fly aloft on the wings of the spirit, to be purged by our Saviour of our sins; by the same token, the Eagle's plunge into the fountain became symbolic of baptism. We find these notions in the Physiologus and in all the bestiaries, which so influenced the heralds and knights of the Middle Ages. Bartholomew the Englishman, for example, repeats these fabulous stories of the 'egle, whiche hath princypalite amonge foules,' and mentions also its liberality to other birds in sharing its prey, as a King that takes heed of his subjects.[5]

When Charlemagne was crowned Emperor of the Romans by the Pope on Christmas Day 800, it was a logical step for him to adopt the Eagle as a symbol of the restored imperium, while its important Christian symbolism emphasised his special relationship with the Papacy and his title of Protector of the Holy Places bestowed on him by the Patriarch of Jerusalem. Richerus, monk of Reims, writing nearly two hundred years later, stated that Charlemagne had a bronze Eagle placed on the gable of his great palace at Aachen. The Emperor Henry III (1039–56) had the sceptre on his seal surmounted by an Eagle; and according to William of Tyre, at Mölsen in 1080 the Emperor's banner bore the Eagle, and in the twelfth century the Eagle was embroidered on the imperial gloves.

THE DOUBLE-EAGLE

The two-headed Eagle has an ancient pedigree, possibly pre-Islamic in origin. It was used as a decorative motif in the countries of the Middle East, before being adopted in the twelfth century as the emblem of the Seljuk sultans, from whom it found its way through Byzantium to the Holy Roman Empire.[6]

De Heraudie (*c.* 1300) states that 'le Roy d'Alemaigne porte l'escu d'or a un egle de sable ove double bek. Et ove double bek pur le graunt seignourie, qar touz les roys de cristientee deveroient par droit estre en sa subjectione, c'est assavoir s'il soit emperoure'.[7] Matthew Paris, writing about fifty years earlier, gives the arms of the Emperors Otto IV (d. 1218) and Frederick II (d. 1250) as, *Or a Double-Eagle displayed sable.* Although at times in his text he seems a little uncertain whether the Imperial Eagle is single or double-headed, he always depicts it as a Double-Eagle. Walford's Roll (*c.* 1273) states definitely that the arms of 'l'Empereur de Almaine' were '*d'or ung egle espany (displayed) a deux testes sable*' while those of 'le Roy d'Almayne' were '*de or a un egle de sable.*'[8]

The children of the Emperor Frederick II bore some interesting variants of these arms. Matthew Paris gives the arms of Henry fitz Emperor (the eldest son, who died in 1242) as, *Party per pale or and vert a Double-Eagle sable,* while the second son, Conrad, King of Sicily from 1250–54, bore *Or a Double-Eagle sable and in chief a Crescent gules enclosing a small Roundel also gules.* Frederick's illegitimate son, Enzio, King of Sardinia from 1238 until his deposition in 1249, bore *Party per pale vert and or a Double-Eagle sable.* His other illegitimate son, Manfred of Apulia, King of Sicily from 1258–66, bore *Or a*

Arms of the Holy Roman Emperor
(Coll. Arms ms. Vinc. 172. f. 11)

Double-Eagle sable, over all a Fess argent.[9] It is hardly surprising, therefore, that John de Bado Aureo, writing a century or more later, should conclude that 'principally the Emperour should bere in his arms an Egle cloven (i.e. double-headed) and splayed in a felde of golde'.[10]

By 1443 the Double-Eagle became definitely established on the Great Seals of the Holy Roman Emperors, and there is an excellent painting in the College of Arms of the Great Seal of the Emperor Francis I, which was pendant from his letters patent dated 2 August 1767, creating (Sir) John Talbot Dillon, M.P., the traveller, critic, and historical writer, a Baron of the Holy Roman Empire.[11] It was not long before the rulers of the Russian Empire also adopted this imperial emblem, which can be seen on the Great Seal of Catherine the Great, pendant from her letters patent, dated 13 February 1769, creating Thomas Dimsdale, 'English Gentleman and Doctor of Physic', who inoculated the Empress against the smallpox, a Baron of the Russian Empire.[12]

172

Nevertheless, in spite of its religious and imperial associations, we find the Eagle and the Double-Eagle being used as charges in non-imperial arms at an early date. Bouly de Lesdain notes fifty-three examples of Eagles and five Double-Eagles in French seals or enamels between 1127 and 1300.[13] Since that time a number of knightly and gentle families, not all of them illustrious, have borne Eagles, either singly, or in threes or more, or in combination with other charges, while a few have borne Double-Eagles. Because of its glorious associations, one cannot help feeling that, in future, Double-Eagles should only be granted in exceptional circumstances.

(a)

(b)

(a) Arms of the Emperor Frederick II
(b) Arms of Henry Fitz Emperor, son of Frederick II by Isabel, daughter of King John

(c)

(d)

(c) Arms of Conrad, King of Sicily, son of Frederick II by Yolanda, Queen of Jerusalem
(d) Arms of Enzio, King of Sardinia, base son of Frederick II

(e)

(f)

(e) Arms of Manfred, King of Sicily, base son of Frederick II
(f) Arms of Henry, King of the Romans, son of Frederick II by Constance of Aragon
(drawn by Miss A. Urwick)

THE ALERION

This is really an Eagle by another name but, as a result of historical accident and misunderstanding, the name has become restricted to a dismembered Eagle, lacking beak and legs and sometimes even drawn with the displayed wings slightly detached. It may well have originated from a faulty rendering of the real thing. It is generally regarded as a charge in the arms of Lorraine, but the seal of Robert, brother of Matthew Duke of Lorraine (1148–76), bears a whole Eagle holding a sword.[14] Walford's Roll (c. 1273) gives the arms of Henry III, Duke of Lorraine, as 'd'or a une bende de goules a treis egles d'argent en la bende'. The birds of Lorraine are also blazoned as Eagles in the Clipearius Teutonicorum, the Wijnbergen Roll, and other medieval sources.[15] It is not clear at what date the Eagles in the arms of the Dukes of Lorraine became Alerions, but they are now regarded as the classic example of these.

Almost unknown in English armory, the Alerion appears more widely in the arms of several European families. Three Alerions are borne by the families of Lallier of Soissonnais and Véelu de Passy of Brie, while five are borne by Alléon du Lac of Forez and six by Chasay of Anjou. Thirteen families bear Alerions charged on a Bend or Bends, a Chief and a Chevron; three bear a Chevron between three Alerions; and six bear a Cross between four Alerions; while quite a number of European families bear Alerions combined with other charges. Perhaps the most famous of European families to bear this creature is that of Montmorency. The seal of Bouchard de Montmorency, in 1177, shows a Cross between four Alerions azure,[16] but the basic arms of the family later became *Or a Cross gules between sixteen Alerions azure*. Different branches of the family difference their arms, often with some minor charge on the Cross.

THE CALADRIUS

This therapeutic, if occasionally alarming bird was not employed in armory until the early fifteenth century, when it is mentioned in Mowbray's French Treatise in the section on birds borne in arms – 'quel oysel est chalendre' – and its characteristics and properties are discussed. The thirteenth century bestiarist, Bartholomew the Englishman, gives a good account of this bird:

> As the philosopher sayth, the birde that hyghte Kaladrius is whyte of colour and hath no parte of blacknes. And the nether parte of his legge clenseth and purgeth dymnes of the eyen. His kynde is suche, when a man is holde in greatte sykness this byrde Kaladrius tornethe awaye his face fro him that is seke and than without dowte the man shal dye. And if the syke manne shall escape, the byrde Kaladrius setteth his syght on him and beholdeth hym, as it were faunynge and playsynge. And this byrde is other than the byrde that hight Calandra, that syngeth as a thrustelle.

Possibly the latter bird is what we now call the Calandra Lark.[18]

Other bestiarists have improved upon the bare account given by Bartholomew, and the commoner version is that the Caladrius, having drawn the sickness out of the patient, flies up towards the sun, the heat of which consumes the sickness and restores the man to health. The moral drawn from this is that in like manner Jesus Christ, on whom there is neither spot nor wrinkle, came down from heaven and turned his face away from the Jews, but looked with favour upon the Gentiles, healing them of their spiritual infirmities. A bird of such remarkable qualities was, naturally, of considerable interest to our ancestors, and representations of it, sometimes perched upon a sick-bed and sometimes flying towards the sun, are to be found in several churches in Western Europe and in many medieval manuscripts. One minnesinger even likened his lady love to the Caladrius, declaring that it was a question of life or death whether her face was turned towards him or away.[19]

A Caladrius giving a doomed invalid the cold shoulder (drawing by Miss A. Urwick based on two early medieval bestiaries)

Various theories have been advanced as to the identity of the enigmatic Caladrius, but one of the difficulties has been that few people have actually seen one. The merchants who sold them were reluctant to let their customers inspect the bird, because so many invalids tried to get a free cure by confronting one and then departing without buying it. In consequence it does not figure as a charge in English armory – a pity, because it would be very appropriate for a physician.

THE GRIFFIN

This most decorative and symbolic of heraldic creatures is depicted in European armory with the foreparts of an Eagle, with ears, and the hind-parts and tail of a Lion; but in classical times the body and all four legs were those of a Lion. It is, I believe, a peculiarity of English armory that the male Griffin lacks wings and has sharp spikes or quills arising in scattered bundles all over its body. A Griffin, or Gryphon, when blazoned as such, *tout court,* is always the winged form, but oddly enough is often depicted with male characteristics.

The Griffin naturally appears in all the bestiaries, from the earliest times. Bartholomew the Englishman writes about the 'Grype hyghte Griphes' which 'dwelleth in those hylles that ben called Hyperborei, and ben mooste enemyes to horses and men and greveth them moste'.[20] Indeed, it was generally held that a Griffin could carry a fully armed man and his horse in its claws, or a pair of plough-oxen, and fly away with them. For this reason the Griffin should always be drawn as a creature of enormous strength and vigour: a weedy Griffin with spindly legs is unthinkable.

As so often, the best comment on the Griffin was made by Sir Thomas Browne, whose *Pseudodoxia Epidemica* was written in 1645.

> That there are Griffins in Nature, that is a mixt and dubious Animal, in the fore-parts resembling an Eagle, and behind the shape of a Lion, with erected ears, four feet and a long tail, many affirm, and most, I perceive, deny not . . . . Notwithstanding we find most diligent enquirers to be of a contrary assertion . . . . As for the testimonies of ancient Writers, they are but derivative, and terminate all in one Aristeus a Poet of Proconesus; who affirmed that near the Arimaspi, or one-eyed Nation, Griffins defended the Mines of Gold. But this, as Herodotus delivereth, he wrote by hear-say; and Michovius who hath expressly written of those parts, plainly affirmeth there is nether Gold nor Griffins in that Country, nor any such Animal extant . . . . Lastly, concerning the Hieroglyphical authority, although it nearest approach the truth, it doth not infer its existency. The conceit of the Griffin properly taken being but a symbolical phansie, in so

175

Griffin supporters of the arms of Baden (drawn by Otto Hupp for the Münchener Kalendar, 1928)

Opposite page
Antelope badge of Sir John Beauchamp. (Buccleuch ms. Wrythe Garter Book, f. 80)

intollerable a shape including allowable morality. So doth it well make out the properties of a Guardian, or any person entrusted; the ears implying attention, the wings celerity of execution, the Lion-like shape courage and audacity, the hooked bill reservance and tenacity. It is an Emblem of valour and magnanimity, as being compounded of the Eagle and Lion, the noblest animals of their kind; and so it is applicable unto Princes, Presidents, Generals, and all heroick Commanders; and so is it also born in the Coat-arms of many noble Families of Europe.[21]

It is not to be wondered at, therefore, that the Griffin is one of the most popular of charges in European armory. Renesse lists two hundred and ninety examples of single Griffins, eleven of two Griffins, three of four Griffins and one coat semee of Griffins; while he has nineteen further pages of Griffin's heads, and three of parts of Griffins, making a pretty formidable total.[22] The College of Arms manuscript, Vincent's Ordinary, compiled in the early seventeenth century, records by that time sixty-two examples of Griffins segreant (i.e. ram-

176

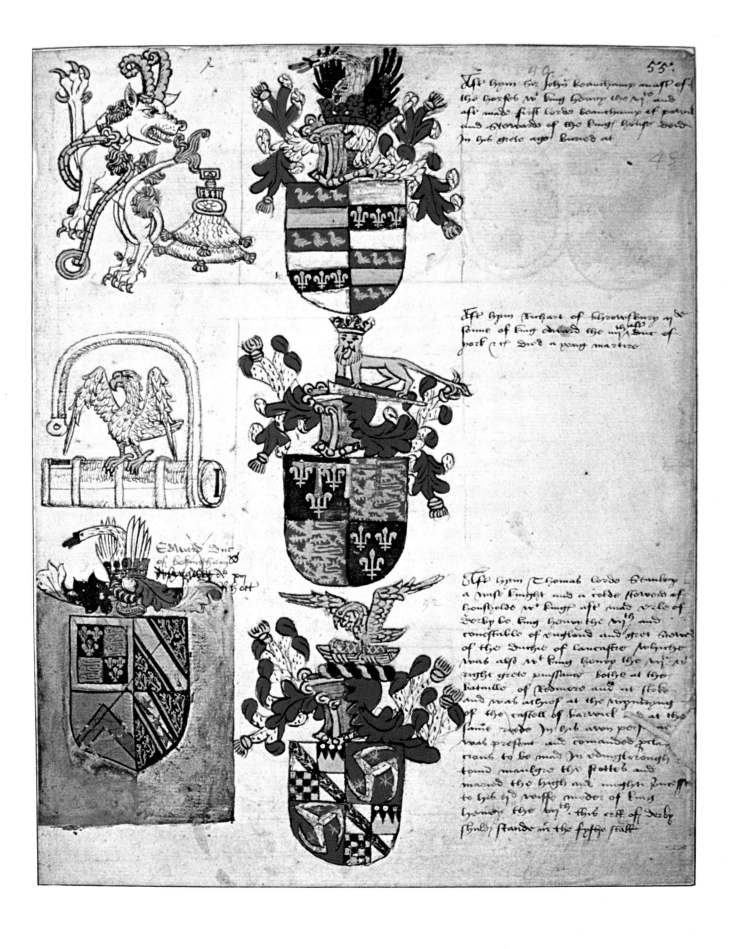

Aft hym Sir John beauchamp mast of
the horses wt kyng henry the vj th and
aft made first lorde beauchamp of powik
and stewarde of the kyngs howse decd
In his olde age buried at

Aft hym Richard of Shrowsbury yt
sonne of kyng edward the iiij th duc of
york ct ct died a yong martir

Aft hym Thomas lorde Stanley
a Iust knyght and a nobl steward of
houshold wt kyng aft made Erle of
Derby by kyng henry the vij th and
constable of england and grete stewa
of the duche of lancaster Whiche
was also wt kyng henry the vij at
ryght grete pussanc bothe at the
bataille of Redmore and at Stoke
and was atyeuf at the wynnyng
of the castell of barwik ct ct at the
same tyme In his owen pson ct
was present and comanded grete
ranc to be mad In worcestr ough
town maufre the folks and
mened the high and myght prince
to hit the noble ordr of kyng
henry the vij th this erle of derby
shuld stande in the fyfth stall

pant), twenty-four examples of Griffins stantant, three of Demi-Griffins, and seventy-three of Griffins Heads in English arms alone, and this does not include crests or badges.

In spite of its later popularity, the Griffin was a fairly slow starter in European heraldry, and Bouly de Lesdain records only one example, the seal of Jean de Laval, a Flemish Lord, in 1267, a Fess with a Griffin segreant over all.[23]

In English heraldry the earliest Griffin appears in the *Heralds Roll* (c. 1270–80), where the attributed arms of 'le Roie de Guyffonye' are given as *Or a Griffin segreant gules*.[24] The earlier heraldic treatise, *De Heraudie* (c. 1300), quotes as an example of the Griffin the attributed arms of Alexander the Great, 'le Roy Alexandre porta l'escu de goules ove un griffonn d'argent'.[25] The *Caerlavrock Poem* (1300) gives the banner of Sir Simon de Montague, Lord Montague, one of the great captains of his day, as *Azure a Griffin segreant gold*.[26] Thenceforward Griffins appear, in one roll of arms after another and in seals, in gradually increasing numbers, but it is not until the fifteenth century that they tend to be fairly widely used.

John de Bado Aureo wrote in 1394 of the Griffin borne in arms, and the Welsh version of his treatise written a few years later, the *Llyfr Dysgread Arfau*, says that 'a Griffin borne in arms signifies that the first to bear it was a strong pugnacious man, in whom were found two distinct natures and qualities', those of the Eagle and the Lion.[27] It was appropriate, therefore, that King Edward III, one of the great generals of his age and the very pattern of chivalry, should use a Griffin on one of his Privy Seals.

By Tudor times Griffins were becoming more widely used and we find several examples of them in Prince Arthur's Book and in the Book of Standards. Two of the most interesting are the badges of Cardinal Wolsey and Sir Hugh Vaughan. The Griffin supporting the banner of Thomas Wolsey, Cardinal Archbishop of York, is red with gold wings, beak and claws, the arms being impaled with his arms of office as Archbishop of York, with his Cardinal's hat above the banner.[28]

The Griffin badge of Sir Hugh Vaughan, of Littleton, Co. Middlesex, is particularly interesting. Hugh Vaughan started life as a Gentleman Usher of King Henry VII and, in 1492, when he wished to take part in some jousting, the other contestants would not accept him, saying, 'he was no gentylman nobled to bere armes'. Vaughan thereupon produced a patent of arms granted by John Wrythe, Garter King of Arms, on 3 April the previous year. The others, however, would not accept this and the matter was taken before King Henry, who supported Garter's grant and authorised Vaughan to take part in the jousts. He therefore challenged his principal opponent to single combat and, by accident, killed him.[29] Vaughan retained the confidence of his sovereign and filled several positions of importance under both Henry VII and Henry VIII. In 1508 he was a Privy Councillor and obtained the grant of a quartering to his arms, a new crest, and for supporters (rare indeed for anyone other than peers) *two Griffins double-queued party gules and azure, platée argent and fretty or*. Sir Hugh Vaughan evidently had a passion for heraldic display, for six years later he obtained from Garter and Clarenceux a grant of a third new crest and also a badge and standard. The badge was a Griffin segreant, like the supporters, holding in the dexter claw a sword erect.[30]

THE OPINICUS

This is really the Griffin of classical Greece, and it is only since the sixteenth century that the heralds have distinguished between them, but the difference has now become sufficiently well established for us to treat them as separate creatures. The difference is that the forelegs as well as the hind-legs of the Opinicus are those of a Lion (the Griffin's forelegs being those of an Eagle),

Attributed arms of Alexander the Great, one of the Nine Worthies of the World, in whose reign medieval heralds believed armory to have originated (drawn by Miss A. Urwick)

Griffin on the Temple of Apollo at Didyma, in south west Turkey, circa 300 B.C. (drawn by Miss A. Urwick)

177

The lord thomas wulsey
Cardinal legat de latere
archebishop of yorke
and Chanceler of
Inglande

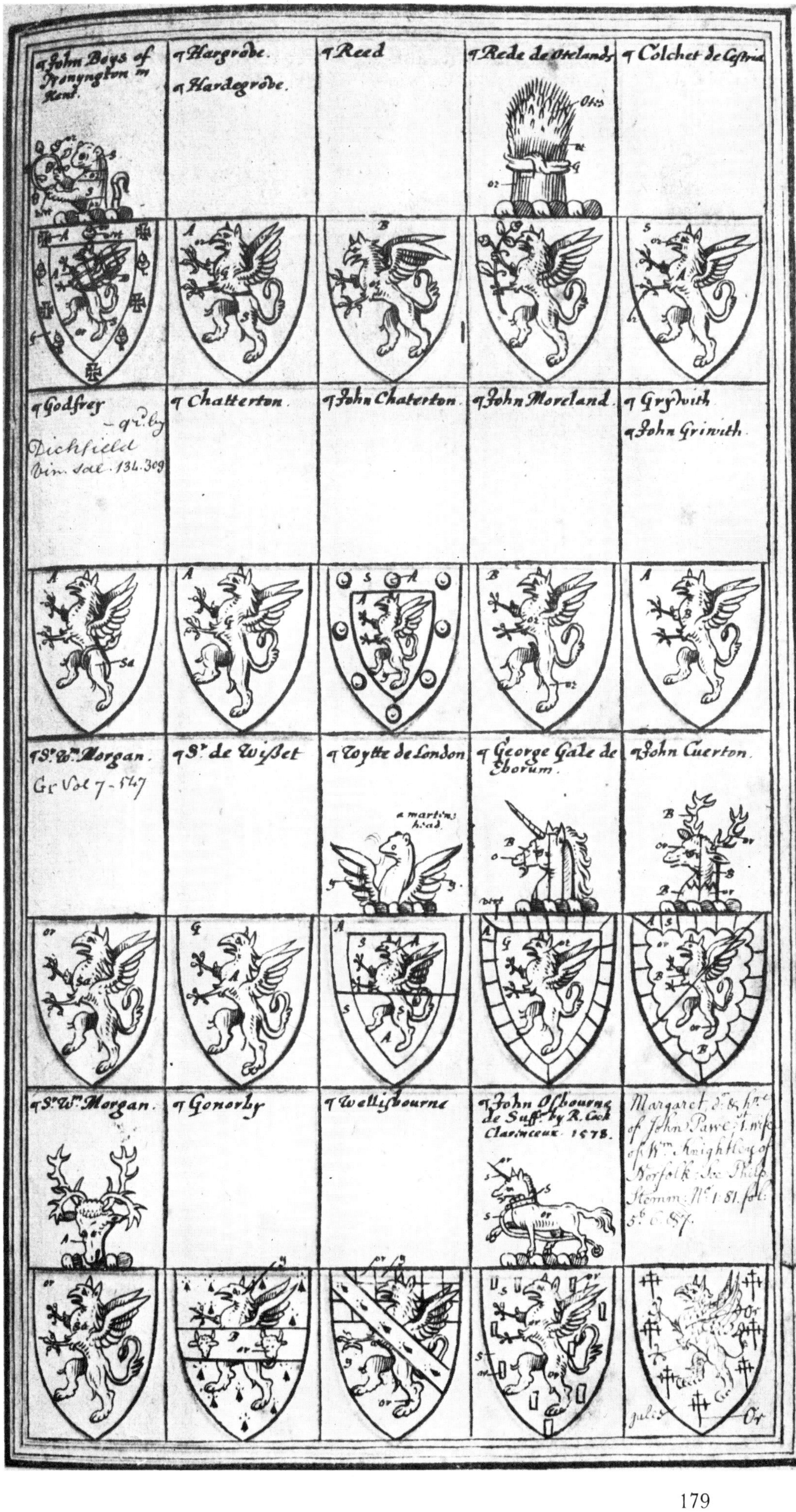

John Boys of Fronyngton in Kent.

Hargrove.

Hardegrove.

Reed

Rede de Otelands

Colchet de Cestria

Godfrey — qr. by Dichfield Vin. sal. 134. 309

Chatterton.

John Chatterton.

John Moreland.

Grywith

John Grinith.

Sr. Wm. Morgan. Gr Vol 7 - 547

Sr. de Wisset

Toytte de London

George Gale de Eborum.

John Cuerton.

a martins head

Sr. Wm. Morgan.

Gonorby

Wellisbourne

John O Chourne de Suff. by R. Cok Clarinceux. 1578.

Margaret dr. & heir of John Pawe. 1 wife of Wm. Knightley of Norfolk. See Philip Stemm. N: 1. 81. fol. 5.6. C. 87.

179

Page from an Ordinary of Griffins (Coll. Arms ms. Vincent's Ordinary)

Opinicus crest of the Worshipful Company of Barber Surgeons of London (drawn by Miss A. Urwick)

and its tail is thin and shortish with a very small tuft at the end, rather like a camel (the Griffin's being the long, lashing tail of the Lion).

Nevertheless there has been, and still is, some variety in the way the Opinicus is depicted in heraldic art. The earliest appearance of it in English armory is as the supporters of the arms of the Worshipful Company of Plasterers of London, granted on 15 January 1556 by Clarenceux King of Arms, and they are blazoned as *two Opinaci vert purfled or, beaked sable, the wings gules.* This is an interesting rendering of the plural of the beast.[31]

Four years later, on 10 July 1561, William Hervy, Clarenceux King of Arms, granted 'an Opinagus golde' as a crest to the Company of Barber Surgeons of London.[32] It is difficult to discover any kind of a common link between these two ancient City livery companies, and there is no clue as to the symbolism of the creature, unless we take it as a variant of the Griffin and credit it with similar sterling qualities.

It is not until modern times that the Opinicus appears again in English armory. Sir Frederick Treves, Bt, the famous surgeon whose successful operation for appendicitis on King Edward VII, in 1902, earned him world-wide renown and a baronetcy, was granted arms on the 28 July 1902 which included a chief gules charged with a Lion of England, and as crest *an Opinicus statant or wings elevated and addorsed purpure, resting the dexter paw on a fleam fesswise argent.*[33] The fleam was an ancient form of lancet, and allusion here is obviously to the Barber Surgeons Company. The latest grant is that to the British Association of Oral Surgeons, on 30 June 1962, where an Opinicus rampant is one of the charges in their arms, and here too the affinity with the Barber Surgeons Company is clear.[34] It should be noted that only Griffins are 'segreant' when they are shown rampant.

The Phoenix

Known to Herodotus and the ancient world, the Phoenix naturally excited the wonder of the medieval bestiarists, to whom it served as a vehicle for allegory and moralisation. The Cambridge Bestiarist, whose work was so felicitously translated by the late T. H. White, devoted a lengthy section to it.

> Fenix, the Bird of Arabia, is called this because of its reddish purple colour. It is unique : it is unparalled in the whole world. It lives beyond five hundred years. When it notices that it is growing old, it builds itself a funeral pyre, after collecting some spice branches, and on this, turning its body towards the rays of the sun and flapping its wings, it sets fire to itself of its own accord until it burns itself up. Then verily, on the ninth day afterward, it rises from its own ashes.

He then goes on to make the point, at some length, that the symbolism of this bird teaches us to believe in the Resurrection.[35]

Guillaume le Clerc (1210–11) says that the Phoenix dwells in India, but Bartholomew the Englishman suggests otherwise.

Phoenix badge of Verney of Pendeley (drawn by Miss A. Urwick from Coll. Arms ms. I.2, f. 55)

> Fenix is a byrde, and there is but one of that kynde in all the wyde world. Therfore lewde men wondren thereof, and amonge the Arabyes there this byrde fenix is bredde . . . . The philosopher speketh of this byrde and sayth that fenix is a byrde without make [sic. mate?] and lyveth three hundred or fyve hundred yeres, when the whiche yeres ben passed she feleth her own defaute and feblenes, and maketh a neste of ryghte swete smellynge styckes that ben ful drye, and in sommer when the westerne wynde bloweth, the stickes and the neste ben sette on fyre with brennynge heate of the sonne, and brennethe stronglye; thanne this byrde fenix cometh wylfully in to the brennyng neste, and is there brent to asshes, and within three daies a lyttell worme is gendred of the ashes, and wexeth littell and lyttell and taketh fethers and is shape and tourned to a birde.

180

Bartholomew had a more scientific approach to his work and usually avoided moralising, as in this case.[36]

Sir Thomas Browne, as usual, brings us firmly down to earth. 'That there is but one Phoenix in the world, which after many hundred years burneth it self, and from the ashes thereof ariseth up another, is a conceit not now or altogether popular, but of great Antiquity; not only delivered by humane Authors, but frequently expressed also by holy Writers . . . . All which notwithstanding, we cannot presume the existence of this Animal; nor dare we affirm there is any Phoenix in Nature.'[37]

Notwithstanding Sir Thomas, the heralds have held it in high regard, and this bird, which symbolises heavenly and earthly love as well as the Resurrection, has played a most distinguished part in royal heraldry. It first occurs as a Badge of King Henry VII, and is to be seen on a misericord in the Henry VII Chapel in Westminster Abbey. It was then used as a Badge by Jane

Phoenix badge of Queen Jane Seymour (drawn by Miss A. Urwick from Coll. Arms ms. I.2, f. 15)

181

Seymour, the third wife of King Henry VIII, in the form of a Phoenix, with wings expanded and crowned gold, rising from flames proper, between four roses, one red and one white on each side, upon a Mount vert encircled by double castle walls, in front of the upper walls an Oak Tree proper crowned gold. The note in the College of Arms manuscript states that 'this Badge was given her by the Kinge her husband And standeth in dyverse wyndowes abowt the Pallace of Whitehall'.[38] Queen Elizabeth I used, as one of her Badges, a Phoenix, with the motto *Semper Eadem,* which a contemporary herald described as 'a true type or figure of her Princely selfe, which whilest she lived was the only Phenix living in the whole world'.[39] Tudor hyperbole cannot, however, get over the remarkable coincidence that Elizabeth's great rival, Mary, Queen of Scots, also used a Phoenix as her Badge, which she had inherited from her mother, Mary of Lorraine, with the motto '*En ma fin ma commencement*'.

The Phoenix is, however, a rare charge in English and Continental heraldry and is borne by only a few noble and gentle families. A good early sixteenth century example is the badge of Ralph Verney, of Pendley in Hertfordshire, illustrated in trick in the Book of Standards.[40]

THE TRAGOPAN

Tragopan crest of Lord of London (drawn by A. Cole from "Wrythe's Book of Knights", British Museum Add. ms. 46354, f. 236)

It fell to that redoubtable armorist, the late Hugh Stanford London, to rescue the Tragopan from the limbo into which it had sunk.[41] The one and only example of this impossible bird in English heraldry occurs in a grant of arms made in the early years of Henry VIII's reign, by Clarenceux Benolt and Garter Wriothesley to Robert Lord alias Laward, of London. The creature is depicted as a Demi-Eagle with wings displayed, and arising from the top of its head two ram's horns.[42]

THE MARTLET

This most widely used of heraldic charges is, in essence, a conventionalised compound of the swift, the swallow and the house martin, those elegant little birds which, to our more perceptive eyes, are readily distinguished. The medieval observers not only telescoped these three birds into one, but threw in one or two other misconceptions as well.

Bouly de Lesdain noted eighty examples of the Martlet in French seals and enamels between 1127 and 1300, the earliest being the arms of Guillaume de Mello in 1185, while his successor Dreux de Mello, Constable of France, bore three Martlets in pale combined with another charge difficult to identify. In 1189 Hugues V, Vicomte de Chateaudun, bore Barry an orle of Martlets.[43]

A slightly earlier literary example of Martlets in armory occurs in Chrétien de Troyes' *Le Chevalier de la Charette*, composed before 1172, where one of the onlookers at the tournament in which Lancelot acquitted himself so nobly, describing the shields of the contestants, says 'yonder shield is of English workmanship and was made at London; you see on it two Swallows which appear as if about to fly, yet they do not move, but receive blows from the Poitevin lances of steel; he who bears it is poor Thoas'.[44]

Arms of William de Valence, Earl of Pembroke (drawn by Miss A. Urwick)

The Martlet was variously rendered as martlet(e), merlot, merle, esmerlot, merlion; and often oisel or oiselet meant Martlet rather than just a bird in general.[45] (Professor Gerald J. Brault's *Early Blazon* has a most valuable note on it.) *De Heraudie* states that 'quant il y ad un merle en un escu, c'est un merle; quant il passe iij sount merlés'.[46]

The *Llyfr Dysgread Arfau,* the Welsh version of Bado Aureo's *Tractatus de Armis* (1394), says

Martlets borne in arms signify that the bearer acquired nobility by his bravery and prowess or by his intelligence, and that he had but little wealth nor means of subsistence at first, but lived on his acquisitions like something that lacked foundation, for the Martlet is painted in arms without feet, like something that is without foundation. And those who bear these birds dwell in courts of lords or Kings, and they live on the bounty of their lords. Yet they are noble. It is not by wealth and riches alone that nobility is acquired, but by deeds of prowess and other good habits.[47]

Much the same view is expressed in the French heraldic treatises of the early fifteenth century, but while Nicholas Upton (1446) also subscribes to this notion, he is in some confusion about the bird. 'Merlions', he says, 'be byrdes . . . . nat moche bygger than ossels (i.e. blackbirds) and because they be smale of body and of smale strength, therfor they flee (fly) at smale byrds, and by iij or iiij together in company . . . . woll take a swanne'.[48] It looks as if Upton was muddling the Martlet with the Merlin, the 'faucon émérillon' of modern French, for the swifts, swallows and martins are the least aggressive of birds, and have never been known to attack other birds, let alone swans in flight. Sometimes, and more understandably perhaps, it looks as if the writer was thinking of the common or garden blackbird. Even some modern heralds are a bit shaky on their ornithology.

One of the best known of the early examples of the Martlet in English heraldry occurs in the arms of William de Valence, titular Earl of Pembroke (d. 1296), who was the son of Hugh of Lusignan, Count of La Marche, by Isabella of Augoulême, widow of King John, and thus half-brother of King Henry III. He differenced the arms of his family, Barry argent and azure, with an orle of red Martlets, and these arms are to be seen to this day on his tomb in Westminster Abbey. Far and away the most attractive representation of heraldic Martlets is in the Luttrell Psalter, which has a picture of Sir Geoffrey Luttrell, of Irnham in Lincolnshire, seated on his horse in full armour, with surcoat and horse-trapper of his arms and being handed his war-helm by his wife and his shield by his daughter-in-law.[49]

13
Dragons and
Fabulous Reptiles

T HERE are in heraldry some half a dozen chimerical creatures of reptilian form, but they are basically serpents and lizards. The Basilisk and Cockatrice, the Amphisboena, Dragon and Wyvern, the Amphiptère and Hydra were all originally flying serpents, while the Salamander is unmistakably a lizard. The Dragon is the largest of all fabulous creatures; but some of the others are quite small – the Basilisk is but some six inches long and the Amphisboena the size of an earth-worm. There was much confusion throughout the Middle Ages over the appearance of these creatures; thus, not only are they depicted with widely varying characteristics, but there was also a tendency to confuse one with the other. A good example is the twelfth-century seal of Raimund de Montdragon, where his creatures, though clearly intended to be Dragons, differ greatly from the conventional Dragons of the sixteenth century and later, but his name makes it clear what they were intended to be.

THE BASILISK OR COCKATRICE

The Basilisk, as its name implies, is the undisputed little king of serpents and of the whole brood of monstrous, chimerical reptiles. The Cockatrice, although delineated in post-Tudor heraldic art as a separate genus with a cock's head, is in origin the same creature, as Bartholomew the Englishman (*c.* 1240) made clear.

> The Cockatrice hyghte Basiliscus in grewe [Greek] and Regulus in latyn, and hathe that name Regulus of a lyttell kynge, for he is kynge of serpentes, and they ben afe[a]rde and flee when they se hym : for he sleeth theym with his smelle and with his brethe : and sleeth also al thyng that hath lyfe with brethe and with syghte. In his syghte no foule ne byrde passeth harmeles, and thoughe he be ferre fro the foule, yet it is brente and devoured by his mouthe, but he is overcome of the wesell : and men brynge the wesell to the cokatrice denne, where he lurketh and is hid. For the father and maker of all thying lefte no thinge without remedy. And so the cokatrice fleeth when he seeth the wesel, and the wesel pursewith and sleeth hym. And the cokatrice is halfe a fote long, and hath white speckes : And the cokatrice sleeth that that he cometh nyghe, as the Scorpion . . . [although] the bytynge of the wesell is deathe to the cokatrice . . . . nevertheless the biting of the cokatrice is deathe to the wesell. And that is soth, but if the wesel ete rewe [the herb rue] before.

184

Bartholomew concludes with an interesting and little-known property of the cockatrice, for 'his ashes be accounted good and profytable in werkynge of Alkamye, and namely in turnynge and chaungyne of mettalle'.[1]

This view of the Basilisk or Cockatrice was held throughout the Middle Ages and well into the sixteenth century. William Caxton's *Myrrour and Descrypcyon of the World* (first printed in 1481) says that 'there ben the Basylicocks which have . . . . the head like a cock and body of a serpent. He is king of all serpents, like as the lion is king above all beasts . . . . The moustele (weasel) is a right little beast and slayeth the Basylicock and in long fighting biteth him out of measure'. He also subscribes to the other accepted ideas about the creature.[2] Gerard Legh and John Bossewell give almost identical woodcuts of the creature displayed, but whereas Legh blazons it as a 'Cockatrice', Bossewell calls it a 'Basiliske'; yet another writer, John Guillim, says 'the Cockatrice is called in Latine Regulus, for that he seemeth to be a little king amongst Serpents, not in regard of his quantity, but in respect of the infection of his pestiferous and poysonfull aspect, wherewith he poysoneth the aire. Not unlike those devillish Witches, that do work the destruction of silly infants, as also of the Cattell of such of their neighbours, whose prosperous estate is to them a most grevious eye-sore'.[3]

Sir Thomas Browne observed that 'many opinions are passant concerning the Basilisk or little King of Serpents, commonly called the Cockatrice: some affirming, others denying, most doubting the relations made thereof'. He pointed out that

> certainly that which from the conceit of its generation we vulgarly call a Cockatrice, and wherein (but under a different name) we intend a formal identity and adequate conception with the Basilisk; is not the Basilisk of the Ancients, whereof such wonders are delivered. For this of ours is generally described with legs, wings, a Serpentine and winding tail, and a crist or comb somewhat like a Cock. But the Basilisk of elder times was a proper kind of Serpent, not above three palms long, as some account; and differenced from other Serpents by advancing his head, and some white marks or coronary spots upon the crown, as all authentic Writers have delivered. Nor is this Cockatrice only unlike the Basilisk, but of no real shape in Nature; and rather an Hieroglyphical fansie, to express different intentions, set forth in different fashions. Sometimes with the head of a Man, sometimes with the head of a Hawk, as Pierins hath delivered; and as with addition of legs the Heralds and Painters still describe it.[4]

We shall, in fact, see that the heralds 'described' this creature with considerable freedom. The Book of Standards records the badge of John Cursson (Curzon), of Croxsall in Derbyshire, which is shown in trick with a Cock's head, wings

Basilisk as illustrated in John Bossewell, *Works of Armoria*, p. 60[b] (drawn by N. Manwaring)

Badge and standard of John Curzon of Croxsall (Coll. Arms ms. I.2, f. 91)

and legs and the hindparts of a Dragon, with the tail ending in a serpent's
head. One's inclination is to identify the creature as a Basilisk or, in more
recent terms, as an Amphisian Cockatrice, but in a record of Henry VIII's
French war it is stated that John Cursson 'enteryng into France xvj June,
V Henry VIII (1513) bayryth in hys standert a cockatrice displayed goulls
with a hed in his tayll, his fette and his wattelles assur'. The badge of Master
Hogan is depicted in the Book of Standards like the more conventional heraldic
Cockatrice, without its amphysian head, and in the expedition of 1513 it is
recorded, as one would expect, the he 'beyryth a cockatryce goulls'.[5] On the
other hand, Sir Gilbert Dethick, Garter King of Arms, a good scholar and
sound armorist, granted on 5 July 1556 to Henry Northey, of Bocking in
Essex, a crest of *a demy Basilisco in his proper coller membred and beaked
sable, open mowthed the breath yssewyng.* The creature is drawn like a
Cockatrice and tricked as gold and vert, the wings, comb and wattles gules.[6]

In 1578 Robert Cooke, Clarenceux, confirmed the arms of Edward Buggin,
of London, *Sable a Cockatrice displayed silver crowned and beaked gold*, but
instead of his old crest, a Wolf sejant on a hillock vert devouring and slaying
a Fox by the throat both proper, he granted a new crest of a Cockatrice statant
wings elevated, crowned and beaked or.[7] One of the more notable of English
families to bear a Cockatrice is that of the Lords De la Warr, of whom Thomas
West, twelfth Lord De la Warr, was knighted at Dublin by the Earl of Essex
in 1599. In 1610 he was appointed Governor and Captain-General of Virginia,
which he organised to his satisfaction the next year, and then returned to
England. He again went to Virginia in 1618, 'but sailing from thence dies,
together with thirty more, not without suspicion of poison'.[8] His armorial
bearings are recorded in the College of Arms, in a beautifully painted vellum
manuscript entitled *Arms and Descents of the Nobility,* which shows the sinister
supporter of his arms, the blue-green Cockatrice.[9]

A more interesting example of the Cockatrice in English armory is the
supporters of Field-Marshal Sir George Nugent, Bt., G.C.B. His long and
distinguished career in the Army included service in America, Holland, the
West Indies, and finally he became Commander-in-Chief in India. He was
created a baronet in 1806 and in 1807 King George III, by royal warrant,
granted him supporters to his arms as 'a further mark of our Royal Favor as
may evince the sense We entertain of his Merit . . . . whereby his Faithful
and Zealous exertions in Our service may be conveyed to posterity'.[10]
In England only peers, Knights of the Garter and Knights Grand Cross
of Orders of chivalry are entitled to supporters, and since Sir George Nugent
was not at that time a Knight Grand Cross of the Order of the Bath, this was a
particular mark of royal favour. It is the kind of gracious action which might
well and usefully be exercised by modern sovereigns, for it lies solely within the
royal prerogative.

As the Cockatrice had a somewhat unsatisfactory reputation in medieval
religious symbolism[11] it is difficult to see what kind of duties it could have per-
formed in an armorial context, for its virtues are hard to discover. Possibly its symbolic importance lay in the fact that the Basilisk was the king of all serpents,
just as the Lion was the king of beasts and the Eagle the king of birds – and
a king is a king irrespective of his habits or morals. Whatever the reason, some
twenty English families bear Cockatrices in their arms, and some ten Continental families. In other European countries one finds the creature blazoned
as a Basilisk.

THE DRAGON AND WYVERN

In English, Scottish and Irish armory since the sixteenth century, the Dragon
is depicted with four legs and the Wyvern with two; but this distinction is not
generally made in the armory of most European countries, where the two-

legged creature is still called a Dragon, in keeping with medieval practice. Vincent of Beauvais, the great encyclopedist of the early Middle Ages (*c.* 1190–1264) said that some Dragons have feet, 'but this is rare'. The Dragon was originally conceived of as a flying serpent, with a long, sinuous neck and long, lashing tail.

Isidore of Seville (*c.* 630) described the Dragon in some detail, and he served as a mine from which most of the medieval bestiarists quarried their information. The compiler of the Cambridge Bestiary spoke of it as 'the biggest of all serpents, in fact of all living things on earth', and commented that the Devil, who is the most enormous of all reptiles, is like the Dragon.[13] A typical medieval description of the creature, that of Bartholomew the Englishman, tells us that the Dragon 'bredeth in Inde and in Ethiopia' and is the 'most gretest of al serpentes'. It has 'a creste with a littell mouth, and draweth brethe at smalle pypes and streyghte, and rereth his tong and hath teethe lyke a sawe, and hath strength, and not onely in teeth but also in his taylle, and greveth both with bitinge and with styngynge, and hath not so moche venyme as other serpentes'. Bartholomew goes on to describe how it attacks and kills elephants. He also tells us that the Dragon

> is a full thyrsty beaste, in somoche that uneth [unless] he may have water ynough to quench his great thurste: And openethe his mouthe therfore agenst the wynde, to qyenche the brennyng of his thurste in that wise . . . . Sometyme he settethe the ayer on fyre by heat of his venym: so that it semeth that he bloweth and casteth fyre oute of his mouthe, and somtyme he bloweth out outragious blastes and therby the ayre is corrupte and infected, and therof cometh pestilente evyls. And they dwell somtyme in the see, and somtyme swym in ryvers, and lurke somtyme in caves and in dennes, and slepe but selde (seldom) but wake nygh all waye.

Bartholomew also mentions their 'ryghte sharpe syght' and describes their method of fighting by biting and stinging with their tails.[14]

What, one may well ask, has made the Dragon so popular in European heraldry, as a charge in a shield of arms, as a crest, or as a badge or armorial supporter? Dragons in various positions, or their heads or wings, are borne either alone or in combination with other charges by some two hundred English families, and some three hundred European families.

Although the Dragon was widely regarded as the very embodiment of evil, it was also conceived in ancient Greece and Rome as beneficient. Dragons were sharp-eyed dwellers in the inner parts of the earth, wise to its secrets and revealing them in oracles. They were powerful creatures to invoke as

Two modern Welsh dragons: the Badges of H.M. the Queen and The Prince of Wales

guardian genii. Their protective and terror-inspiring qualities made them suitable for use as warlike emblems from very early times. The Dragon was the emblem of the Dacians, from whom the Romans adopted it in Trajan's time, and just as the Eagle was the emblem of the legion of ten cohorts, so the Dragon became the emblem of the cohort.[15] Bas-reliefs of the Dacian Dragon – which was of solid form, and supported by a pole from the middle – can be seen on Trajan's Column; the Roman Dragon, which was made of cloth, is carved on the arch of Septimius Severus. Later the purple Dragon became the emblem of the Byzantine emperors.

The Dragon was also known to the Celtic peoples of western Europe in pre-Christian times, and ornaments, with stylised dragon-like motifs, were worn by the native Britons under the Roman occupation. As the emblem of the cohorts, which were stationed in various parts of Britain, the Dragon would be well-known and feared by the inhabitants; so that when the legions left for good in 410, it was natural for the Romanised British leaders to adopt as their own an emblem which had affinities with their own traditions. It is not without significance, as Major Francis Jones, Wales Herald Extraordinary, has pointed out, that the Welsh word *draig* (dragon) was used figuratively to denote a leader, hero, chief or prince. All the earliest Welsh references associate the Dragon with war-leaders and with fighting.[16]

Whether or not 'King' Arthur, or his father Uther Pendragon, used a Dragon as his emblem is unimportant from an armorial point of view; what does matter is that this was generally believed to be so, from the earliest Middle Ages. Geoffrey of Monmouth's *Historia Regnum Britanniae* was to be found in the libraries of the nobility and the heralds throughout the Middle Ages, and it is itemised in the library list of Robert Glover, my predecessor as Somerset Herald in 1570. Geoffrey records that Uther saw a vision of 'a star of marvellous bigness and brightness', from which a ray stretched forth whereon was a ball of fire in the likeness of a Dragon. Uther consulted the famous wizard Merlin and, in the light of the latter's prophesy, 'bade two Dragons be wrought in gold in the likeness of the Dragon he had seen upon the ray of the star. And when that they had been wrought in marvellous cunning craftsmanship, he made offering of the one unto the chief church of the See of Winchester, but the other did he keep himself to carry about with him in the wars'.[17] In all the medieval rolls of arms and heraldic treatises which mention them we find the attributed arms of Uther Pendragon given as, *Or two Dragons addorsed vert crowned gules.*

The West Saxon invaders of Britain, whom Pendragon's son Arthur defeated at the famous Battle of Mount Badon about A.D. 500, but who subsequently recovered to drive back the British about a century later, were using a Dragon standard themselves at the Battle of Burford in 752. We read of the Dragon standard again at the Battle of Assingdon in 1016 between Edmund Ironside and Canute.[18] Also, the Bayeux Tapestry has a vivid scene of the stricken King Harold being cut down by Norman knights as he stands at his command-post beside the Dragon standard of Wessex. Here, the Dragon appears to be modelled, rather than painted on a flag, and to be fixed to its staff by the nose; it has two short legs and small wings.

Bouly de Lesdain notes five examples of the Dragon on French seals and enamels before 1300, the earliest being the mid twelfth century seal of Raimund de Montdragon, a Provençal baron.[19] The creatures, engraved as combatant or face to face, are clearly intended to be a canting allusion to his name, but they are a far cry from the conventional Dragons of the sixteenth century and later, and, if anything, resemble Basilisks with human heads. They are, of course, two-legged, but their bodies appear to be feathered and their tails end in small Dragon's heads; their human heads have beards composed of serpents which each dragon is holding with one foot. The reverse of the seal has a

Attributed arms of Uther Pendragon (drawing by Miss A. Urwick based on the Rede Copy of *De Studio Militari*)

Seal matrix of Raimund de Montdragon (Bibliotheque Nationale, Paris, Seal Collection B.51244)

189

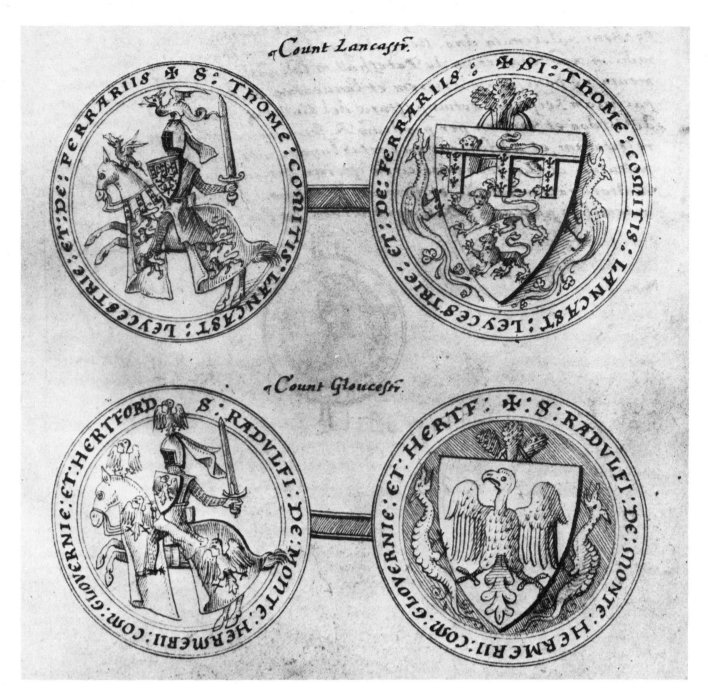

Seals of the Earl of Lancaster and the Earl of Gloucester, from the Barons' Letter to the Pope, from a drawing by Augustine Vincent (Coll. Arms ms. Vinc. 425, f. 5)

delightful picture of Raimund on his knees swearing fealty to his lady, which is very much in the contemporary spirit of the troubadours and the Courts of Love. The family of Montdragon subsequently bore for their arms a single such human-headed Dragon, gold on a red shield. Lest one should think that this is an exception, there is also the seal of Dragonet de Montauban, of which two examples survive from 1229 and 1249. Thereon are two human-headed Dragons, face to face and similarly grasping their beards with one foot.[20] Rietstap's *Armorial Général* lists another French family, that of Anthon, which bears *Or a Dragon with a human face gules*.

King Richard Coeur de Lion is said to have used a Dragon standard in 1191 when on crusade in the Holy Land, and Henry III used it as a battle flag when on campaign against the Welsh in 1245.[21] Apart from these royal heraldic uses of the creature, the Dragon is also found as a decorative adjunct in many English baronial seals, sometimes at the foot below the equestrian figure and sometimes on each side of the shield, rather like supporters. Three of the earliest are those of William de Aubeney, Earl of Arundel and Sussex (*c.* 1180), Geoffrey Bucointe of London (late twelfth century), and Robert fitz

190

Walter, Lord of Baynard's Castle beside London, and one of the **Magna Carta** sureties (d. 1235). The seals of the seven Earls and nintely-seven **Barons**, appended to the Barons' Letter to the Pope, of 12 February 1300/1, include twenty-two in which Dragons appear, but only in one or possibly two are they used as heraldic crests; in the remaining twenty they appear as decorative adjuncts on each side of the shield of arms.[22] One of the most interesting of these seals is that of Henry of Lancaster, Lord of Monmouth, son of Edmund Plantagenet, Earl of Lancaster, in which the Dragon is definitely used as a heraldic crest.[23]

The first mention of the Dragon in a heraldic treatise is by John de Bado Aureo (1394), who describes some of its fabulous characteristics. The interesting point is, however, that the late fifteenth century English translation has a spirited painting in the margin of a green Dragon with only two legs, and this is firmly labelled 'the Dragon'. [24] The *Llyfr Dysgread Arfau* possibly by the same author, begins the section on birds borne in arms with this creature:

> Now that we have discussed the animals we shall speak of birds and, as wise naturalists maintain, those who adopt birds as their charges (in arms) are not as steadfast and grave as those who assume four-footed creatures. First of all we shall speak of the Dragon. A Dragon borne in arms signifies a strong, mighty and fierce man, eager for battle: for the Dragon is so thirsty that scarcely can water quench its thirst. Thus it always has its mouth open to overcome the heat and thirst.[25]

Nicholas Upton puts the Dragon at the end of his section on birds and before the fishes. He follows the bestiaries pretty closely, but does not add anything of importance regarding the Dragon's armorial significance.

The earliest appearance of the Dragon in an English roll of arms is in the Great, Parliamentary, or Bannerets Roll, compiled by the heralds in about 1312 and blazoning the arms borne by 1,110 contemporary earls, barons and bannerets. Among them we find: 'Sire Johan de Folebourne de or a un cheveron de sable et ij wyvres de sable', and 'Sire Edmon de Maulee de or a une bende de sable en la bende iij wyvres de argent'. As far as I know, this is the earliest use in heraldry of the term 'wyver', which is derived from Old French 'wyvre' and Middle English 'wyver' and means a serpent. Unfortunately the shields are not drawn or painted, so we do not know how they were represented armorially.[26]

The four-footed Dragon begins to make his appearance around 1400 or a little earlier. The Boucicault Book of Hours, composed between 1400 and 1415, contains a painting of Marshal Boucicault as St George spearing the Dragon, which is depicted with four legs.[27] In England the earliest example appears to be the seal used by the Kings of England, from Henry IV to Henry VII, for the principality of North Wales; *three Lions passant guardant in pale their tails cowed, supported on either side by a four-footed Dragon sejant addorsed holding up an Ostrich Feather labelled.*[28] Henry IV was crowned on 13 October 1399 and, as he was never Prince of Wales, his Seal for North Wales must be of later date than this.

It is interesting that *The Book of Standards* depicts the banner of North Wales supported by a two-footed Dragon, but the royal arms supported by a four-footed Dragon.[29] These Welsh Dragons were always red with gold underparts. By the sixteenth century we find the quadruped Dragon becoming increasingly popular and differentiated from the two-footed beast, which hence-forth became known as the Wyver and eventually Wyvern.

A delightful Dragon is that in one of the badges of Robert Ratclyffe, Earl of Sussex, K.G., who succeeded to the earldom in 1529 and died in 1542. It is a four-footed Dragon held by the neck by a human hand.[30] Another

The Ratclyffe Dragon (drawn by Miss A. Urwick from Coll. Arms ms. Vinc. 172, f. 27)

191

The Augmented Royal Badge of Wales, as authorised in 1953

decorative crest, which probably goes back to an early period, is that of the family of Moyle, of Bake, in St Germans, Cornwall: this is *Two Demi-Dragons sans wings addorsed and the necks entwined, the dexter gules, the sinister or.*[31] Possibly one of the more curious dragons is that granted as a crest, in 1903, to Sir Edwyn Dawes, K.C.M.G.: *in front of a Demi-Battleaxe erect or, surmounted by a Dragon sans wings and legs the tail nowed sable charged with five Besants fesswise, three Cinquefoils also gold.*[32]

The supporters of Andrew Stewart, third Lord Ochiltree, are generally blazoned as Dragons, but in all the contemporary early seventeenth century manuscripts in the College of Arms they are depicted with only two feet and with a serpent's head at the end of their tails.[33] The creature would thus seem more exactly described as an Amphisboena, but it is pleasanter to follow medieval practice and blazon it as a Dragon with a head in its tail.

One of the oddest interpretations of the creature is in the arms of Isaac Teale, of Hanover Square, London, granted to him on 26 February 1723 by John Anstis, Garter King of Arms, and Sir John Vanborough, Clarenceux King of Arms (the famous architect). The arms are blazoned as *Argent a Python regardant and in chief three Teals all proper,*[34] but the beast is drawn exactly like a Wyvern!

THE HYDRA
There is only one Hydra in English heraldry and he is a very modern addition to the armorial bestiary, being granted in 1927 to Alexander Crispin, Lord of the Manor of Dodbrook in Devon, as a crest, *a Hydra statant proper.* The creature is drawn like a modern English heraldic Dragon, but with seven heads; it is green all over, including the wings, and has a red tongue and claws.[35]

Rietstap's *Armorial Général,* however, gives seven European families as bearing a Hydra in their arms. One bears a Hydra with seven heads, another bears one with three heads, and the Marquis de Belsunce bore the creature with one head cut off and bleeding at the neck.

Hydra as illustrated in John Bossewell, *op. cit.,* p. 8 (drawn by N. Manwaring)

192

THE SALAMANDER

The salamandra hath that name, as Isidore sayth, for he is stronge and mighty ayenst brennyng, and among al venemouse bestes his might is the mooste of venyme. For other venemouse beastes noyethe one and one, and this noyeth and sleeth many at ones. For if he crepe on a tree, he infecteth all the apples, and sleeth them that eate therof, and if he falleth in to a pytte he sleeth all that drynke of the water. By this venym this beaste is contrary to brennynge, and amonge beastes onely this beaste quencheth fyre and lyeth in the brennynge fyre withoute consumpcion and wastyng, and also without smertynge and ache and brennethe not in fyre, but abathethe and swagethe the brennynge therof.

Bartholomew the Englishman goes on to say that the 'salamandra is like an ewte in shap and is never more seen but in moche reine, for he fayleth in fayre wether . . . . Also they bene dyverse in maner of goynge and passing, for some crepe and glyde a way wygglynge and crokedly, and some alway stretche and go forthe ryghte'.[36] Guillaume le Clerc says much the same, but adds a little moralising, which explains why the beast's symbolism appealed to the imagination of the medieval heralds:

> This beast signifies
> The man of sense and holy life,
> Who is so filled with perfect faith
> That he puts out around him
> The fire and heat of lust
> And the burning heat of vices.[37]

The Bible story of Shadrach, Meshach and Abednego, who were cast into the burning fiery furnace, but emerged completely unharmed, would of course be well known to the medieval heralds and the parallel with the Salamander would readily spring to mind, making the creature a very suitable charge for armorial purposes. But the erotic poets also drew inspiration from the Salamander, making it an apt allegory for the lover who revels in the fires of love or, alternatively, laments the fact that, unlike the Salamander, he cannot escape being burnt up by his passion.

One of the earliest Salamanders to be employed in an armorial capacity is the crest of Sir James Douglas, Earl of Douglas and Avondale. He succeeded to the earldom on the murder of his elder brother by King James II of Scotland in February 1451/2. In 1454 he formally defied the King and took the field with 40,000 men, but his insurrection failed and he fled to England. There he was received with great favour by King Edward IV, who created him a Knight of the Garter about 1461, and his crest (on a Cap of Estate azure a Salamander gold breathing fire) can be seen to this day on his Garter

Opposite page
The Salamander badge of King Francois I of France, above a fireplace in the Chateau of Blois, Loire-en-Cher, France. This is one of the finest and most beautiful examples of the beast in armory. (Photograph by Editions Chantal, Paris)

193

THE
COMPLEAT
GENTLEMAN:

Fashioning Him absolute in the most
Neceſſary and Commendable Qualities,
concerning Mind, or Body, that may be
required in a Perſon of Honor.

To which is added the

GENTLEMANS EXERCISE

OR,

An exquiſite practiſe, as well for drawing
all manner of Beaſts, as for making Colours,
to be uſed in Painting, Limming, &c.

By HENRY PEACHAM, Mr. of Arts,
Somtime of Trinity Colledge in *Cambridge.*

———— *Inutilis olim*
Ne videar vixiſſe. ————

The Third Impreſſion much inlarged, eſpecially in the
Art of Blazonry, by a very good Hand.

LONDON,
Printed by E. Tyler, for *Richard Thrale,* at the ſigne of
the Croſs-Keys at St *Pauls* Gate, 1661.

194

Stall Plate.[38] He may have adopted it in allusion to his survival from the flames of King James's wrath. Some twenty years later Douglas joined the Duke of Albany in an invasion of Scotland, but was taken prisoner in 1484 and sentenced to become a monk at Lindores Abbey, where he died four years later. Another member of this great family, William Douglas, twenty-seventh Earl of Angus, a notable historian and antiquary, joined in a plot in 1592 to establish the Roman Catholic religion in Scotland, but it failed and his estates were forfeited. He retired to the Continent, where he died in 1611. He bore for his crest a Salamander proper enveloped in flames and breathing fire.[39] The interesting thing about these early Salamanders is that they were drawn rather like short-legged dogs.

In the early seventeenth century arms and crest were granted to Alexander Gill, High Master of St Paul's School. The crest was a Salamander gules spotted gold, passing through flames proper.[40] Gill was famous as a schoolmaster, a latinist, critic and divine, who, like many worthy fathers, had a son who was in constant trouble with the authorities for somewhat unruly and mildly seditious activities. From the seventeenth century onwards, Salamanders increase in English armory and some thirty families bear them in one way or another; but only some nineteen Continental families bear them. The most famous Salamander of them all, however, was the badge of King Francis I of France (1515-47) and the artist he employed has produced one of the most beautiful and lively renderings of the creature over the great fireplace in the Chateau of Blois. Another example can be seen in the Chateau of Chenonceaux, the home of Diane de Poitiers, the beautiful mistress of King Henry II of France.

Notes

Part I

Chapter 1. The Beginninge and Grownde of Armes

1. *The Song of Roland,* tr. Dorothy L. Sayers (Penguin Books, 1957), p. 111. The version which has come down to us probably dates from about 1100, but it is based on material from a much earlier period.
2. Ibid., LL; 3093, 3266, 3548.
3. *The Alexiad of Anna Comnena,* tr. E. R. A. Sewter (Penguin Books, 1969), p. 173.
4. *Eneide des Heinrich von Veldeke,* in the Staatsbibliothek, Berlin. An illustration of this is printed in Berchem, Galbreath, and Hupp, *Beitrage zur Geschichte der Heraldik* (Berlin, 1939), pp. 2-3.
5. *The Alexiad,* op. cit., p. 416.
6. *Gesta Stephani,* tr. K. R. Potter (Medieval Texts, London, 1955), p. 24. I am indebted to Mr. Michael Maclagan, Portcullis Pursuivant of Arms, for drawing my attention to this passage.
7. Sir Anthony R. Wagner, *Heralds and Heraldry in the Middle Ages,* (London 1939), p. 12.
8. The evidence of his first Great Seal should be considered in the light of the 'Itinerarium Regis Richardi', in *Chronicles and Memorials of the Reign of Richard I* (Rolls Series), vol i, p. 197, which points strongly to two Lions combatant. See also Bartolo di Sasso Ferrato, *De Insigniis et Armis,* ch. 14 and 31, which was probably based on earlier practice.
9. Coll. Arms MSS.: R. 21, f. 13v-14; and Grants of Arms, Oxford, vol i, f. 138-142 (for Browne); and R. 21, f. 145v, and 2 G.4, f. 2, and D. 13 (for Guildford). I am indebted to Mr. A. Colin Cole, Windsor Herald of Arms, for drawing my attention to these interesting and significant grants.
10. Sir H. Nicolas, *History of the Battle of Agincourt* (Tabard Press reprint 1970). The principal banners displayed by Henry V during the battle were the English Royal Arms, the Trinity, St George, St Edward, and probably St Edmund.

Chapter 2. The Heralds as Military Staff Officers

1. C. R. Humphery-Smith, 'Heraldry in School Manuals of the Middle Ages', *The Coat of Arms,* vol. vi, p. 118, being a translation of Brit. Mus. Add. MS. 3744.
2. *Gesta Francorum et Aliorum Hierosolimitanorum,* tr. Rosalind Hill (Medieval Texts, London, 1962), p. 46. I am indebted to Miss Hill for pointing out to me the significance of *preco.* See also Sir Anthony Wagner, *Heralds of England* (London, 1967), p. 22.
3. Regine Pernoud, *Eleanor of Aquitaine,* tr. Peter Wiles (London, 1967), p. 78.
4. Ramon Lull, *Le Libre del Ordo de Cavayleria* (E.E.T.S., vol. 168).

5. A. R. Wagner, *Heralds and Heraldry in the Middle Ages* (O.U.P. 1939), p. 42, quoting. *Parties inèdites de l'oeuvre de Sicile hérault d'Alphonse V roi d'Aragon,* pp. 107-115.
6. *Chronique de Jean Lefévre seigneur de Saint-Rémy* ed. Francois Morand, Societe de l'histoire de France (Paris, 1876-1881), tome i, pp. 267-8.
7. Sir H. Nicolas, *History of the Battle of Agincourt* (Tabard Press reprint 1970), p. 257.
8. Coll Arms MS 2nd M.16, Barnard's Roll of Badges, ff. xvi-xix.

CHAPTER 3. TOURNAMENTS AND THE HERALDS

1. *L'histoire de Guillaume le Marechal,* ed. Paul Mayer, (Société de l'histoire de France), lines 4971-4976. See also S. Painter, *William Marshal* (London, 1968), ch. iii.
2. Chrétien de Troyes, *Arthurian Romances,* tr. W. W. Comfort (Everyman's Library, no. 698), pp. 339-344.
3. *Le livre des tournois du roi René,* ed. E. Pognon (Verve, Paris, 1946), pp. 42-3.

CHAPTER 4. ARMORY AND SYMBOLISM

1. *The Ancrene Riwle,* tr. M. B. Salu (Burns & Oats, London, 1955), pp. 173-4.
2. *The Book of the Ordre of Chyvalry,* ed. A. T. P. Byles (E.E.T.S., vol. 168, 1937). This is the text of William Caxton's publication, *Book of the ordre of chyvalry or knyghthode* (c.1484), which was a translation of a French version of Ramón Lull's *Le Libre del ordo de Cavayleria.*
3. *Sir Gawain and the Green Knight,* ed. J. R. R. Tolkien and E. V. Gordon (London, 1967), p. 18.
4. Geoffrey of Monmouth, *History of the Kings of Britain,* tr. S. Evans, rev. C. W. Dunn (Everyman's Library), p. 188.
5. Chrétien de Troyes, *Arthurian Romances,* tr. W. W. Comfort (Everyman's Library), pp. 150, 343.
6. Cambridge University Library MS. E.e. iv. 20, f. 160v-61v.
7. *Le blason des couleurs en armes, livrées et divisées par Sicille hérault d'Alphonse V roi d'Aragon,* ed. Hippolyte Cocheris (Paris, 1860).
8. E. J. Jones, *Medieval Heraldry* (Lewis, Cardiff, 1943), pp. 17-19.
9. Randle Holme, *The Academy of Armory and Blazon* (Chester, 1688).
10. Bodleian Library MS. Eng. Misc. D.227, f. 104 : John Blount's translation of *De Studio Militari.*
11. Bodleian Library MS. Laud. Misc. 733, f. 2.
12. L. Bouly de Lesdain, *Les plus anciennes armoiries françaises,* Archives Heraldiques Suisses, vol V (1897), pp. 69-79, 94-103.
13. E. J. Jones, op. cit., pp. 241-2; also C. R. Humphery-Smith, 'Bartholus's Treatise on Insignia and Arms' *Coat of Arms,* v. VII, p. 201.
14. Bodleian Library MS. Laud. Misc. 733, f. 9 : a late 15th-century English translation of John de Bado Aureo's *Tractatus de Armis.* See also A. R. Wagner, *Heralds and Heraldry in the Middle Ages,* p. 73.
15. T. H. White, *The Book of Beasts* (Jonathan Cape, London, 1954) p. 136.
16. Bodleian Library MS. Eng. Misc. D. 227, f. 175[v] : John Blount's translation.
17. Coll. Arms MS. 2nd. M. 16, f. xvi-xix.
18. British Museum Add. MS. 40742. See also A. R. Wagner, *C.E.M.R.A.* (London, 1948), p. 106.
19. *The Works of Sir Thomas Browne,* ed. G. Keynes (London, 1928), vol. II, pp. 378, 380.

PART II

CHAPTER 5. SOME HERALDS AND THEIR LIBRARIES

1. A. R. Wagner, *Heralds of England,* op. cit., pp. 66-68; also *Heralds and Heraldry,* 2nd edn. (O.U.P., London, 1956), pp. 59-61 and Appendix C.
2. A. R. Wagner, *Records and Collections of the College of Arms* (Burkes Peerage Ltd., London, 1952).
3. Coll. Arms MS. L. ll, part ii, pp. 1-29. 'Armes in Trick and Callendar of Bookes.'
4. Brit. Mus. Lansdowne MS. 58, ff. 103-105.
5. See also A. R. Wagner, *Heralds of England,* op. cit., p. 171.
6. A. R. Wagner, *Heralds and Heraldry,* op. cit., p. 110.
7. *The College of Arms: 16th Monograph of the London Survey Committee* (London, 1963), p. 120.
8. A. R. Wagner, *Heralds and Heraldry,* op. cit., pp. 78-81.

CHAPTER 6. EARLY MEDIEVAL TREATISES ON HERALDRY

1. Cambridge Univ. Lib. MS. Ee.iv.20, ff. 160v-161v. It has been transcribed in full, with an invaluable critical introduction, by Dr. Ruth J. Dean, 'An Early Treatise on Heraldry in Anglo-Norman', in *Romance Studies in Memory*

of *Edward Billings Ham,* ed. U. T. Holmes (California State College Publications, No. 2, 1967), pp 21-29. We are all in Dr. Dean's debt for calling our attention to this earliest of all heraldic treatises.

2. I am much indebted to Professor Gerard J. Brault, who kindly gave me a preview of his article on *The Relationship Between the Heralds' Roll, Grimaldi's Roll and the Dean Tract,* in which he discusses its date.

3. Professor Gerard J. Brault, *Early Blazon* (O.U.P., 1972), p 209; and *Eight Thirteenth Century Rolls of Arms in French and Anglo-Norman Blazon* (Pennsylvania State University Press, 1973), Camden Roll nos. 50, 94, 108, 182. I am informed that Giraldus Cambrensio also uses this term in describing the French Royal Arms.

4. E. J. Jones, *Medieval Heraldry* (Lewis, Cardiff, 1943), Appendix 1, prints a complete transcript of it. See also C. Pama, 'Bartolus' Treatise Six Hundred Years Old', *The Coat of Arms,* vol. v. pp. 55-56; and C. R. Humphery-Smith, 'Bartholus' Treatise on Insignia and Arms', *The Coat of Arms,* vol. vii, pp. 200-202.

5. *The Tree of Battles of Honoré Bonet,* tr. G. W. Coopland (Liverpool University Press, 1949), with an invaluable introduction on the author and his treatise.

6. *The Book of Fayttes of Armes and of Chyualrye,* tr. and printed by William Caxton (1490), from the French original by Christine de Pisan, ed. with an introduction by A. T. P. Byles (E.E.T.S., 1932).

7. E. J. Jones, *Medieval Heraldry: Tractatus de Armis, by Iohannes de Bado Aureo (An enquiry into the authorship of a Fourteenth Century Latin Treatise),* pp. 9-16. He adduces further arguments to support this view, which have not been touched on here.

8. E. J. Jones, *Medieval Heraldry* (Lewis, Cardiff), op. cit., pp. 3-94.

Chapter 7. Later Medieval Treatises on Heraldry

1. A. R. Wagner, *C.E.M.R.A.,* op. cit., p. 66. It is there described as the 'Bruce Roll', but its name was later changed.

2. Bibliothèque Nationale, Paris, MS. Français 5936.

3. L. C. Douet d'Arcq, 'Un traité du blason du XV siécle', in *Revue Archeologique,* 1st series, vol. xv (1858), pp. 257-274 and 321-342.

4. Bibliothèque Nationale, MSS, Fr. 5939, Fr. 14357.

5. Bibliothèque Nationale MS. Fr. 2692.

6. Deputy Keeper of the Public Records, *48th Report* (1887), Appendix, pp. 267, 272, 275.

7. F. P. Barnard, *The Essential Portions of Nicholas Upton's De Studio Militari, translated by John Blount* (Oxford, 1931), p. xiii. Most of my quotations from the De Studio Militari are from Blount's version.

8. Brit. Mus. Add. MS. 30946.

9. Brit. Mus. Harl. MS. 3504; Arundel Castle MS. 'Heraldry'.

10. Brit. Mus. Add. MS. 34648; printed in full by E. J. Jones, in *Medieval Heraldry,* op. cit., pp. 213-220.

11. James Dallaway, *Inquiries into the Origin and Progress of the Science of Heraldry in England* (London, 1793), p. 151.

12. Dennys MS. 10

13. Brit. Mus. Harl. MS. 2259. This is discussed by H. S. London, 'Some Medieval Treatises on English Heraldry', *The Antiquaries Journal,* vol. xxxiii, pp. 174-182; also A. R. Wagner, *Additions and Corrections to C.E.M.R.A., Aspilogia II* (London, 1967), p. 274.

14. Brit. Mus. Harl. MS. 6097.

15. Coll. Arms MS. 'Treatise on Heraldry circa Henry IV'.

16. Bodleian Library MS. Ashmolean Rolls 4; printed in C. R. Humphery-Smith, 'Heraldry in School Manuals of the Middle Ages', *Coat of Arms,* vol. vi., pp. 163-70.

17. Coll. Arms MS. F. 14, ff. 1-48.

18. Brit. Mus. Add MS. 3744.

Part III

Chapter 8. The Heavenly Host in Heraldry

1. An invaluable introduction to the medieval iconography of the Angels is provided by G. M. Rushforth, *Medieval Christian Imagery* (London, 1936); and M. D. Anderson, *The Imagery of British Churches* (London, 1955); while Louis Réau, *Iconographie de l'art chrétien* (Paris, 1957), and Gustav Davidson, *A Dictionary of Angels* (New York, 1967), are fascinating and essential guides to this esoteric subject. John Vinycomb, *Fictitious and Symbolic Creatures in Art with special reference to their use in British Heraldry* (London, 1906), pp. 25-56, remains the classic on its heraldic aspects.

2. *Colossians,* i, 16.

3. Gustav Davidson, op. cit.,

4. John Guillim, *A display of Heraldrie* (London, 1611), p. 82.
5. Randle Holme, *The Academy of Armory and Blazon* (Chester, 1688), bk II, ch. i, p. 13.
6. Corpus Christi College, Cambridge, MS. 16, f. 45v, Shield no. 8. See *The Mathew Paris Shields* (*c.* 1244-59), ed. T. D. Tremlett, in *Rolls of Arms of Henry III*, (Harleian Society vol. 113, 1967), p. 61. See also A. R. Wagner, *C.E.M.R.A.,* op. cit., p. 3.
7. The Lambeth Apocalypse, Lambeth Palace Library MS. no. 209, f. 53. This is discussed by O. E. Saunders, *English Illumination* (Florence, 1928), vol. i, p. 69.
8. *Cat. Seals British Museum,* ed. W. de G. Birch (London, 1892), no. 4748.
9. Corpus Christi College, Cambridge, MS. 16. f. 45ᵛ.
10. Brit. Mus. Harl. MS. 2168, f. 9ᵛ. Also ed. by Oswald Barron as 'A Fifteenth Century Book of Arms' (*The Ancestor,* vol iii, p. 206).
11. See Emile Mâle, *L'art religieux de la fin du moyen age en France* (Paris, 1908). Also Louis Réau, *Iconographie de l'art chrétien,* op. cit., and G. M. Rushforth, *Medieval Christian Imagery,* op. cit., pp. 402-6.
12. Coll. Arms MS. M.10. f. 125.
13. Brit. Mus. Harl. MS. 6163, f. 1. See Joseph Foster, *Two Tudor Books of Arms* (De Walden Library, 1904).
14. Gerard Legh, *The Accedens of Armory* (London, 1562) pp. 13-14.
15. [Dame Juliana Berners] *The Boke of St. Albans,* ed. W. Blades (London, 1899, facsimile of the 1486 edition).
16. Bibliothèque de l'Arsenal, Paris, MS. no. 288, f. 15. See also the Pierpont Morgan Library MS. 88, f. 179 : a Book of Hours, Metz Use, of the first half of the 14th century.
17. Brit. Mus. Seals, xxxvi, 243. See *Cat. Seals Brit. Mus.* ed. W. de G. Birch, (London), vol. ii (1887), no. 2827.
18. Brit Mus. Cotton MS. Cleopatra D. viii, f. 1ᵛ. I am indebted to Mr. John Goodall, F.S.A., for drawing my attention to this poem.
19. Louis Réau, op. cit., ch. ii. pp. 508-12; and Emile Mâle, op. cit., pp. 97-100; also G. M. Rushforth, op. cit., pp. 255-7.
20. Coll. Arms MS. 1st M.5. The Arms of Christ are on f. 1ᵛ and 2. They have not hitherto been published in colour from this manuscript.
21. Brit. Mus. Harl. MS. 2169. The Arms of Christ are on f. 66, 67. This was published by J. Foster in *Two Tudor Books of Arms,* op. cit., pp. 107, 109; also by Oswald Barron, as 'A Fifteenth Century Roll of Arms', in *The Ancestor,* vol. ix, pp. 176, 178.
22. Bibliothèque Nationale, Paris, MS. Fr. 14357; also Fr. 5939.
23. Brit. Mus. Harl. MS. 2999, f. 61v.
24. Cambridge Univ. Lib. MS. ii. 4. 26, translated and edited by T. H. White in *The Book of Beasts,* op. cit.
25. Brit. Mus. Add. MS. 19352, f. 124ᵛ.
26. The illustration is reproduced in S. Dufrenne, *L'illustration des psautiers grecs du moyen age* (Bibliothèques des Cahiers Archéologiques, Paris, 1966), pt i, Psautier du Mont Athos, Pantocrator no. 61, p. 30 (f. 109ᵛ). I am much indebted to Mr. John Goodall, F.S.A., for drawing my attention to this fascinating picture.
27. O. Shepard, *The Lore of the Unicorn* (London, 1930), p. 49. This is an essential book for any study of the beast. There are those who hold that Unicorns are little larger than goats, and in the Theodore Psalter and the Mount Athos Psalter they are about that size which makes this improbable legend a trifle more probable.
28. Coll. Arms MS. B. 29 f. 20-27 (*C.E.M.R.A.,* p. 10).
29. Fitzwilliam Museum MS. 297.
30. Col. Arms. MS. L. 14, pt i, f. 26.
31. Brit. Mus. Harl. MS. 2169, f. 32 (no. 2).
32. N. Moore, *The History of St. Bartholomew's Hospital* (London, 1918), ch. ii, p. 3.
33. Ibid, ii. 16.
34. *Cat. Seals Brit. Mus.* Birch vol. ii. op. cit., no. 1457.
35. Coll. Arms MSS. L. 8, f. 35 (Copy of Randle Holme's Book, so evidently in use by the reign of Henry VI); L. 10, f. 66 (early Tudor); D. 16, f. 2v, Visitation of Sussex 1662 (in this, which is an official record, he holds an Orb in the left hand and the Sword by the blade). These Arms are also depicted in several other MSS. in the College of Arms. The Arms at present used by the Bishops of Chichester have the Orb; but for some strange reason the figure is now usually blazoned as a 'Prester John sitting on a tombstone'.
36. Coll. Arms MS. Ulster Office Records, Visitations 1568, 1607, 1618, pp. 22-3.
37. Bodleian Library MS. Eng. Misc. d. 227, f. 104 : Nicholas Upton, *De Studio Militari,* tr. by John Blount in the early 16th century.
38. Coll. Arms MS. Vincent 187, f. 31 : Arms of Archbishops, Bishops, Abbeys

and Priories in England.

39. Coll. Arms MS. B. 22, f. 82ᵛ.
40. Brit. Mus. Harl. MS. 2169, f. 32. Printed by J. Foster, *Two Tudor Books of Arms,* op. cit., pt i, p. 38.
41. Coll. Arms MS. WZ, f. 117.
42. Coll. Arms MS. G.18, f. 59.
43. A. C. Fox-Davies, *The Book of Public Arms* (London and Edinburgh, 1915), p. 250.
44. Brit. Mus. Add. MS. 17006, f. 8 : 'Missale Romanum cum calendaris praemisssis'.
45. Brit. Mus. Harl. MS. 6163, f. 1 (no. 3); also in Coll. Arms MS. M. 10, f. 125 (no. 3).
46. Brit. Mus. Cotton MS. Nero C. iii, f. 40ᵛ : Nicholas Upton, *De officio militari et insigniis armorum,* written about 1446. Another good example is in Bodleian Library MS. Laud. Misc. 733, f. 42 : *Tractatus de armis,* by John de Bado Aureo, a copy made later in the same century, where the cross is flory. There are many other examples of these well-known arms.
47. *Froissart's Cronycles,* tr. out of the French by Sir John Bourchier, Lord Berners (reprinted Blackwell, Oxford, 1927), vol. i, pt ii, pp. 335-6.
48. *Sir Gawain and the Green Knight,* ed. J. R. R. Tolkein and E. V. Gordon; 2nd edn ed. Norman Davis (O.U.P., London, 1968), pp. 18, 95.
49. Coll. Arms MS. L. 10, f. 68.
50. Coll. Arms MS. Vincent 187, f. 53.
51. Coll. Arms MS. D. 13, f. 140.
52. *Cat. Seals Brit. Mus.* ed. W. de G. Birch (London), no 2213.
53. Coll. Arms MS. M. 3, f. 67.
54. Coll. Arms MS. Grants lxxx, f. 192-4. See also J. Bromley, *The Armorial Bearings of the Guilds of London* (Warne, London, 1960), pp. 168-72, which discusses the origins of these Arms, and the doubts which have been cast on the identification of the figure.
55. *Isaiah,* vi, 1-7.
56. Bodleian Library MS. Bodleian 968, f. 175.
57. Coll. Arms MS. Grants (i.e. 89) xxxix, f. 225.
58. *Genesis* iii, 24.
59. *Exodus,* xxv, 18-20; xxvi, 1, 31; xxxvii, 7-9.
60. *Ezekiel,* i, 4-28; x, 1-22.
61. Coll. Arms MS. I.78, f. 106-9.
62. Coll. Arms MS. K. 7, f. 97.
63. Brit. Mus. Royal MS. 19 B.XV, f. 21v, 37.
64. Bodleian Library MS. Canon Lit. 151, f. 7, 45v, 70, 94.
65. Bodleian Library MS. Canon Class, Lat. 274, f. lv.
66. Coll. Arms MS. 1st M. 5, f. 5v.
67. Brit. Mus. Add. MS. 18850, f. 228v.
68. The original is with the Drapers' Company. See also J. Bromley, *The Armorial Bearings of the Guilds of London,* op. cit., pp. 72-5.
69. Brit. Mus. Add. MS. 21926, f. 2.
70. Comte T. de Renesse, *Dictionnaire des figures héraldiques* (Brussels, 1895), pp. 345-51.
71. *Revelations,* xvi, 13-14.
72. Bodleian Library MS. Douce 180, f. 87-8.

CHAPTER 9. HUMAN MONSTERS IN HERALDRY

1. T. H. White, op. cit., Appendix (pp. 230-68), gives an invaluable appreciation of the growth and development of this early literature.
2. An excellent example of the 12th century bestiaries is Cambridge Univ. Lib. MS. Ii.4.26, translated and edited by T. H. White, op. cit.
3. Alexander Neckham, *De Naturis Rerum,* ed. T. Wright (Rolls Series 34, London, 1863).
4. Bartholomaeus Anglicus, *De Proprietatibus Rerum,* written in the 12th century and translated into Middle English by John of Trevisa in 1397. The English version, printed in London in 1582, is based on Trevisa's translation.
5. T. H. White, op. cit., p. 261.
6. Ibid, pp. 51-2.
7. For instance, Bodleian Library MS. E. Mus. 136, f. 20v; and Bodl. 764, f. 25. The latter makes a pair with British Museum Harley MS. 4751.
8. Randle Holme, *The Academy of Armory and Blazon* (Chester, 1688), bk ii, ch. x, p. 212.
9. Randle Holme, op. cit., ch. ix, p. 174.
10. Coll. Arms MS. 2nd L. 12, f. 13.
11. Coll. Arms MS. 1st M. 5, f. 5; also B. 23, f. 67.
12. Brit. Mus. Add. MS. 40742, f. 11.
13. Coll. Arms MS. 2nd M. 16, f. xvii.

14. Coll. Arms MS. Vincent 152, f. 99, 106.
15. Coll. Arms MS. E. 16 'Armes and Descents of the Nobility', f. 12v.
16. Coll. Arms MS. L. 14, f. 202.
17. Coll. Arms MS. I. 2, f. 95; there is another example on f. 96. It is curious that the Radcliffes had a Mantyger badge like Hastings, but also had a Bull's Head with a coronet round its neck as a crest.
18. Ibid, f. 112.
19. Coll. Arms MS. G. 5, f. 20.
20. Coll. Arms MS. D. 25(ii), f. 31v.
21. Sir William Pole, *Collections towards a Description of the County of Devon* (London, 1791), p. 499. See also Coll. Arms MS. Grants cxv, f. 288-9.
22. Randle Holme, op. cit., ch. x, p. 212.
23. Coll. Arms MS. 2. D. 5, f. 164; and C. 13, f. 197.
24. Coll. Arms MS. Old Grants 2, f. 172-3.
25. Coll. Arms MS. Misc. Grants i, f. 133; and C. 3, f. 26v.
26. Coll. Arms MS. K. 2, f. 102; also 2. D. 14, f. 14.
27. Coll. Arms MS. Grants xxix, f. 31-4.
28. Coll. Arms MS. Grants xxxi, f. 73-6.
29. Coll. Arms MS. Standards I. 2. f. 222.
30. Comte T. de Renesse, *Dictionnaire des figures héraldiques* (Brussels, 1895), vol. iii, p. 130.
31. Coll. Arms MS. Vincent 88, f. 139.
32. Gerard Legh, *The Accedens of Armory* (London, 1597), p. 112.
33. T. H. White, op. cit., p. 36.
34. Bartholomaeus Anglicus, *De Proprietatibus Rerum*, the Trevisa rendering (London, 1825), ch. xviii, p. 33.
35. Randle Holme, op. cit., ch. x, p. 204.
36. *Remembrancia City of London, 1579-1664* (London, 1878), p. 422.
37. Coll. Arms MS. Misc. Grants iv, f. 4; also EDN. 56, pt A, f. 183.
38. Coll. Arms MS. R. 21, f. 38.
39. Coll. Arms MS. C. 17, f. 16.
40. Lawrens Andrewe, *The noble lyfe and natures of man, of bestes, serpents, fowles and fisshes that be most knowen* (c. 1597). I am indebted to Mr. John Bunting for drawing my attention to this charming reference.
41. Bartholomaeus Anglicus, op. cit., ch. xviii, pp. 345-6.
42. Comte T. de Renesse, op. cit., vol. iii. pp. 363-6.
43. W. de G. Birch (ed), *Cat. Seals Brit. Mus*, op. cit. no. 7110.
44. Corpus Christi College, Cambridge, MS. 16, f. 32v.
45. Brit. Mus. Harley MS. 4379, f. 32v.
46. Brit. Mus. Add. MS. 24686, f. 13; and Bodleian Library, All Souls College MS. 6, f. 71.
47. Jean d'Arras, *Chronique de la princesse,* tr. and ed. A. K. Donald (E.E.T.S.).
48. *The Romans of Partenay, or of Lusignan; otherwise known as The Tale of Melusine* ed. Rev. W. W. Skeat (E.E.T.S.).
49. Sir E. Bysshe, *Nicolai Vptoni, De Studio Militari, etc.* (London, 1654), p. 174; also Bodleian Library MS. Eng. misc. d. 227 (John Blount's translation) and John Guillim. *A Display of Heraldrie* (London, 1610), p. 183.
50. Coll. Arms MSS. Box 21, no. 16 (Clare Roll 4714); and Vincent 225, f. 35; also W. de G. Birch, op. cit., no. 10809.
51. Coll. Arms MSS. L. 14, pt. 2, f. 249; and L. 8, f. 45.
52. Coll. Arms MSS. Vincent 152, f. 98; Vincent 16, f. 2v and I. 8, f. 45v.
53. Coll. Arms MSS. H. 18, f. 38v (Visitation of Dorset, 1531); 2 L. 6, f. 10v.
54. Coll. Arms MSS. K. 2, f. 102 (Visitation of Leicestershire 1681-3); 2 D. 14, f. 14.
55. Coll. Arms. MSS. EDN. 56, f. 57v; EDN Alphabet; also Society of Antiquaries MS. 443, no. 65 (Wriothesley's Roll of Grants, c. 1540).
56. Coll. Arms MS Grants ix, f. 237.
57. Coll. Arms MSS. D. 13, f. 83v; Old Grants R. 21, f. 43; Misc Grants 7, f. 506. Also John Guillim, *A Display of Heraldrie,* 5th edn. (London, 1679), p. 188.

CHAPTER 10. LIONS AND KINDRED CREATURES

1. L. Bouly de Lesdain. *Les plus anciennes armoiries Francaises,* Archives Héraldiques Suisse, vol. v (1897), pp. 69-79, 94-103.
2. E. P. Evans, *Animal Symbolism in Ecclesiastical Architecture* (London, 1896), p. 81.
3. Sir Thomas Browne, *Pseudodoxia Epidemica,* ed. G. Keynes as *The Works of Sir Thomas Browne,* vol. ii. p. 377.
4. T. D. Tremlett, *The Matthew Paris Shields, c. 1244-59,* in *Rolls of Arms, Henry III* (Harleian Society, 1967), p. 8.
5. Brit. Mus. Harl. MS. 2259, f. 69.
6. Brit. Mus. Harl. MS. 2169, f. 40; also College of Arms MS. M. 10, f. 67.
7. C. W. Scott-Giles, *Motley Heraldry* (Tabard, London, N.D.), p. 15.

8. W. de G. Birch, op. cit., nos. 12663, 12665.
9. Bowditch MS., f. 2.
10. W. de G. Birch, op. cit., no. 10684.
11. W. de G. Birch, op. cit., nos. 10717, 12247.
12. John Bossewell, *Works of Armorie* (London, 1597).
13. Coll. Arms MSS. Misc. Grants 5, f. 41; G. 10, f. 60; F. 1; f. 281v; EDN. 56 A, f. 135; also Queens Coll. MS. H. 39. 140, f. 82. I am indebted to Mr A. C. Cole, Windsor Herald, for capturing this beast for me.
14. H. Stanford London, 'The Ghost or Shadow as a Charge in Heraldry', *Archaeologia*, vol. xciii, pp. 125-49.
15. H. Stanford London, 'Glover's and Walford's Rolls', *Rolls of Arms, Henry III*, Soc. Antiqs., (London, 1967), pp. 119-20.
16. T. H. White, op. cit. pp. 14-15.
17. Coll. Arms MS. L. 14, pt 2, f. 380.
18. Col. Arms MS. D. 13, f. 2

CHAPTER 11. SOME FABULOUS BEASTS OF HERALDRY

1. John Bossewell, *Workes of Armorie* (London, 1597), p. lllv.
2. Brit. Mus. Add. MS. 40742, f. 2.
3. Coll. Arms MS. I.2, f. 82.
4. H. Stanford London, 'Minor Monsters VIII', The Alphyn and The Ypotry II, *Coat of Arms*, vol. iv. p. 140.
5. T. H. White, op. cit., pp. 18-29.
6. Coll. Arms MS. Vincent 183, f. 90.
7. Coll. Arms MS. Vincent 152, f. 98.
8. H. Stanford London, 'Minor Monsters II, The Bagwyn', *Coat of Arms*, vol. iii, pp. 142-3.
9. *The Works of Sir Thomas Browne*, op. cit., vol. ii, pp. 167-70.
10. T. H. White, op. cit., p. 33.
11. Coll. Arms MSS. Vincent 163, f. 181; and C. 38, f. 40.
12. Brit. Mus. Add. MS. 40742, f. 12.
13. Coll. Arms MSS. Vincent 152, f. 104; and E. 16, f. 56.
14. Coll. Arms MSS. WZ, f. 207; Vincent 88, f. 21; and I.2, f. 60.
15. H. Stanford London, 'Minor Monsters III, The Calygreyhound', *Coat of Arms*, vol. iii, pp. 179-81, discusses this beast in more detail.
16. Sir William St. John Hope, *The Last Testament and Inventory of John de Vere, 13th Earl of Oxford*, *Archaeologia*, vol. 66, pp. 284, 327, 328, 337, 340, 341, 348.
17. Coll. Arms MS. I.2, f. 134.
18. Coll. Arms MS. 'Concerning Officers of Arms, etc.', f. 34.
19. Douet d'Arcq, *Sceaux des Archives*, no. 3458.
20. John Bossewell, op. cit., p. 66.
21. Brit. Mus. Harl. MS 2169, f. 45v; and Coll. Arms MS. L. 8, f. 41.
22. Coll. Arms MS. C. 7, f. 114.
23. Brit. Mus. Harl. MS. 6563.
24. Coll. Arms MS. Grants xc, f. 252.
25. Bodleian Library MS. Laud. misc. 733, f. 7v.
26. Coll. Arms, MS. I.2, f. 64.
27. Coll. Arms MS. L. 14, f. 191.
28. Coll. Arms MS. 2. H. 5, f. 51.
29. Coll. Arms MS. E. 12, f. 42v.
30. Coll. Arms MS. Grants cxxix, f. 316.
31. Coll. Arms MSS. Vincent 152, f. 103; and L. 14, f. 190.
32. Coll. Arms MS. I.2, f. 58. See also Edward Richardson, *The Monumental Effigies and Tombs in Elford Church, Staffordshire* (London, 1852).
33. Coll. Arms MS. G. 8, f. 40v.
34. Coll. Arms MSS. L. 2, f. 88; and Misc. Grants 5, f. 219.
35. E. J. Jones, op. cit.
36. Coll. Arms MS. Vincent 183, f. 90.
37. Coll. Arms MSS. Grants cxxii, f. 69.
38. T. H. White, op. cit., p. 48.
39. Coll. Arms MS. 2. L. 12, f. 13.
40. John Guillim, op. cit., p. 179.
41. Coll. Arms MS. I.2, f. 29.
42. H. Stanford London, 'Minor Monsters IV, The Pantheon', *Coat of Arms*, vol. iii, pp. 220-5.
43. Coll. Arms MS. Misc. Grants iv, f. 37v.
44. Coll. Arms MSS. I.2, f. 63; and H. 20, f. 39.
45. Coll. Arms MS. 2. L. 12, f. 15v.
46. T. H. White, op. cit., p. 52.
47. Coll. Arms MS. 'Concerning Officers of Arms, etc.' f. 34.
48. C. W. Scott-Giles, *Shakespeare's Heraldry* (London, 1950, reprinted Heraldry

Today 1971), pp. 115, 164.

49. Coll. Arms MS. Vincent 152, f. 92v.
50. T. H. White, op. cit., p. 61.
51. H. Stanford London, 'Minor Monsters V, The Theow, Thoye or Thos', *Coat of Arms,* vol. iii. pp. 268-72.
52. Coll. Arms MS. Vincent 152, f. 107.
53. Brit. Mus. Harl. MS. 5504, f. 121v.
54. Coll. Arms MSS, Misc. Grants iii, f. 47; and Grants ii, f. 485.
55. *The Bestiary of Guillaume le Clerc,* tr. G. C. Druce (privately printed, Ashford, 1936).
56. E. P. Evans, op. cit., pp. 95-109.
57. T. H. White, op. cit., p. 20.
58. Brit. Mus. Add. MS. 40851.
59. Brit. Mus. Cotton MS. Nero C.iii.
60. J. H. Stevenson, *Heraldry in Scotland* (Glasgow, 1914), vol. ii, p. 397.
61. Coll. Arms MS. I.2, f. 133.
62. H. Stanford London, 'Minor Monsters I, The Yale', *Coat of Arms,* vol. iii, pp. 90-2.
63. Brit. Mus. Add. MS. 18850, f. 256v.
64. Brit. Mus. Add. MS. 40742, f. 10. See also H. Stanford London, 'Minor Monsters VIII, The Alphyn and the Ypotryll', *Coat of Arms,* vol. iv. p. 141.
65. Coll. Arms MSS. G. 7, f. 4; Misc. Grants i, ff. 83-4; and Grants ii, f. 639. See also Wagner, *Heralds and Heraldry* op. cit., p. 163; and H. Stanford London, *College of Arms Monograph* (London, 1963), pp. 131, 264.
66. Coll. Arms MS. Vincent 183, f. 71v.

CHAPTER 12. EAGLES AND FABULOUS BIRDS

1. L. Bouly de Lesdain, op. cit.
2. Aspilogia II, *Rolls of Arms.* Henry III, ed. Tremlett and London (O.U.P. 1967).
3. Coll. Arms MS. 2nd. L. 12.
4. Sir E. Bysshe, *Nicolai Uptoni. De Studio Militari* (London, 1654), pp. 1-259.
5. Bartholomeus Anglicus, *De proprietatibus rerum,* tr. John de Trevisa (edn. Thomas Berthelet, London 1535), pp. 163-4.
6. T. S. R. Boase, *Castles & Churches of the Crusading Kingdoms* (London, 1967), p. 104.
7. Cambridge Univ. Lib. MS. Ee.iv.20, f. 161v.
8. *Aspilogia* II, pp. 15, 45, 60, 67, 68, 72.
9. *Aspilogia* II, p. 31, 68, 76, 77.
10. Bodleian Library MS. Laud. Misc. 733, f. 8.
11. Coll. Arms MS. I. 36 f. 31.
12. Coll. Arms MS. I.40, f. 42.
13. L. Bouly de Lesdain, op. cit., p. 97.
14. L. Bouly de Lesdain, op. cit., p. 72.
15. *Aspilogia* II, p. 178.
16. L. Bouly de Lesdain, op. cit.
17. Coll. Arms MS., 2nd L. 12, f. 26v.
18. Bartholomew Anglicus, op. cit. p. 172.
19. E. P. Evans, op. cit., pp. 145-7. See also M. D. Anderson, 'History and Imagery' in *British Churches* (London, 1971), pp. 65, 249.
20. Bartholomeus Anglicus, op. cit., pp. 171, 333v.
21. *The Works of Sir Thomas Browne,* op. cit. vol. ii, pp. 189-91.
22. Comte T. de Renesse, op cit., vol. ii. pp. 65-92.
23. L. Bouly de Lesdain, op cit., p. 78.
24. Coll. Arms MS. Vincent 165, f. 131.
25. Cambridge Univ. Lib. MS. Ee.iv.20., f. 161v.
26. C. W. Scott-Giles, *The Siege of Caerlaverock* (Heraldry Soc., 1960), p. 13.
27. E. J. Jones, *Medieval Heraldry.*
28. Coll. Arms MS. Vincent 169, f. 30.
29. Sir A. Wagner, *Heralds and Heraldry,* op. cit., pp. 79-80.
30. Coll. Arms MS. Vincent 169, f. 31-2.
31. Coll. Arms MS. Grants, i, f. 417.
32. Coll. Arms MS. 2nd. C. 24, f. 201.
33. Coll. Arms MS. Grants lxxiii, f. 72.
34. Coll. Arms MS. Grants cxxv, f. 118.
35. T. H. White, op. cit., p. 125.
36. Bartholomeus Anglicus, op. cit., p. 169v.
37. *The Works of Sir Thomas Browne,* op. cit., vol. ii, pp. 191-2.
38. Coll. Arms MSS L. 14 (pt. ii), f. 27-8, 383; and I. 2, f. 15.
39. Coll. Arms MS.
40. Coll. Arms MS, I. 2, f. 55.
41. H. S. London, 'The Tragopan', *Coat of Arms,* vol. iii, pp. 311-2.
42. Coll. Arms MS. EDN. 56, f. 40; Brit. Mus. Add. MS. 46354, f. 236; and Soc.

Antics. MS.443.
43. L. Bouly de Lesdain, op. cit., p. 74.
44. Chrétien de Troyes, op. cit., p. 343.
45. G. J. Brault, *Early Blazon* (London, 1972), pp. 241-2.
46. Cambridge Univ., Lib. MS. Ee. i.v. 20, f. 161v.
47. E. J. Jones, *Medieval Heraldry*, op. cit. p. 47.
48. Bodleian Library MS. Eng. Misc. d. 227, f. 174; John Blount's translation of Nicholas Upton.
49. Brit. Mus. Add. MS. 42130, f. 202v.

CHAPTER 13. DRAGONS AND FABULOUS REPTILES

1. Bartholomew Anglicus, op. cit., 318. See also T. H. White, op. cit. and in particular his footnote on p. 169.
2. *Mirror of the World,* tr. 1480 by William Caxton from the French *Image du Monde* and printed by him 1481 (E.E.T.S., E.S. 110), p. 79. I am indebted to Mr. John Bunting for this reference.
3. John Guillim, op. cit., p. 260.
4. *The Works of Sir Thomas Browne,* op. cit., vol. iii, pp. 174-5.
5. Coll. Arms MS. I. 2, f. 91, 107; and Brit. Mus. Cotton MS. Cleopatra C.v, f. 62v and f. 59v.
6. Coll. Arms MS. Misc. Grants iv. f. 37v.
7. Coll. Arms MS. Grants ii, f. 511.
8. G.E.C., *Complete Peerage,* under this name.
9. Coll. Arms MS. E. 16, f. 38v.
10. Coll. Arms MS. I. 37, f. 312-13.
11. E. P. Evans, *Animal Symbolism in Ecclesiastical Architecture* (London, 1896), p. 163-70.
12. Vincent of Beauvais, *Speculum Naturale,* xxi, 29.
13. T. H. White, op. cit., pp. 165-7.
14. Bartholomew Anglicus, op. cit., p. 327.
15. W. A. Phillips, 'Dragon', *Encyclopaedia Britannica,* 11th edn., vol. viii, pp. 466-8. His article well repays reading.
16. F. Jones, Wales Herald Extraordinary, *The Princes and Principality of Wales* (Cardiff, 1969), pp. 168-9. I am most grateful to my brother Herald for much of my information on Dragons in early Britain and Wales.
17. Geoffrey of Monmouth, *History of the Kings of Britain,* tr. S. Evans (Everyman Library, no. 577), pp. 170-2.
18. A. W. Vivian-Neal, *The Dragon of Wessex,* Somerset & Dorset Notes & Queries, vol. xxii, pp. 244-9 – a most useful article on the subject.
19. L. Bouly de Lesdain, op. cit., p. 75; also Bibliothèque Nationale, Paris, no. B. 51244.
20. L. Blancard, *Iconographie des sceaux et bulles . . . . des archives departmentales des Bouches-du-Rhone* (Paris, 1860), p. 68, plate 33, nos. 2 and 3.
21. W. A. Phillips, op. cit., p. 467.
22. 'The Barons' Letter to the Pope', *The Ancestor,* vol. vi, p. 185; vol. vii, p. 248; vol. viii, p. 100.
23. Coll. Arms MS. Vincent 425, f. lv; also W. de G. Birch (ed.), *Cat. Seals Brit. Mus.,* no. 11211.
24. Bodleian Library MS. Laud. Misc. 733, f. 7v.
25. E. J. Jones, op. cit., pp. 33-4.
26. N. H. Nicolas (later Sir Harris Nicholas), *A Roll of Arms of the Reign of Edward the Second.*
27. Musee Jacquemart-André MS., 'Heures du Marechal Boucicault'.
28. W. de G. Birch, op. cit., vol. ii, no. 5559.
29. Coll. Arms MS. I. 2, f. 2 and 13.
30. Coll. Arms MS. Vincent 172, f. 27.
31. Coll. Arms MS. 2 C.1, f. 370v.
32. Coll. Arms MS. Grants lxxiv, f. 14-15.
33. Coll. Arms MS. Vincent 172, f. 154v.
34. Coll. Arms MS. Grants vii, f. 238-40.
35. Coll. Arms MS. Grants xcv, f. 9.
36. Bartholomeus Anglicus, op. cit., p. 310v.
37. *The Bestiary of Guillaume le Clerc,* op. cit., p. 79.
38. W. H. St. John Hope, *The Stall Plates of the Knights of the Order of the Garter, 1348-1485* (Westminster, 1901), plate lxxii.
39. Coll. Arms MS Vincent 172, f. 135v.
40. Coll. Arms MSS. EDN. 57, f. 134; and Misc. Grants iv, f. 67v.

Glossary
of Heraldic Terms

Achievement: The full armorial honours of an armiger, e.g. shield, crest, wreath, mantling, and helm, with supporters as appropriate.

Addorsed: Placed back to back, e.g. as in the attributed arms of Uther Pendragon.

Alerion: Eagle displayed, but without beak or feet.

Annulet: A ring.

Argent: Silver, usually depicted as white in heraldic art. Abbreviation is '*a*' or '*arg*'.

Armed: When the teeth, tusks, horns, or claws of a beast, whether real or fabulous, are of a different colour from its body, it is blazoned as 'armed' of such a metal or colour. Similarly with birds of prey, but other birds are blazoned as 'beaked and membered'.

Armiger: One who is entitled to heraldic arms.

Armory: Now usually comprised within the general term 'heraldry', it refers more specifically to the art and science of the devices borne on the shield and its accompaniments.

Arms: Strictly the devices painted on the shield, it now tends to be used more loosely.

Attired: When the antlers of a stag or hart are of a different colour from its body, it is blazoned as 'attired' of such a metal or colour.

Augmentation: An honourable addition to arms, granted for special services.

Azure: Blue. No particular shade is laid down and the artist can interpret it fairly freely, so long as it is recognisably blue at a glance. Abbreviation is 'az' or 'B'.

Badge: A distinct device, which is never borne on a shield or as a crest – although many of the fifteenth and sixteenth century badges were later also used as crests or supporters. Usually employed as a mark of ownership, or worn on the liveries of retainers.

Banner: A flag borne on a lance or staff. Originally rectangular in shape, of greater height than width, it later became square. It was the distinctive flag of a knight banneret and indicated his military rank.

Bar: One of the ordinaries, being a horizontal band, narrower than a Fess. Usually used when two or three are charged upon a shield.

Barry: When more than three Bars, the shield is said to be 'Barry' of so many bars (now always an even number) of alternating tinctures.

206

Base: The lower part of the shield.

Bend: One of the ordinaries, being a diagonal band from the dexter chief to the sinister base of the shield. The opposite diagonal is the Bend Sinister.

Bendlet: A diminutive of the Bend.

Bendy: Divided bendwise into an even number of Bendlets, usually more than three.

Bezant: A gold roundel, so named from the gold coin of Byzantium.

Billet: An oblong, rectangular charge of any tincture.

Billety: When the field or a charge, or crest, or supporter is powdered with Billets.

Blazon: The technical description in words of armorial bearings.

Bordure: One of the ordinaries, being a narrow border around the edge of the field.

Brisure: A mark of Cadency.

Caboshed: The head of an animal such as a bull, stag or deer, depicted full-faced without any neck being visible.

Cadency: A system of heraldic distinctions for differentiating the arms of cadet branches of a family.

Canting Arms: Armorial devices or compositions which allude in a punning way to the bearer's name.

Canton: A rectangular addition to a shield of arms, smaller in size than the Quarter and usually in the dexter chief, which is placed over any existing charges which may be on the original arms.

Cap of Estate, or Cap of Maintenance: An early symbol of high rank, originally borne by princes and peers of the realm. Subsequently more widely used, but still uncommon.

Charge: Anything, whether living or inanimate, placed or charged upon the field of a coat of arms.

Checky, Chequy: The field, or a charge, coloured in small squares of alternate metal and colour, like a chessboard.

Chevron: One of the ordinaries, like an inverted 'V'.

Chevronel: The diminutive of the Chevron.

Chevronny: Divided chevronwise into an even number of chevronels, of alternative tinctures.

Chief: One of the ordinaries, being the upper part of the shield; also used to indicate the position of a charge, e.g. 'and in chief two . . . .'.

Cinquefoil: A conventionalised flower of five equal petals. In early heraldry usually synonymous with the rose and often so called.

Close: When the wings of a bird are depicted as folded shut against the body. Also applied to a helm with the visor closed.

Coat of Arms: Originally the linen coat worn over the armour on which was painted the armorial device of the wearer, and often called in medieval terms the 'coat armour'. Nowadays synonymous with the shield of arms.

Combatant: When two creatures, especially Lions and the more ferocious beasts, are depicted facing each other and rampant, with outstretched paws as if fighting. Creatures in more pacific poses shown face to face are blazoned as 'respectant'.

Compartment: The support, often drawn as a grassy mound, on which the supporters stand.

Compony: Term used to describe a Bordure divided into squares of alternative tinctures.

Cotise: The smallest diminutive of the Bend, Fess, Pale, or Chevron, and almost always accompanying them on both sides, e.g. 'a Bend cotised'.

Couchant: Term used for blazoning an animal lying down with its head held up; but a Stag or Hart thus is blazoned as 'lodged'.

Counter-Changed: When the field is party of two different tinctures, and a charge superimposed over the whole field has the colours reversed: e.g. 'Per pale argent and sable a Chevron counterchanged'.

Couped: Term used to describe a head or limb of a creature which is cut off cleanly at its base (cf. 'erased' below).

Courant: Running.

Cowed: When a beast is shown with its tail between its legs.

Crescent: This is self-evident, but in armory the points are always shown pointing upwards. Otherwise it must be blazoned as a Moon decrescent (when waning and the horns point to the sinister) or increscent (when waxing and the horns point to the dexter).

Crest: The device which is set upon the helm. It is quite wrong to apply this term to the coat of arms or shield. Around the base of the Crest (originally to conceal the join) is placed a wreath of the colours (the two, or sometimes more, principal metals and colours of the arms); sometimes instead of a wreath there is a Crest Coronet, and more rarely the Crest is set upon a Cap of Estate.

Cross: One of the ordinaries and invariably with the arms perpendicular and horizontal; when the arms are diagonal it is a 'Saltire' (q.v.). The Cross can be differenced in an almost limitless variety of ways, by making its outline indented, engrailed, raguly, etc., or by terminating the arms flory, moline, potent, and so on. The standard text-books on heraldry usually devote several pages to this subject, and the diminutives of the Cross, such as the Crosslet.

Crusilly: Powdered with Crosslets.

Dance: A zigzag Bar with fairly wide indentations, hence 'Dancetty'. Not to be confused with 'Indented' when the indentations are much smaller and consequently more numerous.

Demi: Usually the upper half of any creature, shown from the waist upwards; but sometimes used for inanimate objects.

Dexter: The right side. When applied to a shield it refers to that part which would be towards the right side of the man carrying it, thus the portion on the viewer's left.

Difference: Differencing marks introduced into the basic family arms to distinguish one cadet branch from another.

Displayed: When an eagle or other bird is depicted with its belly to the viewer and with both wings spread out on either side.

Embattled: When a partition line or the outline of an ordinary is shown like the battlements of a castle.

Engrailed: A partition line or an ordinary shown with semicircular indents with the points outwards.

Erased: Term used to describe the head or limb of a creature which has a ragged base, as if torn off.

Erect: Upright.

Ermine: One of the furs; white, powdered with small black Ermine tails or 'spots', drawn in various conventional ways.

Ermines: The reverse of Ermine.

Erminous: A gold fur powdered with black Ermine tails. The reverse is known as 'Pean'.

Escutcheon of Pretence: A small shield placed in the centre of the husband's shield to indicate that his wife is an heraldic heiress.

Estoile: A star, normally of six wavy rays. Not to be confused with the Mullet.

Fess: One of the ordinaries, being a broad horizontal band across the middle of the shield.

Fess-Point: The middle point on the shield. By the same analogy a charge depicted horizontally is said to be 'in fess'.

Field: The basic surface of the shield on which the charges are placed. When blazoning, the field is always stated first.

Fimbriated: Edged.

Fitchy: With the lower end of a Cross pointed.

Fleur de Gley: Originally the yellow Iris, and applied in early heraldic treatises, such as *De Heraudie,* to the gold flowers in the French royal arms, but they could also be of any tincture. The term is not met with after c. 1300.

Fleur de Lys: Originally the white Lily, and applied in early heraldic treatises to the white flowers attributed to the Virgin Mary, but later the term was used also for the flowers in the French royal arms, and subsequently to any conventionalised flower of this form and of any tincture.

Flory: Embellished with Fleur de Lys, or powdered with them.

Formy: Of a Cross, with the ends of the arms considerably wider than at their junctions.

Fret: A Saltire interlaced with a Mascle. When the whole field or charge is covered by narrow interlacing diagonal bands, it is 'Fretty'.

Fusil: A Lozenge with the top and bottom elongated. When the field is covered with Fusils it is 'Fusilly'.

Garb: A wheatsheaf.

Gobony: Synonym for Compony.

Gonfanon: A small lance-flag, originally with small streamers from the fly, but also applied loosely to the knights lance-pennon.

Gorged: With a collar, of any kind, round its neck, e.g. the Coronet around the neck of the Unicorn supporter of the Scottish royal arms.

Guardant: When a creature, such as a Lion, is looking at the spectator.

Gules: Red. The shade is not laid down and can vary, so long as it is unmistakably red. Abbreviation is 'gu'.

Gyron: One of the ordinaries, being a triangular sector of the shield, formed by half a Bend line and half a Fess line meeting at the middle of the shield. When this is continued all the way round it is 'Gyronny'.

Hurt: A blue roundel.

Impaled: Said of two coats of arms shown side by side in the same shield.

Indented: When the edge is composed of short straight-sided teeth, or serrations; also used for partition lines.

Invected: The converse of engrailed.

Jessant de Lys: When a Fleur de Lys is issuing from an object, such as a Leopard's Head.

Label: Consists of a narrow band across the top of the shield with three or five tags pendant from it. Used as a mark of cadency for the eldest son during his father's lifetime, and sometimes in the early Middle Ages as a permanent mark of difference.

Lodged: Term used for a beast of the chase when couchant.

Lozenge: One of the subordinaries, being a diamond-shaped figure. When the field or a charge is completely covered with lozenges of alternative tinctures, it is 'Lozengy'.

Mantling: Conventionalised drapery hanging down the back of the Helm, from below the Crest-wreath, and nowadays usually depicted as carried down on either side of the shield. Sometimes called the Lambrequin.

Maunch: An early type of medieval lady's sleeve.

Membered: Technical term for the depiction of the legs and beak of a bird.

Mullet or Molet: Originally intended to represent a spur rowel, and always drawn with five points.

Naiant: Swimming.

Nebuly: With the party line or outline of an ordinary more exaggerated than when 'wavy', rather like the outline of clouds.

Nowed: Knotted, usually of a creature's tail, or a snake.

Ogress: A black roundel.

Or: Gold. Can be depicted as gold or yellow.

Ordinary: The basic geometrical charges used in arms, usually divided into the (honourable) ordinaries and the subordinaries. An ordinary of arms is a collection of arms arranged according to the charges thereon.

Pale: One of the ordinaries, being a perpendicular band down the middle of the shield. If the whole surface is divided in this way with alternately tinctured bands it is 'Paly'.

Passant: Walking, and always depicted side-view.

Paty: Synonymous with Formy.

Pile: One of the ordinaries, being a wedge-shaped figure normally issuing from the top of the shield; it can, however, issue from the sides or base.

Plate: A silver roundel.

Proper: When a creature, flower, or tree is depicted in its natural and proper colours.

Quarter: The quarter part of a shield. Thus, when more than one different coat of arms is marshalled on a shield, through descent from heraldic heiresses, it was placed 'quarterly'. Later the term was applied to any such 'quartering', however many were marshalled together.

Quatrefoil: A conventionalised four-petalled flower, which can be of any tincture.

Rampant: Term used to blazon a Lion when standing erect with the left foot on the ground and the right leg raised, the left forefoot partly raised and the right forefoot fully raised and clawing ferociously.

Reguardant: Term for a beast looking backwards over its shoulder.

Respectant: Face to face.

Sable: Black. Abbreviation is 'sa'.

Salient: Leaping or springing.

Saltire: One of the ordinaries composed of two crossed diagonal arms, like the letter X.

Segreant: Term used for a Griffin when rampant.

Sejant: Sitting.

Semée: Term to describe a field strewn or powdered with small charges, e.g. Fleurs de Lys.

Sinister: The side of a shield towards the left of the man carrying it, thus to the right when viewed from in front.

Sinople: Green in French armory.

Statant: Standing.

Supporters: The human, natural, or fabulous creatures which stand on either side of a shield of arms and support it.

Torteau: A red roundel.

Trefoil: Three-leaved charge with a short stalk.

Tressure: A narrow bordure close inside the edge of the shield, usually found double and, in the case, for instance, of the royal arms of Scotland, enriched with Fleurs de Lys and blazoned as a 'Double Tressure flory counter flory'.
Tricorporate: Having three bodies conjoined to one head.

Undy: Barry wavy.

Vair: Used in the early Middle Ages as a fur lining for cloaks, it became one of the conventionalised furs of heraldry. It was depicted as alternatively white and blue.
Vert: Green. Abbreviation is 'vt'.
Vested: Clothed.
Voided: Term for a charge with most of the centre removed.
Volant: Flying.

Preliminary List
of Medieval
Heraldic Terms

The definition of a heraldic treatise is not quite so self-evident as one might think. Some, like *De Heraudie*, the *Tractatus de Armis*, or John's *Treatise*, are straightforward and confine themselves mainly to the technicalities and practice of armory. Others, like the *L'Arbre de Batailles* or the *Faits d'Armes et de Chevalerie*, are essentially treatises on the laws and art of war, with only a fairly short section on armory. Then there are those that form parts of treatises devoted largely to nobility, ceremonies and the duties of heralds. For the purpose of this provisional list I have included all works containing a reasonably detailed section on armory which have so far come to my attention. I have not here attempted to give references to manuscript copies or printed editions, other than the most important or accessible, as this must be a task for another day. The period covered is roughly 1300–1500, after which the printed works on armory take over. It will be seen that the heraldic treatises produced in other European countries during the Middle Ages are poorly represented, but I hope one day to rectify this and produce a more comprehensive catalogue, which will also include the many other French and English treatises of an armorial nature which have not been represented here as they require further study.

1. "DE HERAUDIE"
    c. 1300, Anglo-Norman.
    Authorship unknown. Included in the *St Alban's Formulary*, compiled shortly after 1382, but internal evidence suggests it was copied from a manuscript of about 1300.
    Complete edition by Dr Ruth J. Dean, 'An Early Treatise on Heraldry in Anglo-Norman', published in *Romance Studies in Memory of Edward Billings Ham,* ed. U. T. Holmes (California State College Publications No. 2, 1967), pp. 21–9.

2. *Bartolo di Sasso Ferrato (Saxoferrato),* 1315–59?
    DE INSIGNIIS ET ARMIS
    c. 1355, Latin.
    Complete edition by Prof. Evan J. Jones, *Medieval Heraldry* (Cardiff, 1943), Appendix I, pp. 221–52, with valuable notes on manuscript sources and other editions.

212

3. *Honoré Bonet, c. 1340–c. 1407*
   L'ARBRE DE BATAILLES (THE TREE OF BATTLES)
   c. 1382–7, French.

Treatise on the laws and art of war, in four parts and a total of 170 short chapters, those on armory being chapters 124–9.

Best English edition with full translation of the text and critical introduction by Prof. G. W. Coopland, *The Tree of Battles of Honoré Bonet* (Liverpool University Press, 1949), with useful references to manuscript sources.

Two splendid manuscript copies are Brit. Mus. Royal MS. 20.C.viii, probably the oldest extant copy and possibly that presented by Bonet to Jean, Duc de Berry, shortly before 1394; and Brit. Mus. Royal MS. 15.E.vi, part 10.

4. *Francois de Foveis* (des Fosses)
   DE PICTURIS ARMORUM
   Mid-fourteenth century.

Known only through references to the author by John de Bado Aureo and in John's Treatise. The indications are that he was probably a Frenchman.

5. *John de Bado Aureo* (possibly Bishop Sion Trevor, but identification not proven)
   TRACTATUS DE ARMIS
   c. 1395, Latin

His treatise is devoted entirely to armory and begins with the origin of arms and the tinctures of heraldry, followed by the beasts, birds, and fish used in arms and their significance. This is followed by twelve kinds of crosses, quarterly shields, and the ordinaries, ending with a short discussion of the English royal arms.

Full text printed by Sir Edward Bysshe in *Nicolai Uptoni; de Studio Militari Libri Quatuor. Johan de Bado Aureo Tractatus de Armis. Henrici Spelmanni Aspilogia,* (London 1654) Part 2. As all the extant copies vary somewhat in detail, it is difficult at present to determine which text is closest to the original. Prof. E. J. Jones, *Medieval Heraldry* (Cardiff, 1943), pp. 95–143 and 144–212, prints two texts of the *Tractatus de Armis,* and in his most valuable introduction deduces that John de Bado Aureo was probably the pseudonym of John (Siôn) Trevor, Bishop of St Asaph. See D.N.B. p. vii, 220.

Many manuscript copies were made from the end of the fourteenth century to the sixteenth century. One of the most delightful is Bodleian Library MS. Laud. misc. 733, a late fifteenth century translation into English by an unknown scribe and beautifully illustrated with marginal paintings of the beasts, birds, and other creatures of heraldry mentioned in the text, and coloured shields of arms illustrating the ordinaries, etc.

6. *Bishop John (Siôn) Trevor* (d. 1410)
   LLYFR DYSGREAD ARFAU
   c. 1405–10?, Welsh.

Professor Evan J. Jones in the Introduction to his *Medieval Heraldry* has identified the author of the *Llyfr Arfau.* As this treatise is almost a verbatim translation of the *Tractaus de Armis* (although there are a few significant variations), he has suggested most persuasively that John Trevor is the same man as John de Bado Aureo, and has adduced strong reasons for it; but since there is still a lingering doubt we should, for the time being, regard this as a separate treatise. Professor Jones gives full source references in his book.

7. *Christine de Pisan* (Pezano), 1364–1429.
   LE LIVRE DES FAITS D'ARMES ET DE CHEVALERIE
   c. 1400, French.

Treatise on the laws and art of war, based partly on Vegetius, Frontinus, Bonet and others, in four books, comprising one hundred and thirteen chapters in all, those on armory being in Book IV, chapters 15–17, and lifted straight from Bonet.

Translated into English by William Caxton as *The Book of Fayttes of Armes and of Chyualrye,* and printed in 1490. The best definitive edition of this is by A. T. P. Byles, with a valuable critical introduction and detailed discussion of manuscript sources and editions (*E.E.T.S., vol. 189, 1932*).

8. *Jean Courtois,* Sicily Herald, d. *c.* 1436.
   LE BLASON DES COULEURS
   c. 1416–36, French.

In his Prologue the author describes himself as Sicily Herald of Alphonso, King of Aragon, Sicily, Valence, Majorca, Corsica and Sardinia, Count of Barcelona, etc., and says that he was then and had for a long time been domiciled at Mons in Hainault. His work was compiled with the 'l'ayde de Dieu, de tous messeigneurs princes, cheveliers, escuyers, et de tous mes frères compaignons, roys d'armes et héraulx'. He describes his treatise as being 'pour apprendre à blasonner toutes armes selon les couleurs et leurs propriétez, et aussi la nouvelle manière de blasonner quant aux noms des couleurs et des métaulx, et celle de maintenant'.

Complete text printed by Hippolyte Cocheris, *Le blason des couleurs en armes, livrees et devises par Sicille herault d'Alphonse V, roi d'Aragon,* (Paris 1860), with a useful introduction.

9. MOWBRAY'S FRENCH TREATISE
   Early fifteenth century, French.

Authorship unknown, but evidently a herald; possibly compiled during the English occupation of Northern France.

Coll. Arms MS. 2nd L.12 is the only known copy. See also Sir A. Wagner, *C.E.M.R.A.,* p. 66, under Bruce Roll; also *Aspilogia II,* Additions and Corrections to C.E.M.R.A., p. 269.

10. BANYSTER'S FRENCH TREATISE
   Early fifteenth century, French.

Authorship unknown, but clearly a herald; probably compiled in northern France during the English occupation.

Coll. Arms MS. M.19 is the only known copy. See also Sir A. Wagner, *Heralds and Heraldry in the Middle Ages* (O.U.P., 2nd edn., 1956), pp. 57–8.

11. *Clément Prinsault*
   (a) PRINSAULT'S TREATISE
   Early fifteenth century, French.

There are at least five manuscript copies of this treatise in the Bibliothèque Nationale, Paris, but only Bibl. Nat. Paris MS.Fr.5936 bears the dedication to Jacques, the son of Bernard d'Armagnac, Duc de Nemours and Comte of La Marche, in which Prinsault claims authorship, although Douet d'Arcq questions this.

   (b) PRINSAULT'S TREATISE (AUGMENTED VERSION)
There is at least one manuscript copy in the British Museum, Lansdowne MS. 882, and four in the Bibliothèque Nationale, Paris, of which one has been published by L. C. Douet d'Arcq, *Un Traité du blason du XV siècle,* in Revue Archéologique, 1st series, vol XV (1859), pp. 257–74, 321–42.

   (c) PRINSAULT'S TREATISE (PASSION VERSION)
At least four manuscript copies are in the Bibliothèque Nationale, Paris, including Fr.5939 and Fr.14357.

12. THE NORMANDY TREATISE
Fifteenth century, French.

Authorship unknown. Typical of the heraldic treatises of this period, containing much miscellaneous matter which would come within the scope of a herald's duties.

Bibliothèque Nationale, Paris, MS. Fr.5930, the armorial portion being at f. 33–63.

13. *Merlin de Cordeboeuf*
CORDEBOEUF'S TREATISE
Mid-fifteenth century, French.

Similar to the last, with a smaller armorial content. Bibl. Nat. Paris, MS. Fr. 5241.

14. L'ART HERALDIQUE
1441, French.

Authorship unknown. Similar to the last, but arranged somewhat differently. Bibl. Nat. Paris, MS. Fr.1983.

15. *Gilles le Bouvier,* Berry King of Arms
LE BOUVIER'S TREATISE
c. 1450, French.

Bibl. Nat. Paris, MS. Fr. 5931. Edited by M. Vallet (de Viriville), *Armorial de France, Angleterre, Ecosse, Allemagne, Italia, et autres puissances, composé vers 1450 par Gilles le Bouvier, dit Berry, premier roi d'armes Charles VII, roi de France* (Paris, 1866).

16. *Diego de Valera* (Jacques de Valere)
VALERA'S TREATISE
Fifteenth century, Spanish.

Brit. Mus. Add MS. 18798 is a French translation by Hugues de Salue, prevost de Fournes.

17. *Nicholas Upton, c. 1400–1457*
    (a) DE OFFICIO MILITARI ET INSIGNIIS ARMORUM, generally known as DE STUDIO MILITARI
1446, Latin.

First published in 1654 by Sir Edward Bysshe, op. cit., Part I. See also Prof. Evan J. Jones, op. cit., pp. xxiii–xxiv; F. P. Barnard, *The Essential Portions of Nicholas Upton's De Studio Militari, translated by John Blount* (Oxford 1931); and Prof G. W. Coopland, op. cit., p. 22–3.

This was a very popular treatise on the laws and practice of war and on armory, and many manuscript copies were made in the fifteenth century and later. One of the most splendid is Brit. Mus. Cotton MS. Nero C.iii, and one of the most delightful is Bodleian Library MS. Eng. misc. d.227, John Blount's translation into English *c.* 1500.

    (b) DE OFFICIO MILITARI : BADDESWORTH'S VERSION
1458, Latin.

Brit. Mus. Add. MS. 30946; Coll. Arms MS. Vinc. 444. Transcribed and rearranged extensively by a certain Baddesworth, who has not yet been identified. Many copies of this version are also known.

18. *Sir Richard Strangways,* d. 1488
STRANGWAYS' BOOK
c. 1447–9, English.

Notes on armory and blazon compiled by Richard Strangways when a law student of the Inner Temple, probably in connection with his studies there. Brit. Mus. Harl. MSS.2259 is the only copy extant.

See also H. S. London, *Some Medieval Treatises on English Heraldry,* The Antiquaries Journal, vol. xxxiii, pp. 74–82; Sir A. Wagner, *Additions and Corrections to C.E.M.R.A.,* in *Aspilogia* II (London, 1967), p. 274.

19. JOHN'S TRETIS ON ARMES
     Mid-fifteenth century, English.

Author's identity unknown, but possibly a lecturer at the Inns of Court, and probably representing the text of his lecture, this essentially a grammar of armory.

Only edition by Prof. E. J. Jones, *Medieval Heraldry* (Cardiff, 1943), pp. 213–20. Only three contemporary copies are known, Brit. Mus. Add. MS. 34648; Brit. Mus. Harl. MS. 6097; and Dennys MS. 10.

20. THE HERALDS TRACT
     c. 1460, English.

Authorship unknown. Clearly inspired by *John's Treatise* which it follows fairly closely. Only copy *Coll. Arms MS.* 'Treatise on Heraldry *circa* Henry VI'.

21. THE ASHMOLEAN TRACT
     Mid-fifteenth century, English.

Authorship unknown, but clearly inspired by *Johns' Treatise,* and has close affinities to *The Heralds Tract.* Complete text published by C. R. Humphery-Smith, *Heraldry in School Manuals of the Middle Ages:* II *The Ashmolean Tract,* Coat of Arms, vol. vi. pp. 163–70.

22. PATRICK'S BOOK
     c. 1465, English.

Plantin-Moretus Museum, Antwerp, MS. O.B., 5.6., transcribed by H. S. London and now Socy. Antiqs. MS. 809. This has close affinities with 19, 20, and 21 above.

23. THE SLOANE TRACT
     c. 1470, English, with begining and end in Latin.

Brit. Mus. Add. MS. 3744. Complete text published by C. R. Humphery-Smith, *Heraldry in School Manuals of the Middle Ages,* Coat of Arms, vol. vi, pp. 115–23. Affinities with four preceding treatises.

24. THE PAKENHAM TRACT
     1449.

Brit. Mus. Add. MS. 28791, f. 5–38. Inspired by the *Tractatus de Armis* of John de Bado Aureo and other sources. See Prof. Evan J. Jones, op. cit., pp. 144–212.

25. THE ASHMOLE TRACT
     Mid-fifteenth century, French.

Bodleian Library MS. Ashmole 764. A collection of divers treatises on heraldry, mainly drawn from earlier authors, but with new matter.

26. *Nicholas Warde*
     Fifteenth century.

Title or description of treatise not known, but Gerard Legh, *Accedence of Armorie* (London, 1562), mentions that 'Nicholas Warde wrote of the whole worke' of armory.

27. *Gille,* King of Arms
LES DROIS D'ARMES
1481, French.
The author was King of Arms of the Emperor Maximilian of Austria and
Count of Flanders. A mixed collection of material of importance to a medieval
herald, concerning the laws of war and tournaments, ceremonies, heraldry, and
armory, the latter inspired by earlier writers. Bibliothèque Nationale, Paris, MS.
Fr.1280.

28. COTTELL'S BOOK
Late fifteenth century, English.
A collection of heraldic notes made by different persons at divers times,
including 'A Tretys of Armes' which has affinities to *John's Treatise,* Brit. Mus.
Harl. MS. 992, formerly belonging to Thomas Cottell of Cornwall.

29. BLASONS DES BATAILLES
Late fifteenth century, French.
Bodleian Library MS. Douce 278. A collection of notes on the duties of
heralds and the laws of war, inspired by the *Arbre des batailles,* and on armory,
which has possible affinities with the mid-fifteenth century English treatises.

30. SEQUIER'S BOOK
Late fifteenth century, French.
Brit. Mus. Harl. MS. 4468. A badly compiled and badly illustrated treatise
on armory, with a general roll of arms.

31. *Franquevie,* Herald of Valenciennes
1485, France.
Brit. Mus. Eger. MS. 1644, being a treatise on armory, with armorial
illustrations.

32. BOKE OF ST. ALBANS
1486, English.
Authorship attributed to Dame Juliana Berners, but this is doubtful. First
printed by Wynkyn de Worde in 1486 as *The Treatyse perteyning to Hawkyng,
Huntyng and Fyshyng with an Angle; and also a right noble Treatyse which
specyfyeth of Blasynge of Armys by Julyans Berners.* The armorial part has
hitherto been considered as being largely based on the *De Studio Militari,* of
Nicholas Upton, but this needs reconsideration.

33. *Jehan Pierre*
TRAITE SUR LE BLASON DES ARMES
1489, French.
Brit. Mus. Add. MS. 26708. A treatise on blazoning arms and on heraldry,
in twelve chapters.

34. *Adam Loutfut,* Kintyre Pursuivant of Arms
LOUTFUT'S BOOK
c. 1494, Scots English.
Brit. Mus. Harl. MS. 6149. Adam Loutfut compiled the book under the
direction of Sir William Cumming of Inverlochy, Marchmont Herald and
later Lyon King of Arms, and it was evidently intended for use as a handbook
on the duties of heralds and matters of concern to them, as well as including
sections on armory. It gives a most interesting picture of the wide interests and
responsibilities of heralds in the Middle Ages.
See also Terence O'Neill, *Adam Loutfut's Book,* Coat of Arms, vol. iv, pp.
307–10; *Queene Elizabethes Academy,* etc., ed. by E. S. Furnival (E.E.T.S.,
Ex.Ser., Vol. viii, pp. 93–104); A. T. P. Byles, op. cit., pp. 1–125.

Index

219

220